DIGITAL EXPRESSIONS

MEDIA LITERACY AND ENGLISH LANGUAGE ARTS

ROBERTA F. HAMMETT & BARRIE R.C. BARRELL

EDITORS

DETSELIG ENTERPRISES LTD.

CALGARY, ALBERTA, CANADA

© 2002 Detselig Enterprises Ltd.

Digital Expressions

National Library of Canada Cataloguing in Publication Data

Main entry under title:

Digital expressions

Includes bibliographic references

ISBN 1-55059-237-8

1. Media literacy. 2. Language arts. I. Hammett, Roberta F. II. Barrell, Barrie R.C. (Barrie Robert Christopher), 1946-

LB1028.4.D53   2002   302.23'071   C2002-910795-4

Detselig Enterprises Ltd.

210-1220 Kensington Rd. N.W., Calgary, AB, T2N 3P5

Phone: 403-283-0900/Fax: 403-283-6947

Email: temeron@telusplanet.net

www.temerondetselig.com

We acknowledge the financial support of the Government of Canada through the Book Publishing Industry Development Program (BPIDP) for our publishing activities.

ISBN 1-55059-237-8

SAN 115-0324

Printed in Canada

<u>**DEDICATIONS**</u>

For Jenica, a child of Disney, whose mediated learning is important to me.

Bobbi

To John and Nick, may the spirit of "the year trip" live on for both of you.

Barrie

Contents

ABOUT THE AUTHORS

Barrie R.C. Barrell is Associate Professor of Secondary English Education, Memorial University. His previous edited books, *Technology, Teaching and Learning: Issues in the Integration of Technology* and *Advocating Change: Contemporary Issues in Subject English*, have brought together over 50 Canadian scholars to discuss the transformation taking place in Canadian education. The focus of *Technology, Teaching and Learning* is the integration of technology into Canadian teaching, learning and school culture. In *Advocating Change*, the English language arts are shown to be evolving as they begin to include and incorporate digital technologies, media studies and other ways of communicating and representing knowledge and information. Informing his university teaching and research are experiences in elementary, middle and secondary schools in remote, rural and urban settings in Canada and the United States. He recently completed a year as Visiting Scholar at the University of Calgary. His research has been published in numerous academic journals and books.

Roberta F. Hammett is Associate Dean for Graduate Programs, Faculty of Education, Memorial University. Her research interests include the literacy implications and applications of computer technologies, teacher education and critical media literacy. She co-edited *Advocating Change* with Barrell and is currently co-authoring a book on feminist pedagogical projects, including a community computer and literacy project funded by SSHRCC. Her World Wide Web address is http://www.ucs.mun.ca/~hammett/

Carl Leggo is a poet and associate professor in the Department of Language and Literacy Education at the University of British Columbia where he teaches courses in writing and narrative research. He is the author of three books: *Growing Up Perpendicular on the Side of a Hill*, *View from My Mother's House* and *Teaching to Wonder: Responding to Poetry in the Secondary Classroom*.

Rebecca Luce-Kapler is an associate professor of Language and Literacy at Queen's University. Her research and teaching arise from a background in writing poetry and fiction and from her experience as an English teacher and professional editor. Her current research focuses on writing processes and technologies. Her book *The Gardens*

7

Where She Dreams will be published early in 2003, and she is the co-author of *Engaging Minds: Learning and Teaching in a Complex World*.

Margaret Mackey teaches at the School of Library and Information Studies at the University of Alberta. She is the North American editor of *Children's Literature in Education* and the author of the recently published *Literacies Across Media: Playing the Text* (Routledge/Falmer, 2002). She has also written many articles about young readers and their texts, both in print and in many other media.

Jill Kedersha McClay is an Associate Professor in the Faculty of Education, University of Alberta, where she teaches graduate and undergraduate courses in language and literacy. Her research focuses on teaching and developing writing abilities, with current studies exploring adolescents' writing in multimedia environments. She is also a YA literature and picture book aficionada.

Valerie Mulholland taught English language arts before joining the Faculty of Education of the University of Regina as a seconded teacher and doctoral student. She teaches secondary methods and curriculum courses.

Helen Nixon is Senior Lecturer in the Centre for Studies in Literacy, Policy and Learning Cultures in the School of Education at the University of South Australia. Her research interests include the pedagogies of global media culture and connections between the new information and communications technologies and changing social constructions of literacy and educational disadvantage. She is particularly interested in how children's out-of-school media and popular culture interests might be used within a critical literacy/English curriculum.

Gurjit Sandhu is a doctoral student in the Faculty of Education at Queen's University. Her research and teaching interests are in the areas of curriculum, culture and identity. Her current doctoral research explores issues of literacy and identity amongst high school girls.

Kathy Sanford is an Assistant Professor in the Department of Curriculum and Instruction at the University of Victoria. Her particular interests are in the areas of literacy, gender, popular culture and the intersection of these in students' lives. She is also involved in researching teacher education. Current research projects include "Boys and Literacy in Western Canada" and "Field-based Teacher Education."

Karen Smith is an assistant professor at the Faculty of Education, University of Manitoba. She instructs teacher education courses in senior years English language arts, language and literacy across the content areas, and arts education. Her special interests include literacy and the Internet, new literacies, and electronic portfolios and online learning. Her homepage URL is http://home.cc.umanitoba.ca/~ksmith/index.html

Peter Weeks recently began teaching technology integration to undergraduate education students at Red Deer College, AB. His previous position was as team leader in charge of technology integration at William E. Hay Composite High School in Stettler, Alberta, teaching grade 9-12 English, Drama and Communications Technology. He is Past President of the English Language Arts Council of the Alberta Teachers' Association and is a co-author of English language arts textbooks for use in high schools.

Chris Worsnop has been a media educator since the mid-1960s. In his later career he has connected his youthful passion for the movies with his professional expertise in curriculum development, implementation and evaluation, to become a freelance consultant in media education, specializing in assessment and teacher training. His books, *Screening Images: Ideas for Media Education* (1999) and *Assessing Media Work: Authentic Assessment in Media Education* (1996) are in broad circulation in the English-speaking world.

Douglas Zook is an assistant professor in the Faculty of Education at the University of Regina. He teaches courses in social studies curriculum and instruction. His current areas of research include media literacy, citizenship education and psychoanalysis.

INTRODUCTION

BARRIE R.C. BARRELL
AND ROBERTA F. HAMMETT

English language arts (ELA) teachers now face an enormous expansion of their subject. In Canada, the regional educational foundations (representing Atlantic Provinces, Western Provinces, British Columbia, Ontario and English Quebec) that oversee and control the writing of the nation's curricula have now included viewing and other ways of representing information and knowledge with the traditional ELA strands of reading, writing, listening and speaking. The situation is similar in the United States, Australia, New Zealand and the United Kingdom. In all these constituencies, media and cultural studies now play a more expanded and important role in ELA teaching. Entering the mix and making classroom literacy events and practices even more complex are curricular requirements mandating the integration of digital technologies directly into classroom praxis. Technology is no longer seen as an add-on to subject knowledge, but rather as a tool for helping mediate, display, critique and create data, information and new knowledge. A third, though less well conceptualized, addition to ELA curricula is critical literacy. The Atlantic Provinces Education Foundation (APEF), for example, states: "Students will be able to respond critically to a range of texts, applying their understanding of language, form, and genre" (n.d., p. 28). Subsequent explanations suggest that, at various levels, students will pose questions of texts, analyze points of view, perspectives, positionings, voices privileged and ignored, values, and instances of prejudice, stereotyping and bias (APEF, pp. 28-29). A result of these curricular changes and additions is that literacy discussions about what knowledge young people might require to make their way in a digital world have been made even more complex. This book centres on the impact popular media and digital technologies have on the reconstructed and expanded English language arts curricula. The inclusion of technology, viewing and other ways of representing challenges and changes the traditional strands of reading, writing, speaking and listening.

With a broadening of the parameters of ELA has come a greatly expanded notion of text. Teachers and students are now expected to "read" not only books but the world and a myriad of analogue and digital texts, online and on cassette, that may include sound, music, static and moving images, and graphics. The linearity of traditional texts is contradicted by the inclusion of hypertext, media and digital representations. Existing writing practices are bracketed by hypertext and hypermedia text constructions. Clear and precise notions of writing are challenged when students begin to compose texts using the tools that information and communication technologies (ICT) put at their disposal to represent identities and creative engagements with the world. Both students and society in general are challenging traditional grammatical conventions by altering, disregarding, reshaping or rewriting them in their digital communications. They are blending iconographic notations into email or ICQ communications. This book supports teachers of English language arts as they juggle multiliteracies and (re)conceptualize how new texts are composed, read, interpreted and taught in a multicultural and dynamic society.

The broader selection of texts and textual experiences mandated in new curricula documents lessen the traditional divide between school texts and pedagogical practices and those enjoyed by students outside school. This book critiques the media and Internet as pedagogical sites, as settings where knowledge and identities are produced. The authors demonstrate to pre- and in-service teachers how the successful and resistant pedagogical practices of the media and Internet function, and how these sites might be investigated, explored and critiqued with students. The chapters in the book demonstrate the questioning and subverting of textual authority and the value of particular texts, messages and genres over others. Following in the traditions of Giroux, McLaren and Lankshear, the authors resist and oppose canonized interpretive authority, seeking to extend and expand the range of textual practices and thus the range of meanings that are produced and legitimated.

TECHNOLOGY, SCHOOL AND SOCIETY

Various information and communications technologies are now common in public schools. Indeed, in classrooms, it is the very absence of computers, like the absence of air or water, that now is noticed. School administrators routinely face calls for additional Internet and Intranet connections. They constantly search for monies to match requests for more and more networked machines able to connect to virtual worlds and to support various forms of technology-mediated learning. The educational establishment is racing to catch up to the integrated presence of the digital technologies that are already deeply embedded in the society it serves. We do not list various cutting-edge technologies for fear they will quickly date our text. However, unlike other technologies that entered the classroom as learning tools and quickly disappeared (radio, television and slides, for example) we venture to say that ICT and the Internet are not going to disappear any time soon. Rather, access and use will become easier and simpler.

The fuss over the Internet is quickly subsiding. At some time in our past history we stopped asking *if* there was a telephone and began asking *where* it was located. The same is becoming true of Internet connections. Travelers are beginning to see access to the Web pop up in public places in much the same way as ATM machines have. Computers with Internet connections for public use have spread from bookstores and coffee shops to local libraries, convenience stores, airports and travel information bureaus.

We believe that young students do not approach technology in the same way that older people do. In western societies, a gap is emerging between those who actually *see* new technologies and those who take their existence and availability very much for granted. As with the lenses in a pair of glasses, they only see the optometry (the technology) when a smudge or scratch elicits their attention. Tapscott (1998) draws our attention to a Net generation that is often oblivious to new technologies; they simply go about viewing, wearing, carrying, connecting or using it.

This is not to say that practices should remain unquestioned. The role of schools and teachers, as the authors in this book see it, is to challenge students to read their world and view their activities more critically. Like print texts, media and Internet texts are engaged in the construction of realities and identities. The critical literacy advocated here by contributors Mulholland and Zook, Nixon, and Hammett would have pre- and in-service teachers, and subsequently their students, explore how subjects are constituted in media and online, what particular social arrangements are represented, and what social ideals are produced. Teachers and students are challenged by contributors like Smith and Nixon to examine the politics surrounding any particular representation and investigate the history and contexts of representations and their interpretations. Teachers and students are invited to explore the discourses that produce and question particular representations and to recognize their conflicting meanings.

Although critical literacy activities like those suggested by Worsnop, Hammett and Leggo invite the critique of representations and the ways texts position us as readers/viewers, it is important that teachers not insist that students respond negatively to the texts that give them pleasure (C. Luke, 1997); rather, the chapters in this book demonstrate how textual investigations give pleasure, particularly when computer technologies play a role in those investigations.

Of course, globalization forms the backdrop in front of which ICT technologies, popular culture, the media and new ELA curricular initiatives are all played out for our young people. The globalization of the communication, information, entertainment, commerce, manufacturing, banking and investment industries now create enormous power brokers that directly influence educational and regional policies. Globalization, especially when combined with the corporate muscle of the multinationals, has great influence on the policies of national states. This powerful force, as Barrell writes, is influencing the vision of curriculum planners.

As Barrell noted in the epilogue, planners are asking if old constructions of literacy will suffice given the realities of the new global economy. In view of the fact that world economic conditions can dramatically impact and disrupt existing social conditions and practices, we need to question what curricular goals are remaining constant and what literacy practices young people need to experience and acquire to make their way in the digital age. Students are entitled to know they have a right to leave a mark on the world and are being equipped to do so. They need assurance that the instruments of the new technologies can help in the releasing of their creative imaginations, as Luce-Kappler and Sandhu and McClay and Weeks suggest in their chapters. Curriculum planners have not turned a blind eye to the economic forces and changes going on in the world. Globalization, as a political and commercial force, has pushed curriculum planners and individual schools to reassess fundamental teaching and learning practices. They return, as the authors in this text do, to ask what are the rich literacies and educational experiences that young people need to experience in a digitized world.

ELA curriculum documents, as an institution and as the shared collective consciousness of local communities, are fundamentally challenged by issues of globalization. Our new ELA teachers sit at the turbulent confluence of globalization, evolving information and communication technologies, new learning theories, multiple intelligence theories, new text constructions and traditional views of praxis, and are expected to plan a personal course of action. Fortunately, the new curricular documents that have resulted from this interplay are quite well defined, and we would argue, quite radical in their breadth and vision. In them, the local gives ground to the regional. Regional, national and transnational positions and interests are juggled against a background of commercial interests and consolidations. Transmission models of teaching are replaced by inquiry and project-based learning, group work is encouraged and interdisciplinary teaching is valued. Representations of student learning now include visual and other non-traditional ways of representing knowledge. Online publishing and broadcasting of student work is encouraged.

TECHNOLOGY IN THE CLASSROOM

With the technical amenities that the digital age now provides, together with the explosion of information accessible in connected classrooms, has come a fundamental questioning about the ways we go about structuring teaching and learning. Seymour Papert (1995) draws a line between "two diametrically opposed visions of the role of new technologies in education. In one vision technology is a means to bolster and improve established practices. In the other, the new technology renders these practices obsolete by creating the opportunity for radically new practices" (p. 2). However, we have to understand that there is lethargy about educational change. Traditional school practices are enduring; they are embedded in a hierarchy of bureaucracies and nostalgic cultural understanding of how "schooling" is to be constructed and practiced. Like the pencil sharpener, the existence of two putty-colored computers in a classroom has become a part of the collective expectations of parents and teachers. Appearances count, but questions about what exactly is being done with the machines are gaining importance. Common sense tells us that poor teachers will use computers poorly and good teachers will find emancipatory ways to use new technologies; however, it is the mandate of faculties of education to intervene and assist pre- and in-service teachers in using and theorizing the use of technologies in their classrooms. As Papert says, technology has the potential to create substantive change and reform in the way we go about teaching and learning.

Public schools, by and large, weathered change remarkably well. They have lived almost unchanged through eras of industrialization and waves of reform. What is radically new this time around, however, is the speed, access and ease of communications and the "mind tools" that computers make available to support the incorporation of new themes of educational research into classroom practices: multiple intelligences (Gardener, 1985; 1999), diverse constructions of texts (Barrell and Hammett, 2002), new ways of representing knowledge and new theories about learning (Jonassen, 1999).

New ICT technologies challenge the monopoly of the curriculum. They threaten the prestige of the school as the sole provider of credentialed information. They make available sources of information that can seem more comprehensive, inclusive and up to date. New technologies break the exclusivity of institutions to control the flow, the type or the structure of information. What is radical, this time around, is the fact that classrooms can now reach outside the school or the community it serves and be information providers to global audiences. They can better participate in the many cultures of the global society. They allow students to participate in the construction and critique of media. Creative productions or scientific findings can now be broadcast beyond the confines of the school, classroom and community, and students can enter into a heteroglossic dialogue about them.

We rest our thinking on the postmodern rejection of inclusive rational frameworks in which, as Maxine Greene (1995) says, "all problems, all certainties cannot be resolved. All we can do...is cultivate multiple ways of seeing and multiple dialogues in a world where nothing stays the same" (p. 16). There are conservative voices that believe they know what knowledge is worth foregrounding and what technologies worth pursuing. They perceive schools as corporate systems and begin to apply management techniques in order to promote predetermined technical skills and particular kinds of knowledge needed to meet present economic imperatives. Others see technology and media as a lens through which the world is seen and that it shapes our perceptions even as we shape technology (Bromley & Apple, 1998; Goyder, 1997;

Franklin 1992). Others voice warnings about the growing gap between society and schooling. As Seymour Papert (1995) remarked to the U.S. House of Representatives Panel on Technology and Education, "the question at stake is no longer whether technology can change education or even whether it is desirable. The presence of technology in society is a major factor in changing the entire learning environment. School is lagging further and further behind the society it is intended to serve. Eventually it will transform itself deeply or break down and be replaced by new social structures," (p. 1).

Linked to and seamlessly integrated with computer technologies are other media technologies. As analogue technologies lose ground to digital newcomers, the computer monitor and the television screen become one and the same, and films and television programs, like music, exist as comfortably on the computer network as in other technologies. Thus the hyperreality of the television and the virtual reality of the computer are blended as seamlessly as Internet and media cultures. The tools of cultural studies, supplementing ICT and traditional English classroom practices, become the necessary means of critique of the multiple and varied texts surrounding young people in the 21st century. This critique can start with the cover of this book. Identity, beginning with gender and race, is not necessarily clear to viewers of the visage. Indeed, the editors of this book, on first seeing the layout, had diametrically opposite readings of the gender yet each could understand the other's conception once articulated. Are two people or one in mirror image portrayed, since the color and shape of the glasses remains the same? What textual practices do viewers bring to their interpretations? What masculinist or racialized codings are noted? How might imaging technologies render the text more "writerly" or "readerly"? Why should it be either?

This book intends to prepare teachers in a range of English-speaking countries to navigate critically the blended fields of ICT, media literacy, English education and cultural studies. Building on the experience of seasoned classroom teachers and university educators, the chapters in this book combine theory with practical applications and examples to engage pre- and in-service teachers in the critique and examination of the practices and texts of intermediate and secondary English language arts. The broad theme of this book is the integration of the wide variety of texts, media, tools, skills and knowledge needed by young people as they graduate from our secondary schools and as they live their lives and construct their identities in an information-rich world.

The authors of the chapters begin with curricular changes and the changing worlds of students; they then describe strategies for responding to those changes. The proposed activities demonstrate a respect for students' abilities and knowledge of new media (Sanford, Mackey) and often advocate inviting students to engage in research of literacy practices (Nixon, Mackey). Early chapters in this volume explore how more traditional activities (writing and poetry study) are enhanced by new technologies. Smith demonstrates how viewing and representing can be incorporated into the curriculum and how such knowledge can be displayed and assessed in electronic portfolios. Worsnop, after providing some history and definitions associated with media literacy, suggests some tools for assessment. We place these near the beginning of our text as a reminder that evaluation is not an afterthought, but an integral part of curriculum conceptualizing and unit planning. As a conclusion to this volume, Mackey lays out clearly the many kinds of texts and literacies students should understand, as they consume and produce them, and she reminds us that students' relationships with texts are or should be positive experiences. Barrell, to end this book, summarizes the impact of global trends on communications, schooling and society in general. We trust that all the chapters will support new and current teachers, as they respond to technology infusion and media profusion, not to put new wine in old bottles (Lankshear & Bigum, 1998), but to design innovative and appropriate activities that will prepare students to react critically in a media-saturated world.

REFERENCES

Atlantic Provinces Education Foundation. (n.d.). *English language arts foundation*. Halifax: Author.

Barrell, B. and Hammett, R. (2002). A critique of a critical social literacy project: Newfoundlanders confront *The Shipping News. Interchange: A Quarterly Review of Education, 33*(2), 139-158.

Bromley, H. & Apple, M. (Eds.). (1998). *Education/technology/power: Educational computing as a social practice*. Albany, NY: SUNY.

Franklin, U. (1992). *The real world of technology*. Concord, ON: Anansi Press Ltd.

Gardener, H. (1999). *The disciplined mind: What all students should understand.* New York: Simon and Schuster.

Gardener, H. (1985). *The mind's new science: A history of the cognitive revolution.* New York: Basic Books.

Greene, M. (1995). *Releasing the imagination.* San Francisco: Jossey Bass.

Goyder, J. (1997). *Technology + society: Best perspectives.* Peterborough, ON: Broadview.

Jonassen, D. (1999). *Computers as mindtools for schools: Engaging critical thinking* (2nd Edition). Upper Saddle River, NJ: Prentice Hall.

Lankshear, C. and Knobel, M. (1997). Literacies, texts and difference in the electronic age. In C. Lankshear, *Changing literacies* (pp. 133-163). Buckingham and Phillidelphia: Open University Press.

Lankshear, C. & Bigum, C. (1998). Literacies and technologies in school settings: Findings from the field. Invited keynote address to the joint national conference of the Australian Association for the Teaching of English and the Australian Literacy Educators' Association, Canberra, Australia. [Online]. Available at: http://www.geocities.com/c.lankshear/litandtechs.html

Luke, C. (1997). Media literacy and cultural studies. In Muspratt, S., Luke, A. & Freebody, P. (Eds.), *Constructing critical literacies: Teaching and learning cultural practice* (pp. 19-49). Cresskill, NJ: Hampton Press.

Papert, S. (1995). Technology in school: Local fix or global transformation? [Online] Retrieved October 2000: http://kids.www.media.mit.edu/projects/kids/sp-talk.html

Tapscott, D. (1998). *Growing up digital: The rise of the net generation.* New York: McGraw-Hill.

Popular media and school literacies

Adolescent expressions

Kathy Sanford

Introduction

What I like best about school is looking forward to going home, maybe some things I do with my friends at school after school's over. My friend tried to start up a skate club, but that didn't work out. Mostly I do things in my room, I play my guitar, play music on the computer, talk to my friends on MSN, sometimes I play computer games, as a last resort, sort of. I play puzzle games where you have to figure things out, sometimes it can be fun, but sometimes it's boring.

These words were spoken by Harley, a 14-year-old boy growing up in a large urban center in Canada. Although he speaks of the importance of school, "You've got to do it because if you don't you're screwed," he finds little of interest or value to him personally. "Teachers have a way of making things not enjoyable," he comments, and he can't think of any classes he likes this year. "Maybe next year," he suggests hopefully, "I'm signed up for drafting, computers, and guitar… there's a new guitar teacher which will be good." But while he finds little from school to connect to his life, he leads a very rich and diverse educational life after school. He uses his electronic keyboard and a computer program to compose music that he later writes lyrics for and plays with his friends, stays connected to his friends through the MSN Messenger chat-line, and occasionally engages in simulation games – but not games "where you're a man with a gun who walks into a room and shoots a bunch of people."

Students in school today, like Harley, have a considerable knowledge of the world and popular or "life" literacies; by the time they reach adolescence the sophistication of their knowledge is often considerably broader and more in depth than their teachers recognize. They are familiar with many complex visual, aural and print-based forms of communication from TV cartoons, sit-coms, game shows, billboards, movies, computer games, Internet as well as a wide array of books and magazines. They have been exposed to the adult world, the global world, the technological world. The full range of adolescent literacy is much more complex, dynamic and sophisticated than what is traditionally encompassed within school-sanctioned literate activity. Adolescents have multiple and overlapping literacies (Phelps, 1998, p. 1). However, their vast wealth of knowledge is seldom drawn upon to develop formal school experiences and learning. While there should be many intersections in the knowledge students develop out of school as they read multiple forms of texts, there are often more gaps than connections. Rather than using their knowledge of language, of story structure, of information-gathering, teachers often choose to begin with students as if they were blank slates, as if each new teacher was the only one responsible for depositing information into the minds of his/her students (Freire, 1972). We seem to be missing "much of the rich and nuanced literate lives they lead outside of what O'Brien (1998) calls school-sanctioned literacy" (cited in Phelps, 1998, p. 1). We should focus on adolescents and the "various forms of literacy through which they inform, define, and transform their lives" (p. 1). Teachers need to become more aware of the connections between youths' engagement with popular culture and their need to form personal identifications, to construct memory, and to pursue their own interests (Alvermann & Heron, 2001, p. 122). However, while students have a great range of skills and understandings, often these literacies are gender-biased, developed through powerful socialization literacies such as popular media images seen in advertising, movies and TV. As they are learning to read various texts, students are also learning how to be in the world, how to understand themselves as male or female. Hinchman (1998) points to the mostly unexplored ties to gender, as well as race and class, in research projects connected to adolescents' literacy. Gender as a social construct is largely ignored in school literacy experiences, but one that is subtly and powerfully exploited in life literacy situations. Many attempts are made by commercial ventures to manipulate adolescents' actions and thoughts by appealing to gendered hopes and desires (Kenway and Bullen, 2001). Adolescents navigate their way through treacherous media messages in an attempt to develop their understanding about the world.

Given the many opportunities and exposures to texts, curriculum developers, theorists, researchers and teachers, however, often make assumptions about the students they are teaching and the skills they bring to the classroom rather than listening to their voices and hearing what they have to say. This chapter will attempt to include those voices, and to draw upon the words and ideas of seven adolescents, ages 11 to 17, male and female students who come from across Canada in urban and rural communities. These adolescents have had very diverse educational experiences and levels of success at school. Sarah and Morgan, as young adolescents, are seldom concerned with school success; while both are competent and capable readers and writers, their positive experiences are measured more by their interest in particular school projects than by the evaluation assigned by the teacher. Luke, Anna, and Blythe have experienced considerable school success (as measured by exam results and awards), and have clear expectations of post-secondary education. Harley and Nella, on the other hand, have not experienced their schooling in such positive terms. Their literacies have been seldom recognized and the messages (in the form of teacher evaluations) have focused more on traditional school literacies than on the literacies in which they are highly competent.

INTRODUCING THE ADOLESCENTS WHOSE VOICES INFORM THIS WRITING

SARAH

Sarah is 11 years old, and is currently attending a school on the rural west coast, although she has also lived in Newfoundland. She likes school for the active things she does like run around, play with her friends, usually at lunch and recess breaks. When she's not at school, she plays with her friends on the beach, practices the piano, bike rides, sometimes watches TV at her granny's house, and does homework. Her computer access at school is very limited and she rarely uses it at home.

MORGAN

Morgan is a 12-year-old girl living in a moderately sized urban centre who reads extensively, watches TV regularly (sit-coms, movies, action/adventure), and is very capable on the computer. She spends many hours on the computer writing stories and illustrating them, stories for school and for giving to family and friends. She uses e-mail or ICQ to stay in touch with current friends as well as friends she left when she moved last year. She uses the Internet regularly to locate information for school projects and her own information (in the past about Beanie babies, now about interesting actors and movies); the latest skill she has acquired is the ability to scan and digitally manipulate a variety of images for projects and for her own amusement. She also likes to create visual images using Corel Draw on the computer. Additionally, she plays sports such as soccer and tennis, and rides her bike extensively. She plays piano and clarinet, using CD accompaniment to enhance her clarinet playing.

HARLEY

Harley is a grade 10 fourteen-year-old in a large urban Canadian city. His use of the computer is highly sophisticated and he has learned on his own to program, write music, and conduct research on the computer, as well as maintain close daily e-mail contact with his friends. Harley also plays music on guitar and keyboards, and has adapted what he has learned in piano lessons to independently learn how to play these other instruments. He also spends time skateboarding with his friends, an activity that largely defines his identity at school as a "skater." Harley is not a "reader" of novels and doesn't often do homework because "it's only worth 5%." Instead, he listens in class and then figures out what he has to do in each assignment. He doesn't usually read from his textbooks, unless he has to study for exams.

LUKE

Luke, 15 years old, has grown up in Newfoundland. He doesn't like school but knows it is necessary; he describes himself as "lazy" and says he doesn't like to work. Nevertheless, he does complete his homework and gets decent grades in school. He likes science and social studies because he says they are interesting, show him what the world is made of, and how it is made. What he likes to do best is read, books like Tom Clancy that combine historical fiction with international politics. "Reading is very enjoyable, I'm reading five books at the moment, so it's pretty important to me." Luke also plays "lots of video games," although he's trying to keep it down because, he comments seriously, "it's not always healthy sitting in front of a computer." While he tolerates school, he thinks he would like it more if it was more interactive, not note-taking and homework – "I'm not fond of that", he says. He looks forward to the end of the day when he can talk with friends to discuss what's happened in the day, voice their opinions (they're into politics), walk the dog, or just meet and hang around.

ANNA

Anna is almost 16, entering grade 11 in school. She lives in a fairly rural and remote community, and has also lived in other small towns and urban centers across Canada. She thinks school is "pretty good, a place where you can learn and get knowledge for life, and for the social times as well." She likes film, drama and music classes best, but also likes her English class as she likes to write. She reads novels when she has time, but during the school year rarely has time to read for her own pleasure or interest. She also likes a variety of sports such as soccer, volleyball and ping-pong, that she plays in her home with family and friends.

NELLA

Nella is 17 and entering her final year of school. She has spent much of her life in a suburb outside a large prairie city, and has acquired a strong network of friends. ICQ is a popular method of staying connected with her friends, as well as telephone and regular note-writing during school. Nella has, until recently, avoided reading and was not a confident reader. In the past two years, however, she had become a keen reader of novels for her own enjoyment, and has become a much more confident reader of school texts as well. Nella's greatest love is watching movies and she has an extensive knowledge of current and older videos. She listens to a wide range of popular music, reads magazines when they are available, and watches informational TV as well as her "favorite" TV shows. She uses the Internet fluently to help her complete school assignments in classes such as social studies, English and biology.

BLYTHE

Blythe is 17 and looking forward to her first year away from home next year when she begins University. She liked school for the most part, a lot of it because of the social part of school. In her final year of school she found a good environment to work in where she could communicate with a lot of people, have friends around and teachers who encouraged them to work together. She reports having had lots of good discussion and opportunities to hear what other people thought about the texts they were reading. She also does some reading on her own, as well as singing in a jazz choir that has enabled her to travel to Europe, but reports spending little time watching TV or movies and using computers mainly for e-mailing her friends and staying in contact.

These students have all come from families who have supported and encouraged their school success. They have had access to a variety of technologies, either at home or at school, and parents who themselves have professional careers where technology and fairly sophisticated literacy abilities are required. It is a safe bet that "significant qualitative differences exist between the technological literacy practices enacted across different homes and worksites: these differences will have inevitable consequences for patterns of scholastic success and failure, other things being equal" (p. 152). Other things are not always equal in classrooms, however. While these seven adolescents interact with popular and school literacies in varied ways, they have a common ground and support for their learning. Many students who come from working class backgrounds, diverse cultures, abilities and interests will not have the same opportunities or outlooks on the world, and these differences will markedly affect academic success and future life options.

However, despite the opportunities afforded them, seldom have these seven students been asked about their acquired knowledge, either at home or at school; often their interests and abilities (or lack thereof) have been assumed. Students' complaints that the opinions of teenagers are not given the respect they deserve is a valid and important concern (Knobel, 1999; Hinchman, 1998). Claims being made of "growing gaps between the experiences and values investments of teacher and student 'generations' respectively" and the lack of connection schools have with emergent technological literacies (Lankshear & Knobel, 1997) need to be carefully considered.

If schools as effective institutions of learning are to be maintained in light of current allegations that technology is rendering schools "obsolete and expensively counterproductive" (Perelman, 1992, p. 135), schools must be shown to be purposeful. Educators need to be clear on the value of schools as sites where teacher/learner relationships are formed, and where literacy is recognized as having "an important function in the development of individual, cultural, and social identities"

(Phelps, 1998, p. 1). Educators also must be clear, to themselves and to the public in general, that today's students are quite different from students of previous eras, "different in important ways from their teachers and different from constructions of the 'ideal student' which underlie current curricula" (Bigum & Green, 1992, p. 119).

SCHOOL LITERACY

School literacies are generally comprised of reading and writing activities, and are most often located in English language arts classes. Reading, as understood by most of western society and the adolescents in this study, is a process of decoding and understanding texts such as novels and short stories. Reading is done most often in English language arts classes, and is defined in various ways. The adolescents represented here connect reading to decoding (Sarah), to personal interest (Luke), and with pleasure and making connections (Blythe). Sarah views reading in a traditional way, as "looking at words on a piece of paper and saying or thinking them, and making a story, or a sentence", while the older adolescents recognizes reading as something more, as encompassing personal meaning-making and enjoyment as important aspects of their expanded notions of reading. "Reading," says Luke, "is something that one does for oneself, looking for information on Internet, books, magazines, as long as you enjoy the experience and learn something." Blythe suggests that reading "doesn't *have* to do with pleasure, but it's better when it is, because you don't get bored, but reading is…it's important, definitely, everything in school has some kind of reading, whether it's instructions in math, or poetry and literature; reading the printed word is the building block, but reading is about taking the printed word and turning it into something that means something to you, an image, sound, or feeling, and you understand it better, it becomes a whole world built on top of that word; it evokes an emotional response."

Writing for these adolescents refers to a limited set of print-text events and activities. Anna describes her notion of writing: "creative" writing of short stories, sometimes poetry, and the writing of essays, while Nella comments that "putting your thoughts on paper, writing words on paper, actual *writing* writing is what you feel, what you think, or a reaction to something." "Real writing" for Luke is "writing from your own imagination, your own endeavors" but it is something he seldom does. Manguel's (1996) definition supports those presented by the adolescents, although he extends the definition beyond print text: "Reading, and by extension, writing, is an act of attributing meaning to multiple sign systems… reading letters on a page is only one of its many guises" (p. 6-7) and he suggests that architects, dancers and astronomers share with book-readers the craft of deciphering and translating signs. However, Street exhorts us to move beyond such naive conceptions of literacy as "reading and writing," "encoding and decoding" subsumed within the "autonomous model of literacy" (1984, 1993). Definitions of literacy evolve as a result of the consensus of members of society, and human activity and cultural tools, such as emerging technologies, influence the ever-changing definition of what it means to be literate (Thakkar, Bruce, Hogan & Williamson, 2001).

Some teachers are reluctant to use film, comic strips, contemporary music and other popular media, and technology in the classroom (Morrison, Bryan & Chilcoat, 2001), fearing "that such a non-traditional approach denies students time during which they could gain additional exposure to the canon" (p. 760). They want their students engaged in rigorous scholastic endeavors and may resist activities that appear frivolous. But is the engagement of alternative texts *really* reading, some might ask? Alvermann & Heron (2001) believe it is, and, like Manguel, suggest that "reading comprehension is a meaning-making process involving both print and non-print texts" (p. 119). They suggest that "what might be easily dismissed as 'frivolous' actually involves multiple literacies embedded in complex communication practices" (p. 122). These multiple literacies are seldom found in school practices, but their use in classrooms would help connect students to the world beyond the classroom.

Adolescents may struggle against becoming engaged in the study of the world, its sciences or its literatures, unless they see how such study pertains to them (Alvermann et al., 1998, p. xix). Language is one, if not the most predominant, of the social practices used by "affinity groups" (Gee, 2002), which has clear implications for the involvement of adolescents in their school learning. The affinity groups of these particular adolescents provide language connections between their personal interests, such as jazz singing, skateboarding, fashion, and politics and the world beyond their own individual lives. Attention to the types of language use that adolescents engage in will help them make connections between school literacies and the relevant literacies of their lives. Witkin suggests that "to scorn the pop culture of teens as unworthy of serious attention is to underestimate not only adolescents' need for peer group identity but also the way popular culture influences 'high' culture" (1994, p. 30). Making connections between pop and high cultures, she continues, "helps me understand what is important to teach; I could not do it without pop culture to supply the entrance and the evidence...one reflects the other" (p. 32). A biographical video of Michael Jordan, for example, has provided Witkin a way to connect the form of biography with other life histories and biographical works of historical and political figures. She uses segments from the popular *Star Trek* television series to introduce classical works of science fiction, encouraging students to critically examine society's goals and possible future directions.

Schooling "always represents an introduction to, preparation for, and legitim[iz]ation of particular forms of social life" (McLaren, 1989, p. 160) and always involves power relations, social practices and privileged forms of knowledge that support a specific vision of past, present and future. These traditional forms of "social life" are continually challenged by today's adolescents and in an effort to maintain a present and future that is known and comfortable, many educators attempt to resist the dramatic changes that are occurring in 21st century literacies and classrooms (Teasley & Wilder, 1997). Many classroom teachers have been denied, or have otherwise refused, opportunities to implement new technologies into their pedagogies in anything other than the most domesticated ways (Lankshear & Knobel, 1997, p. 136).

Papert (1993) suggests that the current generation of students, who have already grown up in a cultural milieu in which video games have a prominent place, have already learned what computers are just beginning to teach adults. School, not surprisingly, he says, strikes many young people as slow, boring and out of touch by comparison. As with all social structures, school needs to be accepted and valued by its participants (Howe & Strauss, 1993). Relevance, which largely determines value for adolescents, is central to popular culture, for it minimizes the difference between text and life. Relevance is the intersection between the textual and the social (Fiske, 1989). Schools are caught in the tension between the need to convey information deemed to be in society's interest and the need to be popular, but it is the job of schools to provide relevant, integrated and meaningful experiences for students that connect school literacies to the students' life literacies.

Sometimes journals are used to help students capture their personal ideas and opinions, although these are implemented in very different ways in English language arts classes, with the focus sometimes being placed on handwriting, sometimes on recording personal thoughts and opinions, and sometimes on gathering ideas for future creative writing projects. Other writing activities identified by adolescents are note-taking and worksheet completion, and while these are reported by the participants as important school activities, they often have little relevance to their lives and cannot sustain their interest. There is little crossover between literacy activities in their English language arts classes and their other classes, and there was initial surprise and puzzlement expressed when they were asked about reading and writing activities in other classes. School literacy, then, is comprised largely of the study of literature and it happens in English language arts classes rather than being shared among all school subject areas. Sarah reported being given traditional activities, "We did book reports on the novels we read in class, we'd put our name and the date, the title of the book, then write what you think will happen, then half way through, write what's happened so far, then at the end we drew four little pictures and the teacher signed it." The reading Morgan described included "stories the teacher read to us, and lots of reading that I did at home." Both Harley and Anna commented on the novels they were assigned to read in their English classes: "We read a few books in English, like *In the Heat of the Night, Midsummer Night's Dream*, and *The Giver*"; "We did novel studies, *Animal Farm* and *The Chrysalids*, a few articles in Socials…" They all commented on writing lots of notes, textbook reading, and completion of worksheets. "Homework" was a big part of the reading and writing activities that these adolescents reported; they spoke dispiritedly of the quantities of homework they were assigned that they saw as pointless and some, such as Harley, found ways to ignore or minimize the homework. Additional writing included Luke's report of "lab write-ups in science and a term paper in history class," Nella's description of "in-class essays and an essay assignment in social studies," Harley's reporting that "in English we wrote a couple of short stories and in social studies we wrote a few reports on things, a report on September 11th, a report on an Israel battle." Anna's writing experiences included "a journal for a bit – it was like, if you were an animal, what would you be and why – but the class didn't like it." In Blythe's final year at school, her writing experiences consisted of "lots of essays and outlining to show you understood what was going on; we wrote responses to our novel studies, but no poetry at all, which was disappointing."

Most often these adolescents reported reading textbooks and writing notes in their content area classes. They demonstrated a similarly limited experience and understanding of "literacy" as noted in the definitions they offered. Literacy for Luke is defined as "someone who can comprehend language and read language." Harley defines literacy as comprehending, "some people can read but can't comprehend, understand the plot, theme, or message the writer is trying to put across." Anna says, "The word I associate with it is 'writing,' literacy – books, people writing and writers, intellectual people." Sarah describes literacy as "being able to read and understand what is being said," and Blythe explains literacy as "being able to understand the concepts that someone is trying to get across to you whether it's Dr. Seuss concepts, or Orwell's *1984* concepts...more than just being able to read and even write, although that's obviously necessary." They did not make any connections to literacies other than print-based unless prompted.

LIFE LITERACIES

Although students do not see their out-of-school activities as "literacy" in any way, there is a growing understanding of the 21st century need to broaden our notions of "text," "reading" and "literacy" (Alvermann & Heron, 2001). Out of school, students engage in a broad range of activities that often require a high level of literacy, demanding the reading of diverse complex texts. Students report reading music, writing scripts and filming, reading political novels, researching on the Internet, scanning texts into digital forms, playing computer "games" and writing in personal journals and diaries. Teachers are often unaware of these activities and do not consider these as legitimate literacy activities.

Students' attitudes towards alternative literacies are very different from their attitudes toward school-based literacy activities (Kenway & Bullen, 2001). While they do not recognize e-mail interaction, creating visual images, or reading magazines as literacy events, students have a much more sustained interest in these activities (O'Brien, Moje, &

Stewart, 2001). They have no formal instruction in these alternative literacies but learn the required skills themselves, by reading manuals, asking friends, experimenting and repetition. The activities they have chosen support personal interests and learning styles, connect to their social lives and peer-group and are related to social and cultural group identities, allegiances and exclusions. Because of adolescents' interest in such activities, there is an excitement about learning, an ability to focus for a long period of time, to practice for long hours, and to rehearse. Talk, in the form of discussion with peers or adults who have knowledge beyond their own, is a critical aspect of learning these literacies (Wells, 1989). "Talking is a form of literacy," comments Harley, "it's kind of like writing, it's a form of communication, for me a better form of communication because it's quicker and easier, face to face or MSN." Information is researched from diverse sources and the students are not reliant on one textbook or the authority of one teacher for this information. And these literacies will have considerable life-long influence over the types of careers and interests that are selected, shaping their ability to critically and creatively act and react in workplace situations (Tannock, 2001). Often it is the out-of-school literacies such as technological aptitude and awareness of media (creation of spreadsheets, ability to interact quickly on computer games, awareness of visual messages, composing using computer programs) that prepare adolescents more for future employment.

The technological and media forms that teachers and parents fear are limiting adolescents' progress and damaging their ability to learn sometimes influence their perceptions of how adolescents spend their time, how they learn best and what interests them. Computer games, e-mail and compact discs are dismissed as frivolous. Parents are informed by "news" items in newspapers, magazines and on television that report the number of hours their children sit in front of the television. Although surveys report that 50% of children watched television for three hours or more in 1990 (Witkin, 1994), no reports are made on the 50% of children who do not watch television for extensive periods. These voices are not represented in media reports. "The media and schools would have parents, who are not able to interpret their children's attraction to video games, believe that children love them because they're easy and hate homework because it's difficult, where in reality the reverse is more often true" (Papert, 1993, p. 150).

Teachers bemoan the fact that their students do not "read" any more and everyone is concerned with decreasing "standards" of literacy. However, when these popular perceptions are challenged, and adolescents are asked about *what* they are reading and writing, and *how* they are reading and writing, another much richer story emerges, one that can inform teaching practices and choice of texts. Sarah reports having just completed reading Phillip Pullman's *A Subtle Knife*, and enjoying animal stories and fantasy. Morgan has recently completed all of Madeleine L'Engle's five stories beginning with *A Wrinkle in Time*, and is beginning to read *The Hobbit*. Luke loves to read novels and books on history – it's what he likes to do best. He just completed Sunzu's *Art of War*, a book from Ancient China. His favorites are Tom Clancy novels that talk about international politics. Anna reports that she's not really into "teen novels," but just recently read *The Pilot's Wife* by Anita Shreve, and is now reading Rohinton Mistry's *A Fine Balance*. Nella has read numerous historical mystery stories, and can't put one down until she's reached the end.

About television, Blythe comments, "I don't watch television; occasionally I'll watch *The Simpsons* or the news, whatever's on." Nella, however, loves to get involved in her favorite television programs, which include *Smallville*, *Higher Ground* and *Ally McBeal*. She also reports enjoying learning things on the Discovery channel. Although broad surveys question students on the amount of time spent watching television, spent playing computer games or "surfing the net," many adolescents' individual lives are very different from the reported norm as their comments reflect. Although media access is widely available, many students do not have regular access to the Internet, and many do not have regular access to global television. Many have different interests. And as Fiske (1989), Hartley (1982), Buckingham (1998) and Sheldon (1998) suggest, adolescents "read" these alternate texts with a critical and discerning eye, often aware of the media manipulation they are subjected to.

It is here where the intersection between school literacies and life literacies can be very powerful, where students can read history from multiple perspectives, can use their fertile imaginations to create new ideas, and to challenge the aspects of society that support inequity and injustice. For example, Nella describes a social studies essay she recently had to write on any aspect of World War II. She chose the experience of women during that time, and located information sources from the

Internet about Russian, American, and Korean women's experiences during the war. Her interest in gender issues intersected with the social studies curriculum and enabled her to create a meaningful text for both herself and her teacher. Other adolescents create meaningful texts and literacy experiences for themselves. Luke comments, "In computer games, there's a story line and if you can get the storyline and enjoy the whole experience, that's like reading, you can comprehend what happened, the theme, the plot, the character interactions..." He continues, "In a sense, video games are like writing, especially the non-linear ones, where you can choose what happens, because you're writing the character's story with everything you do." Anna suggests that "being able to understand rules of a game, other people playing, being able to communicate with them" is a form of literacy. Harley's literacy of learning skateboarding connects to reading the moves other people make and imitating them, "You can see people do it but you don't know how it feels, but after you've done it you know how it feels so you can do it again." Although there are differences between the two, Blythe connects music and the printed word, "like a novel is equivalent to a symphony" and Nella connects literacy to visual texts – "You need to be very literate to understand a lot of television and movies, to really get the meaning from them, for example, even *The Simpsons* and all the references they make, or a movie like *Pearl Harbor,* or *Titanic.*" Morgan finds many literacy experiences on the computer, as she delights in locating information on the Internet for school projects and her own interests, e-mailing her friends, scanning pictures to e-mail to relatives, and composing print and visual texts.

Although for teachers, incorporating popular culture and technology into classroom activities and discussion can be treacherous ground, it can also be a relief to be able to give up the pretense of knowing everything about technology – they can then assume a different stance about knowledge in all subject areas they teach (Lankshear & Knobel, 1997). Morrison, Bryan & Chilcoat (2001), citing several sources, recommend the use of popular culture in all subject areas for three reasons: 1) popular culture is integral to the lives of most adolescents and can diminish the disparity children perceive between their lives in and out of school by legitimizing many of their after-school pursuits (Buckingham, 1998); 2) students learn to become critical consumers of media messages (Alvermann et al., 1999; Dyson, 1997); and 3) popular culture is popular, and students enjoy it (Wright & Sherman, 1999). Lemke (1995) observed that students who are computer users have developed perceptual strategies to deal with the hundreds and thousands of visual images they see in electronic games and information databases in ways that older individuals have not. And while books and printed matter will not go away, the ways of thinking about and with and through text are utterly changed by the new technologies (Purves, 1998). Technology is helping to change our very consciousness.

It is apparent that gaming "has an educative/educational significance both overtly and covertly. Covertly, learning the game, one is being apprenticed to rule-governed activities and to testing ideas about how to work within rule-governed settings" (Lankshear & Knobel, 1997, p. 150). The involvement with computers teaches young people that some forms of learning are fast-paced, compelling and rewarding, and that "gaming is an initiation into modes of practice that are characterized much more by learning, and self/collaborative direction and discovery than about wholesale exposure to teaching and instruction" (Lankshear & Knobel, 1997, p. 151). Teachers, they conclude, are going to have to adapt and become adept at technology.

The electronic text, suggests Lanham (1993) is both "creator-controlled and reader-controlled"(p. 4), therefore reading and writing undergo major transformation. However, no technologies except the blackboard, states Cohen (1987) have had any significant effect on school organization or practice – they have not made schools more modern, more efficient, or more congruent with the world outside! Papert (1993) and Hammett (see this volume) have offered constructive possibilities for how teachers can transform their classroom practices by integrating new technologies into their pedagogy in ways that engage the interests and prior experiences of students while not compromising their communicative competencies of the future. Educators must consider how the relationships between adolescents and technologies affect their learning, and how gender plays a part in the development of these relationships.

GENDERED PERSPECTIVES OF LITERACY

In this discussion of school literacies and out-of-school life literacies, it is important to provide a gendered overlay to the perspectives presented and to broaden the literacy landscape. In addition to the seven adolescents whose perceptions have informed a deeper under-standing of their literacies, adolescents in two middle schools I have recently visited have both shown and told me how gender shapes their views of literacy. They have provided depth and complexity to the stereotypical perceptions about the ways in which boys and girls engage in literacy practices, as the following classroom scenarios show.

There is no doubt that adolescents' gender plays a major role in identity formation as students and as future citizens. Media messages blast at adolescents telling them what to wear, who to like, how to look and what to think. School curricula present ideas still steeped in Eurocentric patriarchal ideology, glorifying the role of males in current and historical events while ignoring the role of women. Media messages such as "Test results show lag in boys' literacy" (*Guardian*, 2000) and "The trouble with boys" (*Guardian*, 2001) conspire, albeit unknowing-ly, to maintain a divisive focus on male and female adolescents regard-less of their true complex characteristics.

Although there are valid connections between students' literacy activities and their gendered orientation, the words of adolescents chal-lenge the simplistic stereotypes of boys' and girls' literacies. While the socialization of children and adolescents encourages them to take up different activities (boys are encouraged in science, math, technology and physical pursuits; girls are readers of fiction, writers, interested in fashion, relationships) there is considerable resistance to the common stereotypes by many adolescents. It is true that, upon cursory observa-tion, girls do read more novels, are more nurturing and concerned with social relationships, and boys do read more non-fiction, are more capa-ble of adapting situations and taking physical risks. Girls create and communicate their ideas using traditional print-based texts, while boys create with technology and digital media. Girls *seem* to be more inter-ested in reading texts such as fashion magazines, that connect to their social world, their friends and that give information about how to pres-ent themselves in their peer groups (Hollows, 2000). Boys, on the other hand, read popular texts such as magazines and newspapers for infor-mation, for example, sports scores, new skateboarding moves and com-puter cheats (Alloway & Gilbert, 1998). Boys appear to see school as important to their futures and careers, while girls use school to sustain present interests and social positions. As Sadker and Sadker (1986) point out, boys are trained to be assertive and girls are trained to be passive, mere spectators relegated to the sidelines of classroom discussion. When these same adolescents are asked about their activities and views, however, more complex pictures emerge (Smith & Wilhelm, 2002).

Many adolescent boys, as they report in interviews, are vocal about their dislike of literacy activities, "My mom would force me to read, but now she doesn't – I hate reading, so I won't read"; "I play sports – I've never read a book that I liked"; "A book, you have to imagine it and you have to read it and reading, I don't like it." Many girls report finding real enjoyment in reading novels, "I love to read animal stories," "It's really relaxing to get into a good book." However, by restricting our view of literacy to reading print text and restricting our view of gender to a binary conception, we would miss the broader understanding of literacy as seen in these scenarios:

I. Four or five boys at recess asked the teacher if they could stay in and play a computer game. They clustered around the computer on the teacher's desk, one boy took the controls and the others coached him, gave him suggestions, words of encouragement and praise. A couple of other boys joined them, and a couple more, and then three girls also joined, but were at the back of the cluster. The male teacher came and joined in and engaged in a conversation about the game with the boys while the girls watched silently.

    These male students are learning how to interact in an "affinity" group (Gee, 2002), to communicate effectively with each other, to take risks, and to think and react quickly and multi-dimensionally. They are becoming adept with various computer functions. The female students are learning other messages, how to learn vicariously, how to be supportive and also what literacies are not meant for them.

II. A grade six class of students was working on a scrapbook assignment where they had been asked to locate international, national or local news items, read them, summarize them and paste them in scrapbooks. There was a box of current newspapers located at the back of the classroom. Several of the boys had chosen to continue reading their books rather than spending this time completing their scrapbooks, and there was a cluster of several girls and a couple of boys at the newspapers. They selected sections, browsed through them, showed each other items, complained about how hard the activity was, cut out items that interested them, and some of the students read the items silently, reading out interesting bits as they came across them. Boys working on this task each took their own section of the newspaper to their desk and worked independently. Although the girls looked like they were not focused on their work, the teacher confirmed that it is the girls who complete the assignments on time while many of the boys who were working independently do not.

Students in this class are experiencing a range of literacy activities that connect school literacies with those of the broader world. They are learning to read a variety of texts in appropriate ways such as skimming, scanning and close reading. The girls are learning to use social communities to complete their work and to infuse enjoyment into their tasks, and to become school-successful.

III. A middle school teacher has decided that his students will focus on reading for the next three weeks, so he has allotted one and a half hours a day to reading books that the students have selected themselves. On this particular day, they have a fifteen-minute time to read, and the teacher has instructed them all to get their books and read. Most of the girls and a few of the boys complied, and began reading silently. One boy in particular did not. He first walked to the back of the class, browsed in the magazine box, came back to his desk empty-handed, then went to the sink at the front, got paper towels and proceeded to clean off his desktop. He finished this task, then sat at his desk and shuffled papers on and in his desk for a few more minutes. After about ten minutes, he finally picked up his novel and began to read. Soon after the teacher told them that it was time to move on to the next activity, but that they might continue reading if they wished. This particular student, and four other boys who took a while settling down, chose to read and continued reading throughout the next thirty minutes with absolute concentration.

The teacher in this case has provided opportunities for all of his students to be successful and to develop an interest in sustained reading rather than pre-judging and penalizing students who need time to prepare for literacy activities.

In each case, our traditional conceptions of literacy are broadened and our stereotypical gendered views are challenged.

WHAT'S TO BE DONE?:
CLASSROOM SUGGESTIONS

Through discussions that educators facilitate in classes, activities requiring critical reading and analysis of multiple texts, and opportunities for students to create "texts" using a diversity of literacies, students will be enabled to become more aware of their own literacy potential and apply it much more broadly than to the English Language Arts classroom. As shown in the previous scenarios, many teachers are attempting to tackle the complex literacies of a new century and incorporate these into their teaching practices. It is through the "life" literacies so familiar to adolescents that a critical element can be infused into school-based activities. Teachers need to learn to look differently at their school-based practices and be encouraged to consider adolescents' prior literacy knowledge.

The use of critical literacy, defined by Young (2001) as "an awareness that the language of texts and the reader's responses to it are not neutral, but are shaped by social contexts and our experiences as people of particular races, ethnicities, genders, and social classes" (p. 5) can assist adolescent readers and their teachers to become more aware of textual constructions. They can be helped to become more aware of how texts portray gender identities and inequities in stereotypical ways (Gilbert, 1997) and through their growing awareness can discover alternative literate positions for themselves. Many (2000) suggests that it is becoming more and more imperative in the world of Internet that "students assume a stance that includes an interrogation of the author, the author's background, perspectives, and expertise. They must be able to understand how an author's knowledge, personal agenda, and subjectivity may have shaped the information they are reading" (p. 66). We can help students to feel more literate and to make more explicit connections between their personal literacies and formal literacies of school. Using a critical approach to pedagogy, Lankshear & Knobel (1997) remind us of important features associated with critical practices. First, critical practices involve the components of analysis and evaluation, and second, "critical pedagogy and critical literacy engage students and teachers collaboratively in making explicit the socially constructed character of knowledge, language, and literacy" (p. 155).

SUBJECT-AREA LITERACIES

Examples of critical literacy activities, offering opportunities for analysis and evaluation and incorporating personal interest, enjoyment, challenge and purpose in meaningful and active ways, can be found in many classrooms. For example, Nella's social studies teacher invited a representative of "fair trade" to address issues with the students regarding a socialist perspective of globalization. Harley's social studies teacher attempted to incorporate discussions regarding "current events" in his class, even though Harley found these "sometimes useful, sometimes not." Teachers need to make the purposefulness of such activities consistently explicit to their students.

Alvermann & Heron (2001) suggest that "the corporate interests of multinational firms appears to offer teachers the perfect opportunity for incorporating students' interests in popular culture while simultaneously developing their critical awareness of mass marketing strategies – a sure-fire way to produce critical readers" (p. 121). Robb (2002) suggests the use of multiple diverse texts in a single unit of study to introduce students to multiple perspectives on specific topics, similar to the approach Blythe described being used by her social studies teacher using three different textbooks and examining how each of these presents information differently.

Inquiry projects such as the one described by Linn, Slotta and Baumgartner (2000) integrate Internet-accessed information with school curriculum. Using computers in their classrooms with Internet access, students and teachers logged into the local University computer, manipulated experimental conditions and viewed the resulting images of a chicken embryo in real time. This project enabled students to engage in scientific practices and to construct their own scientific knowledge through investigation and analysis rather than through memorization.

In addition to developing critical literacy skills, adopting an inquiry stance to texts, that is, gathering information, analyzing and organizing it in order to develop an in-depth understanding of issues, enables adolescents to engage in texts in personally meaningful ways. A wide range of texts, including fiction, non-fiction, poetry, instruction manuals, Internet sites, and chatters, can be selected that enable room for choice in everyday reading. These texts should be selected to represent society in a wide range of stereotypical and non-stereotypical ways (Young & Brozo, 2001). Teaching strategies that incorporate social interactions, opportunities for success, and personal meaning making need to be made part of classroom life.

CRITICAL PRINT-BASED LITERACIES

Other critical literacy activities include the following: 1) comparing the nouns and verbs used in two sports articles, one about a female and one about a male (Young, 2001); 2) discussing the relationship between textual representations on television, in song lyrics, in advertising, and the students' personal experiences; 3) addressing stereotypes perpetuated through the everyday language of students, e.g., "chick," "nerd" and ask students to consider the stereotypical meanings held by such terms; 4) present students with texts that are written in the first person and ask them to assign a character to the "speaker" in each instance, then compare with other members of the class, and discuss what this might indicate about their assumptions (Martino & Mellor, 2000). Chapter two of Lankshear's *Changing Literacies* (1997) provides additional examples of critical literacy experiences that can be incorporated into classroom practice, based on current newspaper texts juxtaposed with diverse alternative texts. Such an approach enables teachers to bridge traditional subject-area divisions, coordinate resources and model an integrated approach to teaching and learning.

VISUAL LITERACIES

A further example of integrating popular media, technology and critical literacy involves cartooning. Students are interested and familiar with the format and able to draw from many life literacy examples in comic books and various forms of cartoons. They can integrate their own personal interests and aptitudes with new learning about multiple perspectives, visual representations of motion and emotion, and print text to support visual text. A middle school class I recently visited in mid-June, nearing the end of the year, was engaged in creating a variety of comics for their final class project. This class, a generally challenging group of predominantly boys, remained focused on their projects throughout the final week of school, attending to the details of form and content of their developing cartoons. Their drawings were meticulous, thoughtfully developed, and completed. Both boys and girls were engaged in this literacy event, and while there were differences noted between boys' selected subjects ("The Sneezing Disaster," "Snowboarding," "Adventures of Square Head" being some of the boys' titles, while girls' titles included "Anna's Birthday," "A Summer Splash" and "Pool Party") all students were equally interested. As Morrison et al. (2001) comment, "given the opportunity to share and create their own comic books, students engage in greater literacy exploration than they otherwise would, due to comics' popular and easily accessible format" (p. 113).

CONCLUSION

As the world becomes increasingly complex and interconnected, educators and schools are challenged more insistently by diverse interest groups, including adolescents themselves, to provide experiences that engage their attention in the present as well as to prepare them for possible futures. Such engagement should provide meaningful experiences as determined by the learner as well as the educator, and change the way literacy is understood and taught in classrooms. By considering the value of "playing" to learn (Gee, 2002) teachers may come to "appreciate the attraction popular media texts hold for youth, and in doing so they may discover ways to foster academic endeavors that invite the types of literacy practices adolescents find most worthwhile" (Alvermann & Heron, 2001, p. 122). It is the ways of making meaning rather than the specific texts used that need to be highlighted. Using popular texts as a connection between present and past cultures is a powerful starting point for classroom teachers. "Teachers who draw on popular culture references," suggests Nella, "make things more interesting and connected – like my social studies teachers sometimes refers to *The Simpsons*, it helps makes things stick, it helps me learn and reminds me of what happened during the day." Cunningham (2000) suggests that "nothing exemplifies the difference between reading and writing as school-based activities and literacy as a society-based practice" more than the growing use of technologies such as the Internet and popular media. It is this difference that needs to be bridged if schooling is to have the powerful impact on adolescents that is critical in this globalized and networked world.

Lankshear & Knobel (1997) identify four related goals for class-room learning: 1) enabling learners to make explicit the relationship between "word" and "world"; 2) providing adolescents with opportunities to "explore the extent to which social practices, ways of doing and being, and forms of knowledge are historical, contingent, and transformable rather than natural, fixed, and immutable" (p. 156); 3) providing opportunities for exploring the social implications of discursive practices and values existing as they are; and 4) providing adolescents with experiences that enhance their awareness of possibilities for the vast range of actual and possible ways of doing and being. If these goals are to be achieved, educators need to be more clearly attuned to the world outside of school and acknowledge the degree of literacy sophistication adolescents bring to the classroom. The traditional spaces that have separated subject specialties need to be melded and the role of subject specialists needs to be reconsidered in light of new literacies that allow simultaneous processing of word, image and sound (Lankshear & Knobel, 1997).

The contemporary challenge faced by educators in relation to literacies needs to be considered in light of new reconfigurations of discourse made possible by alternate texts, particularly at the intersections between informal modes of communication and more traditional academic forms (Shannon, 1995). As Luke recognizes, "It's important to talk with friends, to voice our opinions on things, talk about what happened in the day. We learn from world experience and the news and from history." Luke and the other adolescents quoted in this paper are looking for challenges, for understanding, for insights into the world they are entering. School literacy practices need to encompass the world, to help adolescents with their personal and social development, to find a place in the world. Teachers offering literacy experiences need to encourage the need for respect and for the development of reflective and critically informed approaches to the world. Developing the potential of students, demonstrated through their knowledge of technological literacies and the world, will bring classroom learning into closer contact with the developments and forces operating in the world beyond the school walls, and may achieve the goal of educating informed creative and critical thinkers.

REFERENCES

Alloway, N. & Gilbert, P. (1998). Videogame culture: Playing with masculinity, violence and pleasure. In Howard, S. (Ed.). *Wired-up: Young people and the electronic media* (pp. 95-114). London: UCL Press.

Alvermann, D. & Heron, A. (2001). Literacy identity work: Playing to learn with popular media. *Journal of Adolescent and Adult Literacy, 45*(2), 118-122.

Alvermann, D., Moon, J. & Hagood, M. (1999). *Popular culture in the classroom: Teaching and researching critical media literacy.* Newark, DE: International Reading Association.

Alvermann, D., Hinchman, K., Moore, D., Phelps, S. & Waff, D. (Eds.). (1998). *Reconceptualizing the literacies in adolescents' lives.* London: Lawrence Erlbaum.

Bigum, C. & Green, B. (1992). Technologizing literacy: The dark side of the dream. *Discourse: the Australian Journal of Educational Studies, 12*(2), 4 - 28.

Buckingham, D. (1998). *Teaching popular culture: Beyond radical pedagogy.* London: UCL Press.

Cohen, D. (1987). Educational technology, policy and practice. *Educational Evaluation and Policy Analysis, 9*(Summer), 153-170.

Cunningham, J. (2000). How will literacy be defined in the new millennium? *Reading Research Quarterly, 35*(1), 64-71.

Dyson, A. (1997). *Writing super heroes: Contemporary childhood, popular culture, and classroom literacy.* New York: Teachers College Press.

Fiske, J. (1989). *Understanding Popular Culture.* London: Unwin Hyman.

Freire, P. (1972). *Pedagogy of the oppressed.* Harmondsworth: Penguin.

Gee, J. (2002). Millennials and bobos: Blue's clues and Sesame Street: A story for our times. In D. Alvermann (Ed.). *Adolescents and literacies in a digital world* (pp. 51-67). New York: Peter Lang.

Gilbert, P. (1989). *Writing, schooling and deconstruction: From voice to text in the classroom.* London: Routledge.

Hartley, J. (1982). *Understanding news.* London: Methuen.

Hinchman, K. (1998). Reconstructing our understandings of adolescents' participation in classroom literacy events: learning to look through other eyes. In D. Alvermann, K. Hinchman, D. Moore, S. Phelps, & D. Waff (Eds.). *Reconceptualizing the literacies in adolescents' lives* (pp. 173-192). London: Lawrence Erlbaum.

Hollows, J. (2000). *Feminism, femininity and popular culture.* Manchester: Manchester University Press.

Howe, N. & Strauss, B. (1993). *13th Gen: Abort, retry, ignore, fail?* New York: Vintage Books.

Kenway, J. & Bullen. E. (2001). *Consuming children.* Buckingham: Open University Press.

Knobel, M. (1999). *Everyday literacies.* New York: Peter Lang.

Lanham, R. (1993). *The electronic word: Democracy, technology and the arts.* Chicago: University of Chicago Press.

Lankshear, C. (1997). *Changing literacies.* Buckingham: Open University Press.

Lankshear, C. & Knobel, M. (1997). Literacies, texts and difference in the electronic age. In C. Lankshear (Ed.), *Changing literacies* (pp. 133-159). Buckingham: Open University Press.

Lemke, J. (1995). Local knowledge and the computer. Presentation made at the University of British Columbia, July 1995.

Linn, M., Slotta, J. & Baumgartner, E. (2000). *Teaching high school science in the information age: A review of courses and technology for inquiry-based learning.* Santa Monica, CA: Milken Family Foundation. [Online]. Available: http://www.mff.org.

Many, J. (2000). How will literacy be defined in the new millennium? *Reading Research Quarterly, 35*(1), p. 64-71.

Manguel, A. (1996). *A history of reading.* Toronto: Alfred A. Knopf Canada.

Martino, W. & Mellor, B. (2000). *Gendered fictions.* Urbana, Illinois: NCTE.

McLaren, P. (1989). *Life in schools: An introduction to critical pedagogy in the foundations of education.* New York: Longman.

Morrison, T., Bryan, G., Chilcoat, G. (2001). Using student-generated comic books in the classroom. *Journal of Adolescent and Adult Literacy, 45*(8), 758-767.

O'Brien, D., Moje, E. & Stewart, R. (2001). Exploring the context of secondary literacy: Literacy in people's everyday school lives. In E. Moje & D. O'Brien (Eds.) *Constructions of Literacy* (pp. 27-48). London: Lawrence Erlbaum.

O'Brien, D. (1998). Multiple literacies in a high-school program for "at-risk" adolescents. In Alvermann, D., Hinchman, K., Moore, D., Phelps, S. & Waff, D. (Eds.). *Reconceptualizing the literacies in adoles-*

cents' lives (pp. 27-49). Mahwah, N.J.: Lawrence Erlbaum Associates Inc.

Orwell, G. (1949). *1984.* New York: New American Library.

Papert, S. (1993). *The children's machine: Rethinking school in the age of the computer.* New York: Basic Books.

Pereleman, L. (1992). *School's out: The new technology and the end of education.* New York: Morrow.

Phelps, S. (1998). Adolescents and their Multiple Literacies. In D. Alvermann, K. Hinchman, D. Moore, S. Phelps & D. Waff, (Eds.) (1998). *Reconceptualizing the literacies in adolescents' lives* (pp. 1-2). London: Lawrence Erlbaum.

Purves, A. (1998). Flies in the web of hypertext. In Reinking, D., McKenna, M., Labbo, L., & Kieffer, R. (Eds.). *Handbook of literacy and technology: Transformations in a post-typographic world* (pp. 235-252). Mahwah, N.J.: Lawrence Erlbaum Associates Publishers.

Robb, L. (2002). Multiple text: Multiple opportunities for teaching and learning. *Voices from the Middle, 9*(4), 28-32.

Sadker, M. & Sadker, D. (1986). Sexism in the classroom: From grade school to graduate school. *Phi Delta Kappan, 67*(7), 512-515.

Shannon, P. (1995). *Text, lies and videotape: Stories about life, literacy and learning.* Portsmouth, NH: Heinemann.

Sheldon, L. (1998). The middle years: Children and television — cool or just plain boring? In S. Howard (Ed.). *Wired-up: Young people and the electronic media* (pp. 77-94). London: UCL Press.

Smith, M. & Wilhelm, J. (2002). *Reading don't fix no Chevys: Literacy in the lives of young men.* Portsmouth, NH: Heinemann.

Street, B. (Ed.). (1993). *Cross-cultural approaches to literacy.* Cambridge: Cambridge University Press.

Street, B. (1984). *Literacy in theory and practice.* Cambridge: Cambridge University Press.

Tannock, S. (2001). The literacies of youth workers and youth workplaces. *Journal of Adolescent & Adult Literacy, 45*(2), 140-143.

Teasley, A. & Wilder, A. (1997). *Reel conversations: Reading films with young adults.* Portsmouth, NH: Heinemann.

Test results show lag in boys' literacy. *Guardian,* September 20, 2000.

Thakkar, U., Bruce, B., Hogan, M. & Williamson, J. (2001). Extending literacy through participation in new technologies. *Journal of Adolescent & Adult Literacy, 45*(3), 212-218.

Trouble with boys. *Guardian*, August 21, 2000.

Walker, C., & Foote, M. (1999/2000). Emergent Inquiry: Using Children's Literature to ask hard questions about gender bias. *Childhood Education*, Winter, 88-91

Wells, G. (1989). Language in the classroom: Literacy and collaborative talk. *Language and Education, 3*(4), 251-273.

Witkin, M. (1994). A defence of using pop media in the middle-school classroom. *English Journal*, January, 30-33.

Wright, G. & Sherman, R. (1999). Let's create a comic strip. *Reading Improvement, 36*, 66-72.

Young, J.P. (2001). Displaying practices of masculinity: Critical literacy and social contexts. *Journal of Adolescent & Adult Literacy, 45*(1), 4-15.

Young, J.P., & Brozo, W. (2001), Conversations: Boys will be boys, or will they? Literacy and masculinities. *Reading Research Quarterly, 36*(3), 316-325.

Writers in a Multiliteracy Classroom

A Telecollaborative Novel Project

Jill Kedersha McClay
and Peter B. Weeks

As Billie looked down at her small gold locket, she wished she could tell her mom everything about the past day that had led up to her running away.

I can't believe I'm doing this, Billie thought as she absentmindedly kicked a shattered beer bottle, and as she did her mind drifted back to the night before. (2000, Chapter One, telecollaborative novel, www.clearview.ab.ca)

We tried to have a timeline, like let's try...and have this amount done by the end of next week. The timeline was in pencil. (Randy[1])

I feel that all the arguments and all the fighting and all the hard work and stress we had to put into it, did come out in the end. It was well worth it. (Kristy)

These quotes, from students who initiated, framed and wrote the beginning and end chapters for a telecollaborative novel writing project, intrigued us as we set out to learn about their learning. Gunther Kress (1997) exhorts educators "to explore and implement the consequences of a fully multiliterate environment" (p.150), a call that suggests to us that such a complex and essential contemporary task belongs equally to researchers and teachers. When researchers and teachers work together to understand their students' learning, our work is mutually informing and well grounded in both theory and practice. Kist (2002) is one of many voices calling for descriptions of "new literacy" classrooms. Though we prefer the term "multiliteracies" to "new," we take his point that such descriptions are essential to present and consider. In this chapter, we will describe an online novel-writing project that illustrates one "multi-literacy classroom" and explore implications for collaborative and telecollaborative writing with teenage writers.

The project was the teacher's conscious effort to make sense of the interrelationship between technology, writing and teaching, as he sought to test his own limits and possibly those of his students in using technology to collaborate in writing fiction. Peter was the teacher of the class, and Jill was the researcher drawn to the project by her work with young writers working in new forms and technologies for writing. Here we will weave our perspectives together in the third person for clarity, but will label individual differences and perspectives when warranted. The students' perspectives and commentary stem from Jill's interviews (group and individual) with seven volunteer members of the class after the initial project was completed, while they waited for other classes to contribute to the collaboration.

The project included collaborative writing in several respects: first, the students within Peter's class collaborated to create the novel's plot and storyline and to write the initial chapters. They wrote in small groups and then as a class made decisions and revisions. This writing was hyperlinked and mounted on the school's web page, along with an open invitation for classes in schools throughout the province of Alberta to write a chapter of the novel themselves. The invitation was later taken up by two other classes, thus making an additional tier of telecollaborative writing.

PETER'S TEACHING CONTEXT AND OVERVIEW OF THE PROJECT

Peter teaches in Stettler, Alberta, in a high school of approximately 640 students; the school has invested substantially in technology, and its administration has been supportive of teachers' efforts to integrate technology. Peter is more technologically savvy than many English language arts teachers, who are often stereotyped (unfairly, we hope) as technological foot-draggers, and he took advantage of professional development opportunities supported by both Alberta Learning and the corporate sponsor, Telus, which had created a popular site for educators <www.2Learn.ca>. In conjunction with these and with his work in piloting the new English Language Arts program of studies, he worked to integrate technology into his English LA classes. As he continued to integrate technology, he focused on the questions, "Why use Internet technology in the student writing process?" and "What implications does the Internet have for the possibilities of collaborative writing?"

Peter's class read W.O. Mitchell's *Who Has Seen the Wind?* and he wanted to extend the reading by encouraging the class to explore their sense of place. Since high school students seldom write longer works of fiction in class, Peter proposed that his class, writing collaboratively, would create a narrative that would start in their community and then, through the agency of the characters, be able to travel on to other classes and communities. Peter's class would establish a plot, setting and characters and then post the chapter on their school division website. Using the Telus 2Learn Project Centre, other classes would then be able to join in to write successive chapters. The story would have a plot structure that would allow the narrative to return to its starting place, Stettler, for its conclusion.

His first step was to hold a full class discussion to negotiate the genre, parameters and basic facts about the novel. The students worked hard to build a consensus, and the act of coming to terms with what they actually wanted to write was in itself a positive experience, he felt, as it highlighted some of the opportunities and challenges of writing extended narratives. They agreed to have two main characters, one male and one female, one from town and one from a farm outside town. They brainstormed a plot outline that featured the two teenagers, each running away for a different reason, thrown together through circumstance. In the process, students instinctively leaned toward story elements that would offer juxtaposition. They wanted to create a plot that would be flexible enough for other classes in other schools to take and make their own, yet would allow characters a motivation for the travel and eventual return to the original setting.

Once the basic features were decided upon, the class was split into groups with specific writing responsibilities: Plot, Setting, the Male Character, the Female Character, Dialogue, and finally a Re-write group, who would act as a liaison between groups at first and then eventually coordinate the final draft of the chapter. Most of the drafts flowed from group to group both through email and face-to-face communication. Each group had previously worked together on a research project, so students were comfortable with group members and accustomed to collaborating to produce a product. The original research groups had been student-defined, although Peter allocated specific responsibilities to each group, a decision based on his perception of each group's abili-

ties and observed strengths and weaknesses. The Re-write group was
made up of the strongest writers in the class.

The groups worked diligently. Often, heated discussions would
emerge, as differing artistic visions came to bear on the problems
encountered in the writing process. Each group worked on its area of
responsibility, with the re-writers scampering from group to group. It
was a very dynamic process that eventually spilled out over two classrooms, two computer rooms, and occasionally the hallway. They peri-
odically paused to share their work, both for Peter to check progress and
to ensure that the entire class was aware of the progress.

After a week of work in this manner, the class came to a logjam due
to the nature of the collaborative process. The challenge was to put the
parts together. Although each group was producing a quantity of writing, too much time was needed to liaise among the groups. Each needed revision had to be passed on to every group to allow for continuity,
and this delay slowed the writing process too much. It was clear to both
the students and Peter that these problems had to be solved. The students themselves came up with a solution. They jigsawed their original
groups, making up three new writing "teams," each composed of members from the separate writing groups (Plot, Setting, etc.). Each of these
three teams then wrote a version of the full chapter, building from the
earlier drafts. At this point, the students and Peter were all aware that
they were working against some fairly tight deadlines, as the semester's
end loomed very near.

Once the three separate versions were created, all three were read
aloud to the whole class and the students discussed the strengths and
weaknesses of each draft. The Re-write committee, working in congress
with the whole class, wrote the final version, which was posted on the
division website. The Plot group, who had taken a great deal of ownership for the project, went back to the inkwell and wrote the final page
of the novel, which the class felt would be needed by anyone else who
might wish to author a chapter. An invitation was posted on the website to offer access to the original writers through email to any other
group who wished to join in; the writers were willing to act as editors,
proofreaders or consultants as needed.

The website *www.clearview.ab.ca/novel* had external links to the
school district and the Telus2Learn sites, as well as internal links that
Peter established with Matt, the student who took on many technology

responsibilities. The internal links included photos of the class, explanations of the writing assignment and process, Chapter One, a Chapter One plot overview, character sketches, information about the writing groups and email contacts for them, an invitation to join in the collaborative writing, and the text of the final page of the novel. The site invited viewers to meet the authors and get a sense of what each group added to the process. Internal links to character sketches and other student writing, as well as external links to the school, the school division and Telus 2Learn all served to provide a context of the collaboration and celebrate the process. As the second chapter was created, a linked page was added to the site. Since the time of the initial collaboration, student names and access have been modified on the website to meet Internet security concerns and Freedom of Information regulations.

There was initially considerable interest in the project when the site was posted, and the 2Learn site also promoted the project. Peter fielded inquiries from teachers, but, unfortunately, few teachers felt they could afford the class time that writing a further chapter might require. However, teacher Rhoda Trehearne in Lethbridge, Alberta, did take up the challenge with her grade nine class; they wrote Chapter Two, which was subsequently posted.

STUDENT PERSPECTIVES

Jill's interviews with seven student volunteers (four boys, three girls) from the class confirmed many of Peter's perceptions about how the class viewed the project, and also introduced several other aspects of their thinking for our consideration. The interviews were conducted after the class writing was complete but before the chapter arrived from the Lethbridge students. Their sense of ownership of this collaborative novel was raucously and palpably evident during these interviews.

As the students self-reported, they spanned a broad spectrum of interests as readers and writers, with all seven students acknowledging an interest in reading. Two of the girls were enthusiastic writers. (One of these students later went on to win an award in a provincial writing contest.) Three other students reported sporadic interest in writing. Two boys said that they do not like to write. Only Kristy reported having some previous experience of collaborative writing:

I believe some, when I was younger. We'd just write a little sentence in the story and then pass it on in the class. And we would do that type of thing as a class project, but nothing provincial, like this. (Kristy)

WRITING PROCESS

The students discussed the process and structure of the collaborative writing with appreciation for the organizational challenge of having 27 students collaborate on one coherent narrative. Matt had moved into town in the midst of this project, so he had not read the novel that preceded the writing. As he was technologically skilled, Peter had assigned him to contribute more toward the creation of the web page than to the actual writing. They recognized that Peter had set the process in motion but allowed them choices. Ken explained, "He had a few ideas and then he had us vote on it, and we liked that one the best."

The class agreed that the narrative would be a road novel and set out to provide motivation for the characters. They agreed that a male and female character, Vince and Billie (the girl), who were not friends, would run away from their homes and join together as they drove Vince's truck from town to town. As the two made their way through towns in Alberta, they would learn something in each town. They hoped that students from other towns would write the appropriate chapters for their towns. Kristy's explanation for this intention reveals something of her understanding of narrative coherence as well:

And what we want other schools to do is to say, OK, we are here and get them [Vince and Billie] to do what they need to do in that town to get a learning experience of some sort, and then that school has to send them to the next school....And that's not to say that they came here to drink a pop and then left. I believe that they should learn something because [otherwise] what's the point then? You are just running away to get away from home. But it would probably be an idea if you are going to come back home you should have learned something. (Kristy)

Ultimately, in addition to their first chapter of the proposed novel, the class also wrote and posted a Chapter One plot summary, character sketches, and the last page of the novel, as a way of ensuring that the narrative would not be completely derailed from their intentions. Their "plot overview" link for Chapter One establishes the plot and characters:

PLOT SUMMARY
CHAPTER ONE

The chapter starts off with Billie walking down a road outside Stettler. She's thinking about the problems she has been having with her father and the party that she had attended the night before. The other main character, Vince, is driving down the same road in his truck, thinking back to the problems he has with his parents and to the party he had thrown at his home the night before (coincidentally the same one Billie had attended that same night).

Vince stops to pick up a hitchhiker and realizes that it is Billie. Prior to this occasion, the two characters have lived in different worlds and have not liked each other at all. The two of them start discussing the problems they have with their parents and their experience of the party the night before. They realize that they have many similarities and yet are almost totally different. The chapter ends with Vince and Billie driving down the road to their destination...

Want to meet the Plot writing group?

Want to read Chapter One?

How does the novel end?

BACK TO HOMEPAGE

Commenting on the original organization for writing, in which each group of four or five students tried to focus on a specific element (Plot, Dialogue, Character, etc.) and then weave it all together, these students all reported their frustration, acknowledging that they argued a lot and did not progress well. As Liam said, "We tried to write as a class, but that got us about two sentences a day." Randy added, "We just weren't getting anywhere because we had to run across the room to check with different groups to make sure that it would all fit together, and it was taking so much time."

The conflicts were fundamental and encompassed large-scale and small-scale decisions simultaneously. For example, the Character, Plot, and Dialogue groups all had a stake in the development of the two main characters, Billie and Vince. As the groups vied with competing ideas for what these characters did and said, they were in fact trying to negotiate the large-scale question of the establishment and development of the characters. But the argument sometimes played out on the picayune level, as Kristy reported the Dialogue group argued about the character of Vince:

> *What kind of attitude and what type of tone and the words they were saying and the way they were putting it, and the way they were emphasizing certain words. Well, like, Vince saying "Well, THIS isn't going to freakin' work" or "Well, this ISN'T going to freaking' work." Different ways they said it. (Kristy)*

Along the way, the class rejected some organizational ideas as non-starters. At one point, there were four male and four female students working out the two main characters. A potential teen disaster was averted when the students recognized an unworkable situation:

> *Laura: We thought about having the males do the female character and the females do the male character, but we just decided not to.*
>
> *Loretta (laughing): It was kinda sexist.*

They settled on having the males write Vince's character and the females write Billie's, but Kristy noted that in so doing, they lost the possibility of the other gender's perspective. She had mixed feelings: "I think they [the characters] lost something but also gained something. It may not have the full view but it also has the deep meaning."

The students recognized the need for Peter's intervention to re-organize and felt that this enabled them to move forward. The re-organization into three larger "writing teams" made the process more constructive:

> *Mr. Weeks just broke us down into three writing teams and he would take one or two members from each of the element groups and put us all together and then that way we could all collaborate within one group. And do some writing instead of running across the room and having to double-check everything with the other groups. So at the end of it, we had three chapters and then we just combined them all. (Randy)*

The jig-sawed groups broke the logjam and made progress with the narrative. Then the three groups sought feedback for their writing so that the three narratives could be pared to one:

We read them in front of the class to see what they thought and kind of did a discussion thing of which parts we liked the best and which parts we didn't like, and then the final group took those and actually wrote the stuff and would come back and read it to us. Did we like it? Didn't we? Feedback. (Loretta)

While most of the students saw this negotiation as necessary and productive, Kristy's frustration was more pronounced. She likened the negotiations to "being a lawyer-type thing" with too many negotiators. She acknowledged that her own tendencies were to be individualistic and perfectionist, adding, "…if it doesn't go my way then I perceive that it is not right, but I really think that the way the story has turned out is quite good. After all the work that everyone has done in class."

All seven students voiced satisfaction with the final writing that the class produced, though they also acknowledged the difficulty of collaborative writing. Laura noted, "It is sometimes easier when you do it by yourself, but I think it often turns out better when you do it with a bunch of people." Randy stated the dilemma: "Yeah, because with the group you get more ideas to write and then there are a lot of conflicts of what to write." They felt that the best ideas generally won out in the end, and they noted that some people were fairly forceful about putting ideas forward. There was much teasing about Loretta and Kristy, who were known as strong forces with definite ideas of their own. Loretta had a bout of laryngitis at a key point in the collaboration, which the others made a point of noting with great appreciation. She took the teasing in stride.

Several students commented that there were leaders in their particular groups. Laura explained:

In my little writing group, I think it was [student] who actually wrote it and everyone else was watching over her shoulder. If she wrote something wrong, they would correct her. Like fill in the blank. (Laura)

Liam described his group's leader of the writing as the wordsmith:

We were giving her the ideas, and she would just write it down…She'd come up with the actual words, we weren't actually dictating to her, we would just give her the ideas and she would write it out. (Liam)

They saw the confusion and false starts as necessary to the process. At one point in a group interview when two students were exclaiming about wasted time in the groups, a third cut in, "Give us some slack!" They pointed out that it would have worked better if they had known where they were going from the start, but they all readily acknowledged that this would have been impossible. They joked about incentives (e.g., free pop) for writing on schedule.

SENSE OF NARRATIVE CONVENTIONS
AND AUDIENCES

The students reported their intense focus on the logic and coherence of the narrative. From the initial groups, they realized the need for consistency, so that Billie and Vince behaved and spoke "in character," and so that the settings were appropriate and realistic. They revised constantly to maintain consistency and coherence, to extremes at times: "We had like an hour discussion about, like, Taco Bell wrappers. But there is no Taco Bell in [our town], so we did A&W." (Liam). They made hard decisions to reject interesting ideas that were not consistent with their characters' established personalities. Kristy reported several rejected ideas that she had liked but knew were not suitable:

One idea was that Vince was going to get really drunk and he did, like he threw up on a brand new leather sofa, and Billie was going to stay sober and take him out for a coffee the next morning…But that wouldn't have worked because they are repelling characters and they are totally different, and they don't have the same friends, nothing. Those were some ideas that were really good but wouldn't have worked. No matter how hard we really tried to make it. (Kristy)

The issue of appropriate language and content presented a dilemma for the writers and for Peter. As the students put it, if it is a teen novel, it ought to have swearing and alcohol. But, they reported, Peter reminded them that if they included profanity, there was a possibility that a religiously affiliated school board would not allow its students to write a chapter. The dilemma, they understood, was between realism and adult sensibilities about appropriate language:

Laura: We had to discuss what kind of content to put in. Language. If we used slang dialogue, would we get a Christian school to write with us?

Matt: Like some of that stuff you can't avoid, if you want to make a realistic teenage novel, then you can't do it without…alcohol and all that kind of stuff.

Ken: I think we had a lot of slang that was almost swears.

They compromised in ways that stretched their creativity. Pointing out a passage, Randy explained, "See here, instead of saying they were drinking, it's 'The stench of alcohol and smoke overwhelmed me.' So it's hinting to it but not actually stepping on it." They felt that Peter had bent the rules a bit to allow them to be somewhat realistic in the dialogue. Loretta pointed out an irony: "But the other thing that really bothered me was that there's actually swearing in W.O. Mitchell's *Who Has Seen the Wind?* but we couldn't use it." Ken noted a further irony that even the adult language had been somewhat sanitized, pointing to the passage, "'Holy, what a mess. What happened here?' Molly exclaimed, not half as angry as I expected." He added, "I mean, come on, you guys,…that's not exactly what my parents would say!" They acknowledged that teens would most likely read such language as code, knowing that parents and teens alike would use stronger language in real life.

The students were all aware of the Telus sponsorship of this project, and at least one of these young writers was remarkably sensitive to the question of corporate sponsorship in education. When Kristy talked about potential contributors to this novel, which was deliberately set in Alberta, she sensed that narrative coherence might not be the only limiting factor:

And if someone from Saskatchewan asked us [for permission to add a chapter], I am not sure if we would, because we got the funding to do it for Alberta, and it's…I'm pretty sure Telus is Alberta-based, and I am not sure if they would object or agree to allow it outside Alberta. And we've just originally always thought that it was going to be in Alberta. (Kristy)

VISUAL ELEMENTS

The website included pictures of the students who collaborated in the writing but none within the text of the novel itself. The students considered the possibility of including drawings within the context of the novel itself, but vetoed that idea.

Do we want to have drawings with this? and then we kinda crossed it out because it was going to be difficult. Um...when I am reading a book I don't generally like pictures in it because I like to let my imagination run but with other people who like the pictures, to know exactly what you are talking about. I think that it might be good to have a few pictures here and there. Say, this is Billie's house and this is Vince's house. And like, their truck driving down the highway. Just a few pictures, not many, just enough to give the idea of what it is like... Possibly drawings because then...you can detail it more and it is more personal, I guess. Like I have always preferred drawings over photographs because of the feeling, the heart that people put into it that they take the time to sit down for a few minutes to write it instead of taking two seconds with the click of a button. (Kristy)

The other students concurred. Laura noted, "Drawings still leave a little to the imagination, I think." They felt that if there were to be any photographs, these would best be of the settings and perhaps key moments or items from the novel, such as the truck, Billie's locket, the A&W, or Billie walking down the road.

They were also aware of the possibility that the inclusion of photographs and audio could make the website more difficult for some schools to access if the school's computer facilities were not up to date.

TELECOLLABORATION AND OWNERSHIP
BEYOND THE CLASS

The students were keen to have other classes join in. A class in St. Albert had indicated interest, and they also anticipated a chapter coming from Lethbridge:

Liam: Lethbridge was ready to do it right away so instead of making Lethbridge wait, we went and changed everything so they are going to Lethbridge instead of St. Albert. So we had to change the highway.

Matt: And a few towns, and it wasn't that hard. It really only took about 10 minutes. Me and [Randy] actually did the additions on the web page.

The students saw the project continuing at least into the next academic year (the interviews occurred in May, when the semester's end was in sight), quite possibly beyond their grade 12 graduation, and were willing to commit to continue working on it, hoping that the characters could eventually travel through many Alberta towns. They were eager to see what other groups would do with their initial brainchild, but they were nervous about whether the writing from other classes could measure up to their expectations. As Kristy said of the anticipated Lethbridge chapter:

I am sure that they will do good. I have high expectations and they may not meet those, but I will still be proud of whatever they have. Unless they totally change it, and then I am saying, "Sorry. Bye-bye."

The others were equally determined to keep control of the "collaboration" as it spread to students in other towns. They noted:

Ken: Basically they [the Lethbridge students] are writing what they think is good, and then they are going to send it to us, and we get to say if we like it or don't like it and give them ideas, and so basically the final thing is up to us.

Liam: So if they totally slaughter what we think the character's supposed to be like, we can tell them, "No you have to change this."

Kristy: I am pretty sure that we won't reject one unless it is like really totally different than what we had and Billie just changes like that, or Vince changes like that…Or conflicts with the way they are, or conflicts with the way we set it up.

They knew they had final control, as Matt noted with satisfaction, "They can't put it up on the web page until me or Mr. Weeks puts it up."

Their collaborative spirit worked in tandem with this sense of ownership, however. Kristy reported that the class deliberately laced some narrative possibilities into their chapter:

What we tried to do, which was quite difficult, was to leave hang-

ings, like little foreshadowings, to use later on, and we don't mind if they don't use them or not…And we tried to put as many as we could in there so they could use them later on. [For example,]…with [Billie's] locket. One thing we had was that she could lose her locket later on. [Or] Vince's CDs. We just put that in there because we figured that in the next chapter something could happen to those, or if they ran out of money, he could pawn them, and we gave him a really nice truck, so that if they are really dire for money, they could pawn that off or sell it or something like that.

There were also possibilities for flashbacks and openings for narrative alternatives that other groups of writers might wish to develop:

Or like I know there's a flashback of Billie and Vince when she was fighting with her dad at the whole party and you could flashback and say, well, they forgot to say this about it, and then another school could say that she grabbed the wrong keys to the house and now she can't go to her Uncle Vinny's…because she doesn't have keys to the actual house…And one thing that we did is we left the address book, like she stole her dad's coat that had the money, his keys, and his address book…So she's got money and addresses, she could do…Like we didn't say who was in the address book. (Kristy)

RECOMMENDATIONS FOR COLLABORATIVE AND TELECOLLABORATIVE WRITING PROJECTS

All the students were highly enthusiastic about the project, noting that the month they spent on it felt rushed. They felt that other schools could avoid some of the trial and error aspect of their learning and could streamline the process because many of the decisions were already made. They recommended splitting into smaller groups immediately after the main ideas were agreed upon. The initial class discussion was important, they felt; Matt noted, "…You need the class discussion…you get so many different ideas." Randy reassured teachers or fellow writers that tangents are productive:

That's another thing. Don't worry if they go off on little tangents. It does help. But you've got to make sure that the whole class is more or less going in the same direction, otherwise it doesn't work. (Randy)

Kristy recommended having four or five groups each develop the complete narrative at that point, or having each student write his or her own complete narrative. She acknowledged the difficulty of working with so many versions, but thought that those students could write more consistently in their own styles and preferences. Ken advised:

> *Try to get a variety of people in each of the groups. Like with different beliefs and value systems so different ideas, and then you get less of the conflicts in the end.*

Tʜᴇ ᴄᴏᴍᴘʟᴇxɪᴛʏ ᴏꜰ ᴄᴏʟʟᴀʙᴏʀᴀᴛɪᴠᴇ ᴡʀɪᴛɪɴɢ ᴘʀᴏᴄᴇssᴇs

As the comments of these young writers show clearly, collaborative online writing requires particular skills and processes. Researchers have noted that conventional writing process approaches have underestimated the social complexity of the worlds of student writers (Finders, 1997; Lensmire, 2000; Dyson, 1997); these conventional approaches often fail to take into account productive or necessary procedures for collaborative authoring in multimedia environments. As Peter observed and assisted in their writing, these students developed sensibilities, organizational skills and negotiating strategies that served them well for this project and, perhaps, for future collaborative writing ventures.

Three of the students interviewed reported their commitment to writing. For such students, collaborative writing does not always offer obvious benefits. In this project, however, the interaction of committed and indifferent writers seems to have worked positively for all. Working intuitively, the class developed ways of working collaboratively that would allow space and narrative license to other groups of writers but still require adherence to a coherent narrative vision.

Kristy, by her own account and the acclamation of her peers and Peter, was an excellent and inspired writer. Not surprisingly, she was teased by the others for her seeming intransigence when decisions were made. For Kristy and other students who prefer to write individually, collaborative writing may offer learning of a different sort. She recognized that collaborative writing calls for certain skills and understood that such writing does not allow for completely individual ownership, or an individual writer's "vision" of the work. Despite her frustration with the group process, Kristy noted that she would take the opportunity if one arose to do another collaborative writing venture, though "maybe not with the same individuals." She evaluated her own learning:

> *One of the main things I learned was that everyone is going to have their own point of view and you have to try and find that middle ground. It's just saying you want this, and I want this, but you also want this, we can give her that if I can have this. And that was one of the ways we found middle ground. And we'd debate, and say, you can have this and I'll have this, and this will work that way. And then you can do this part and we can work around that...When you are doing a collaboration novel like this, not everyone's going to be happy with it all the time. (Kristy)*

Loretta and Ken, who described themselves as committed writers, noted that they fought about whose ideas ought to be included. Loretta admitted, "I argued a lot with [Kristy] and I argued a lot with [Ken]. Me and [Ken] almost took it outside a couple of times." When Jill asked whether they felt that the committed writers had been more stubborn about using their own ideas, they interrupted each other to agree:

> *Loretta: I think we were a little bit more adamant about what we wanted. Like we could see what we wanted.*
>
> *Ken: We are more or less used to writing on our own, so once we've got an idea-*
>
> *Loretta: We build on that idea.*
>
> *Ken: We can start building on that idea, and then we got all these other ones, and how do we make that work with mine?*

There was a clear understanding among the seven students that while it is generally easier to write alone, the payoff for the "organizational chaos" of collaborative writing is in a richer product. Liam summarized, "It's easier sometimes when you do it by yourself, but I think it often turns out better when you do it with a bunch of people." The seven students interviewed clearly relied upon a problem-solving approach to their writing. They negotiated, at times loudly, questions of narrative coherence and literary merit. These discussions provided opportunities for students to scaffold the learning of their less writerly classmates. Those writers who were more opinionated and bent on their own creative vision demonstrated in their groups the problem solving that writers typically do individually. In so doing, they helped build the level of commitment that the class as a whole devoted to the project.

The enthusiasm and energy with which these students regarded their collaborative writing was clearly evident in their comments and in their commitment to continue the project by providing advice to future telecollaborators and reviewing potential chapters. They were fully willing to maintain their commitment through the remainder of their high school years. Kristy sent the website to friends and family in Montreal and California, explaining:

I'm quite proud, I guess would be the word, that we stuck to it and didn't give up before we had to get another class into it...(Kristy)

The sense they developed that their writing was innovative and excellent was fuelled in part by the outside attention it attracted: from the corporate sponsor, from the presence of a researcher, from a professional presentation Peter made based upon the project, and from an article that appeared in their local newspaper. Laura announced, "I have the article this big that was in the paper, guys. My mum cut it out. My mum absolutely loved it." While these sources of attention are external, they are also focused, the students were proudly aware, on the reality of their genuine accomplishment.

Through this glimpse at the dynamics of one collaborative online writing project, we have confirmed our initial respect for the learning that can occur when teenage writers tackle an enormous organizational and narrative challenge. Peter initiated the project with the belief that students learn much when the teacher does not try to have all the answers pre-packaged for them, but allows students to construct their understanding. This collaborative writing process, with its false starts and dead ends, clearly inspired worthwhile and rewarding learning for these students. The students repeatedly noted their preference for working through problems to develop coherent solutions in the context rather than having an external process dictated by a teacher. Though adults may consider that such a project is risky for the teacher, the students also felt the risk of the potential for failure, defining failure not in terms of marks but as an inability to carry off their intentions. They recalled an argument when some of them despaired that the project would not work, that it was too close to the end of the semester. Randy had worried, "I was wondering what could have happened? I think we could have all miserably failed this project." Nevertheless, this sense of jeopardy and uncertain outcome was part of the excitement and incentive of the project, as they felt determined to prove that they could carry it off. Kristy summed up her own feeling, which was echoed by several of the others:

> *I am not sure how many of the other kids are going to be in this, but I am very interested and I want to keep working on it to the very end. Beyond like the minute we started working on this I knew it was going to be somewhat big. (Kristy)*

POST-SCRIPT

Chapter Two, written by grade 9 students in Lethbridge, is also available now: <www.clearview.ab.ca> Happy reading!

REFERENCES

Dyson, A. H. (1997). *Writing Superheroes: Contemporary Childhood, Popular Culture, and Classroom Literacy.* New York: Teachers College Press.

Finders, M. J. (1997). *Just Girls: Hidden Literacies and Life in Junior High.* Urbana IL: National Council of Teachers of English.

Kist, W. (2002). Finding "New Literacy" in Action: An Interdisciplinary High School Western Civilization Course. *Journal of Adolescent and Adult Literacy, 45*(5), 368-377.

Kress, G. (1997). *Before Writing: Rethinking the paths to literacy.* London and New York: Routledge.

Lensmire, T. (2000). *Powerful Writing, Responsible Teaching.* New York: Teachers College Press.

www.clearview.ab.ca

www.2learn.ca

END NOTES

[1] All students' names are pseudonyms. Their comments are used with permission.

We acknowledge the support of the Alberta Advisory Committee for Educational Studies and the University of Alberta Faculty of Education for this research.

THE POETICS OF DIGITAL SPACE

REBECCA LUCE-KAPLER
AND GURJIT SANDHU

I was learning, I believe, how to write, as well: not to have a self which, in writing, is projected into images. And not, simply, to permit the production of images, a production unencumbered by mind, but to use the mind to explore the resonances of such images, to separate the shallow from the deep, and to choose the deep.

-Louise Glück

Poetry is the genre that usually provokes the strongest response in English class: sometimes passion because poetry has a way of immersing us into the heart of lived experience; more often fear because poetry is deemed difficult to teach and understand especially within the expectations of schooling. One of the graduate students in our writing group described her poetic experiences in the following way:

My memories of poetry are focussed on Shakespeare's sonnets, some of which I had to memorize. I can still recite them years later without having a clue about their meaning. When I studied poetry in university, things didn't get a lot better; I still didn't understand what I thought was supposed to be a beautiful form of expression. I couldn't get past the underlying message that there was always a correct interpretation of the poem and I had to work to discover it. My best memory of poetry in school came from an independent study of Leonard Cohen where I tried to imitate his writing style. I experimented, reading his poems the way I wanted to and writing some in response. When I presented my project, I had a huge feeling of risk even though everything went well. That's the last time I can remember writing a poem. I feel a bit "ripped off"...I don't know the language well enough to articulate clearly what it is that I feel has happened, I just know that I have been cheated. There definitely is more to poetry than what I was taught.[1]

Jane's story is similar to those told by other graduate and undergraduate education students who were involved in a study that explored several forms of writing – narrative, poetry and hypermedia. As the writers worked together in small groups, the issues around the writing of poetry became clearer – the fear and the uncertainty as well as the rich interpretive potential of poems. When the groups shifted from poetry on a page to creating hypertext interpretations of their writing, we noticed that many of the characteristics of working in such a digital space facilitated their poetic writing. Specifically, many of the writers explained that working with such a medium helped them realize their poem's potential and that they felt a greater sense of control over their expression. Upon realizing this, we looked more closely at what had transpired through the writing of poetry and the transition to the HyperStudio[2] program to understand how using digital media might support and encourage poetry writing in school.

In this chapter, we describe this relationship between the nature of poetry and digital media by juxtaposing our two voices to describe the thinking behind this project and to exemplify how it unfolded. The writing moves between Rebecca's explanation of the context and under-pinnings of the work to Gurjit's development of a poem from paper into HyperStudio with the support of a writing group. At the end, our two voices come together to suggest how teachers can nurture a welcoming context for poetry within a digital space.

GURJIT

The bones of a poem rattled beneath a garb of words. There were images I wanted to create and gaps I needed to leave but instead of giving the poem skin and blood, I smothered the frame like a child playing dress-up. She was a poem with tiny feet shoved deep into the toes of her mother's high heels, tripping and clomping all the way. I dragged my poem that so desperately wanted to be a poem to the writing group meeting.

Amongst peer graduate students, I read what I thought I had written and what I was sure would be conveyed. When we discussed the piece, I realized the layers and lists I used to dress-up my poem were fooling no one. I needed the poem to speak herself. Cadence. Rhythm. Pulse. These were the words I heard, remembered, and repeated to myself when I looked at the poem again. I read and reread, trying to feel the poem's natural pulse, trying to capture the beat in the words and lines.

The idea that poetry had a pulse and that pulse resonated within the writer and the reader captivated me. The poem shifted, matured, and sought ways to speak herself without constantly having to speak. I wanted the gaps and silences to be a space for the reader to pause and wait and anticipate, to be a necessary part of the music. I wanted the poem to move beyond my story and my words. HyperStudio presented me with different ways to imagine the pulse of the poem. Images, colours, textures, and separation of verses, to name a few, created possibilities for a more layered and rich experience. Paths diverged and converged all within the context of one poem.

The following images are four cards extracted from the final version of the "Pulse of the Poem." The poem begins with the outline of a woman's body, linking the image of the body with the imagining of the poem. Clicking anywhere on the card moves the reader to the first verse which makes the connection between body and poem even more apparent to the reader. Similarly, clicking anywhere on the first verse, takes the reader to the second – a short text that slides into five other verses. Each image beneath the second verse connects to yet a different verse, an example of which follows. Readers are free to choose how they will connect the verses. Accompanying images are related to the text, but do not limit or define the reading to one interpretation. Transforming the written poem into a poem in HyperStudio changes the linear structure into a space of movement – changing my story into multiple stories.

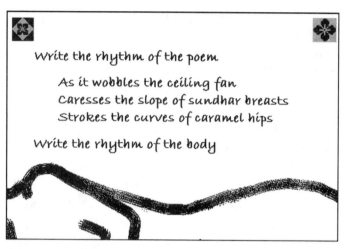

Write the rhythm of the poem

> As it wobbles the ceiling fan
> Caresses the slope of sundhar breasts
> Strokes the curves of caramel hips

Write the rhythm of the body

> pulse quickens
> and beats
> beneath
> the line
> lurching
> and stuttering

Taste blue black ink on tender lips

> Sip and spill forbidden wine
> Over seductive whispers
> And flushing words
> Tingle remains of a reckless mitti

"The Pulse of the Poem" began in the warm recluse of a sunshine and pine farmhouse. Writing in selective isolation, I was never alone. I imagined pages floating down over my desk, resting with the invitation of a tablecloth. One by one they came to this gathering place, sharing in each others' stories, realizing they were a part of one another's story: my mother, lovers old and new, the girl I was, the woman I desire/fear to be. A mug of chai, glass of grape juice, goblet of sherry, and shot of something stronger chimed a greeting in perfect pitch. Splashes throw themselves over the edges of containment, colouring my tablecloth. I swirl the tiny puddles around with the tip of pen, first creating images, then shaping lines, and finally connecting the lines into a story.

THE NATURE OF POETRY

Poetry brings us back to the world. In its rhythms and sounds, its images and stories, poetry can "approximate the actual flavor of life, in which subjective and objective become one, in which conceptual mind and the inexpressible presence of things become one" (Hirshfield, 1997, p. 32). Because we wish our students to understand how literature and poetry bring them to a deeper participation in life, we must find ways that invite them to experience that level of engagement.

Jane Hirshfield reminds us that poetry also connects across time. When we read a poem to ourselves or aloud, our breathing takes on the author's breathing as we speak in the way of the poem's first making. "There is a startling intimacy to this. Some echo of a writer's physical experience comes into us when we read her poem; if the poem is our own, it is our own past that re-inhabits our bodies, at least in part" (p. 8). In poetry, even the spaces are important, the silence as robust as the words. Those silences ask us to pause, to listen. They invite us to join in a beat or two of attentive waiting as for the moment we settle in the poet's contemplation.

Ezra Pound identified three forms of poetic meaning: melopoeia, logopoeia, and phanopoeia (Hirshfield). The first, melopoeia, is the poem's music, its rhythms and sounds. Logopoeia is the intellect of the poem, and the third, phanopoeia, is its imagery. Thinking about poetry in this way reveals the complexity of the form and suggests why we believe it difficult to teach and to understand. In school, the focus is often on the intellect of the poem. We are comfortable with that because it can take the form of questions about the meaning, the significance of the metaphors, the effectiveness of the story portrayed or the phenomenon explored. Often this perspective includes consideration of the imagery (phanopoeia) as a touchstone for underlying meanings. What is considered less often is the power of the images to evoke our imaginations and memories and the melopoeia of poetry. A poem's musical character usually becomes noticed only if the poem is read aloud. Scansion exercises, which attempt to have students identify the pattern of rhythm such as iambic pentameter, seldom bring appreciation for the music of the words and lines.

It is not surprising, then, that students find poetry writing difficult beyond the standard form exercises such as writing limericks. The importance of rhythm, image and ideas all working together to create a unified work is a challenging assignment. And yet, if students can begin to sense the relationships among these three aspects through their own experience, then they are more able to relate to the work of poets and to understand the rich and evocative nature of poetry. Poems can bring us to moments of insight about our experience and place in the world.

GURJIT

In much the same way that I write with and from many voices, the writing groups allowed to me write with and amongst another set of voices. I first brought my writing to a group of two other graduate students, Corrine and Ben,[3] and Rebecca. Corrine shared a piece about different people teaching her how to drive, in particular her father. Ben recorded the landscape of his body as experienced in a dream-state. I traced my body in relation to my mother. We experienced, remembered and wrote differently, but we pulled out threads of similarity, knotting them together in our conversations.

FIRST DRAFT

When I think about writing, I remind myself to keep it simple. The old K.I.S.S. theory. Such a simple word, kiss, and yet the secrets and desires it harbours are complex. Amidst the complexity and sensuality, I write. In coming to understand myself, I imagine the forbidden: the desiring, dreaming, demanding, sexual, and erotic self. She and I, we lay together as one watching the arms of a wobbly ceiling fan throw shadow around the room. I talk to myself in whis-

pers about our risks and chances and I feel the freedom and loss. Reflective and reckless, confident and afraid, loving and leaving and the lines begin to blur.[4]

CONTENT RESPONSE TO FIRST DRAFT

~~When I think about writing, I remind myself to keep it simple. The old K.I.S.S. theory.~~

Sometimes we start with sentences and phrases that lead us to what we really want to say. They are important to the process, but not always included in the final product. Think about how important it is to include the first two phrases. Do they tell the reader something the following lines do not?

Such a simple word, kiss, and yet the secrets and desires it harbours are complex.

"Show" me how it harbours "secrets" and "desires," don't just "tell" me. Give me an image or describe with more detail.

Amidst the complexity and sensuality, I write. In coming to understand myself, I imagine the forbidden: the desiring, dreaming, demanding, sexual, and erotic self.

I don't hear your voice or cadence. Pay attention to your body and memories when you reread the previous lines. What words, images, and movements come to mind?

She and I, we lay together as one watching the arms of a wobbly ceiling fan throw shadows around the room.

This is a beautiful line.

We read. We listened. Our suggestions began with "I like this" and other simple niceties. We eased our talk into what we liked and why, what struck us and why, what didn't quite sound right, and offered interpretations and illustrations of personal connections. Rich with new suggestions, stories, tangents and possibilities, each writer left to work on her or his writing. Ideas came not only from direct response we received, but also from the act of engaging and listening to other's stories. When we returned again although our stories were still different,

---

FORM RESPONSE TO FIRST DRAFT

When I think about writing, I remind myself to keep it simple. The old K.I.S.S. theory. Such a simple word, <u>kiss</u>, and yet the secrets and <u>desires</u> it harbours are complex. Amidst the complexity and sensuality, I write. In coming to understand myself, <u>I imagine the forbidden</u>: the desiring, dreaming, demanding, sexual, and erotic self. She and I, we lay together as <u>one watching the arms of a wobbly ceiling fan throw shadow around the room. I talk to myself in whispers</u> about our risks and chances and I feel the <u>freedom and loss</u>. <u>Reflective and reckless</u>, confident and afraid, loving and leaving and <u>the lines begin to blur</u>.

Your writing is very poetic. Think about how line breaks would accent your ideas. For example, what word do you want to punctuate and leave in the reader's memory before she moves to the next line? Placing that word at the end of a line will help create that effect. What rhythm or pattern do you want to create? Long and breathless? Short and staccato? I have underlined phrases and images that I think are key to your piece. Which words are taking up space? Where is space needed? Play with different breaks and images —delete, include, create — and see what emerges.

---

they took up similar themes of body, embodiment and relationships. They became stories entangled with voices of our own and the voices we brought together.

THE NATURE OF WRITING GROUPS

The members of Gurjit's group responded to different aspects of her work – they noticed the content in their comments about her imagery as well as where the meaning was unclear. They also responded to the musical aspects with their suggestions for line breaks and rhythm. The writing group was an important part of her process, especially for articulating the images and rhythms of the piece that would shape the intellect of the poem.

What is not clear in the above excerpt, although Gurjit alludes to it at the end, is the collective contribution present in poems. While writing groups have been used in classes for some time, especially with the rise of the writing process movement, the focus has been primarily on the individual writer. The aim is to improve each person's piece of writing by asking questions, offering suggestions and presenting the readers' perspectives. What has been acknowledged less frequently is how writing groups, even with an individual focus, will transcend that work to develop a kind of group text that feeds into everyone's work. For example, in Gurjit's group above, themes would arise without being planned or imagery would appear in more than one person's poem albeit in a different context. When I was a member of a particular poetry group for several years, themes, images, discussions and ideas that emerged from group conversation or responses to texts appeared in various guises throughout everyone's poetry. The collective support created by our conversations led to writing that would not have been possible from a writer working alone.

Writing is a complex system that is entangled in the historical, cultural, biological and more-than-human worlds as well as our individual and collective identities. A complex phenomenon like a writing group is greater than the sum of its parts and is a dynamic and adaptive entity. When I write a poem, for instance, I might consider such a text to be a discrete whole, part of a collection of poetry, or I might think about the different aspects of my poem drawing on Pound's characterizations. Further, the writing of that poem connects me to my poetry group who responds to my work and shapes its evolution. The larger literary community also influences our group's work as poets – the writers' guild to which we belong, the world of writers and texts, the publishing industry and so on. In addition, my identity as a poet, as a woman writer, perhaps even as a teacher of poetry shapes the writing of that poem as its creation influences me. While its unfolding is not predictable, I can nevertheless trace the pattern in my evolution as poet and notice the interconnections created through such an activity. This web of relations goes beyond the poem, beyond the poet. Writing, far from being the stereotype of the solitary creator in a garret, is really an immersion into a sea of language whose meanings and character are intertwined with the diversity of human understanding and activity and which marks the rhythm of our existence. As an engagement with language, writing becomes part of that larger system, a system that reveals traces of inter-connection in every word.

Di Brandt described some of the tensions and discoveries in her col-laborative writing projects and how they reminded her of the fluidity of identity and the interplay of "me/not me" that takes place in such work. She challenged the belief that the writer works from a solitary space and explained how working collaboratively illustrated what language really is. "Words being traded back and forth between people, the same words, with slight variations, endless recycling of the same stories and rhythms, each one slightly different from the last, with the transmitter's indelible personal imprint on it, and yet recognizably communal, the same" (1996, p. 82). While one can trace the patterns of rhythm, syn-tax and semantics in the work of an individual writer, it is within the context of a writing group that one can see how this pattern of one writer is dependent upon and crucial to the rhythms and meanings that co-emerge in the group and in the larger literary world. So while we can focus on these characteristics from a single author perspective, seeing that pattern in a larger context changes one's perspective of writing being a solitary practice to one that is necessarily dependent upon the presence of others.

Such interconnections are what Guillén (1993) has called the "intertexuality of significance," where words, themes and contexts min-gle with the writer's intentions and thus are less attributable to specific sources. Such intertextuality in a poem, for example, begins to blur the boundaries between the "fictitious and the natural, the novel and the autobiography, the original and the replicated, the self and the other, written and read, broken and whole" (McHugh, 1993, p. 71). The idea of intertext, Guillén suggested, is to reveal the "social aspect of literary writing, whose individual character, up to a certain point, is located at a specific junction of earlier writings" (p. 247).

Within the writing group, this intertextual nature can become more evident. The participants noted how the texts of published writers that we read, how the work of the others in the group, and the responses to their texts had helped shape their writing. Most found such a process reassuring not only because such interactions enriched their creative work, but also because their conversations with others helped them dis-cover ways to say more distinctly what they wanted to express through their writing, especially the affective nature of their texts. In realizing how other texts could give them forms and practices for writing and the role of the reader in their writing, they developed strategies that they would use in their writing and teaching beyond the group.

GURJIT

As members of the graduate student writing group, we shared and worked through multiple drafts with one another, creating a greater text of understanding and interpretation that bled through our individual pieces. Part of what the group did to push our own thinking and engagement to poetry and our different stories further was to articulate our interconnections in two different ways: efferent response and aesthetic response. Efferent response, as developed by Louise Rosenblatt (1978), is concerned with what details are retained from the actual reading of the text. Aesthetic response is concerned with the reader's lived experiences as they relate to the reading the text. For example, images, words and characters may evoke a certain memory within the reader. Both types of responses are important for interacting with the members of the writing group and with the different poems shared within the

---

PRESENTATION COPY
THE PULSE OF THE POEM

Write the rhythm of the poem
  As it wobbles the ceiling fan
  Caresses the slope of sundhar *breasts*
  Strokes the curves of caramel hips

        pulse quickens
        and beats
        beneath
        the line
        lurching
        and stuttering

Taste blue black ink on tender lips
  Sip and spill forbidden wine
  Over seductive whispers of flushing words
  Tingle remains of a reckless mitti

group. Two different responses by members are included below. The responses reveal not only the efferent and aesthetic connections, but also the rhythm and text that have developed within the dynamics of the group.

EFFERENT RESPONSE TO
PULSE OF THE POEM

Words are not merely words. Each word tells a story and each sentence a history, or rather herstory. Poems have the power and seduction to say more than words can say. What is poetry? It is image and imagination, secrets and screams. It is a way of saying what cannot, should not, dared not be said. Poetry is a way of living, of being. T.S. Elliot wrote, "poetry communicates before it is understood." Pulse of the Poem is about the possibilities of memory, existence, and contemplation that arise through the writing of poetry. It is about so much more.

AESTHETIC RESPONSE TO
PULSE OF THE POEM

I remember such an evening as this. An evening when silence spoke and words were silent. When I heard my pulse beat above the whirling fan, felt every breath squeeze into my chest and then rush to escape me, flushed more red than the wine in hand. It was an evening to remember and one to forget. Saying everything with a glance, lingering fingertips, and knees touching, and pretending to say nothing at all. Dreaming for it, for him, to be more. Desiring that it, that he, be just for this moment. Flushing for the forbidden and resisting the reckless, it was my night too. And the fan continued to whirl and wobble.

I used my experiences from the graduate writing group to guide and participate in a second writing group composed of undergraduate students: Margot, Kate, Crystal and Sarah.[5] We worked and wrote through three different forms of expression: narrative, poetic and hypertext. Narrative, being the most common and familiar form of writing, was introduced first. Next, writers considered poetry with attention to shape and rhythm as a way to move beyond the narrative. Finally, hypertext, probably the least familiar form of the aforementioned three, was introduced as a digital extension for narrative and poetry.

The conversation and interaction during our writing meetings initially began as response to opened ended questions about how one wrote, when and where we each wrote, what writing offered the writer, what did it offer the reader and listener. As we grew more familiar with each other's stories, the discussion took a broader range: from comment and critique on personal writing and the writing of others to personal experiences and dreamy ideas. Sometimes I would bring writing activities in order to practice a different form or tap our creativity. Other times, a participant would begin our discussion by telling the group how she was still struggling over a line and collectively we would tease out possibilities.

I noticed that interconnectivity of one writing group did not remain enclosed in that group. I carried my writing experiences from one group to another, creating threads between two different nodes. Similarly, HyperStudio allows the writer to imagine, create and connect different stories within one text and amongst different texts. HyperStudio made it digitally possible for me to imagine and visualize a poem connected in multiple and different ways. Endings and beginnings blurred so that reading was no longer a simple linear experience. The reader was actively engaged in responses for the reading that evolved. The reading I have tried to evoke here in print form is also meant to blur the moments of beginnings and endings by taking the reader back to an earlier moment in this paper to view the images from the HyperStudio version of the "Pulse of the Poem." Movement, connections and interconnections possible in written form, are enhanced and extended with programs like HyperStudio.

THE NATURE OF THE DIGITAL SPACE

One of the interesting things we learned in working through three forms, ending with hypertext, was that the character of the writing did not change to the degree that we expected. We had thought that the form would challenge the structure of writing and the expectations of readers in ways that did not happen. Perhaps hypertext is not as divergent from other forms as some claim, especially when one considers how some non-electronic writing has been moving toward being more fragmented, interrupted, dialogic and non-linear for some time (Moulthrop, 1995). At the same time, one must consider that the experience in this group had all been with typical forms of writing, and working with hypertext was a new activity for them. Until students have more extensive and early experience with hypertext structures, writing may not change significantly when performed in digital space. The underlying structures and potential of hypertext will need to be more thoroughly understood and played with before we can determine how it might influence or change writing practices in substantial ways.

There were two things about the hypertext writing, though, that we did see: One was that the digital medium was useful in highlighting the nature of poetry, specifically the three aspects that Pound identified – melopoeia, logopoeia and phanopoeia; and second, that the role of the group contributions could be diversified and expanded.

When exploring the nature of poetry, the writers using HyperStudio felt that some of the processes of writing poetry became more concrete. They became more aware of the importance of imagery as they were able to include pictures that emphasized the sensory nature of the poems while creating links between images, words, sounds, etc. that highlighted the importance of line breaks and rhythm. They became more conscious of the musical quality of poetry as the hypertextual links brought prominence to the power of the gap or line break in the creation of rhythm. From attending to these features, they could then begin to discuss how the rhythm and the imagery of a poem create a sense of its intellectual heart.

Several writers, after completing the HyperStudio project, felt that creating links and bringing in other media gave them more control over their texts, an insight that differs from suggestions that hypertext diminishes the decision-making and control of an author. This sense of control, however, was perhaps just a heightened awareness of authorial decision-making – decisions that are less obvious in other kinds of textual work – bringing the writers a greater consciousness to their planning, thinking and creating.

At the same time, the use of links highlighted the gaps in the text and left room for noticing reader interpretation in a way that was not as obvious in paper text. While all poetry invites readers to connect their own experiences and readings to the poem, intertwining with the text, readers and writers are perhaps not as conscious of the invitation as they are when the gap is a physical presence on a screen. While we did not have time to invite the writers to link their own images and responses to the work of their colleagues, that possibility certainly exists when using such a medium. Such a process would further exemplify the role of the reader in aesthetic response.

With many of the writers clearly sensing that they had a great deal of control as authors with HyperStudio, we wondered what would have happened if there are had been more time for concrete evidence of reader response through the creation of additional links. Would this sense of authorship change if others were to connect their readings and interpretations? Foucault (1984) has suggested that as textual understandings change, the author function will disappear "in such a manner that fiction and its polysemous texts will once again function according to another mode, but still with a system of constraint – one which will no longer be the author, but will have to be determined or, perhaps, experienced" (p. 119). The concept of single authorship and individual achievement in school will certainly be an issue that will have to be addressed as such possibilities for writing become more common, requiring a dramatic shift in perception about the processes and products we value in schooling.

GURJIT

Although HyperStudio ultimately gave "Pulse of the Poem" more interpretative and interactive possibilities, it began as model sketched out on paper with pen. I needed to see that there was structure and a way that I could read the poem with some order. Fragmenting the poem was discomforting and I needed to maintain some control over what I imagined the poem to be saying and how I wanted the reader to experience the poem. With the structure in place, I could then let go and leave some gaps for the reader to fill in. I also believe that a guiding structure invites the reader into the poem, but does not confine the reader so that s/he is always an observer of my story. Rebecca refers to this approach as a "liberating constraint" (Davis, et al., 2000). There are

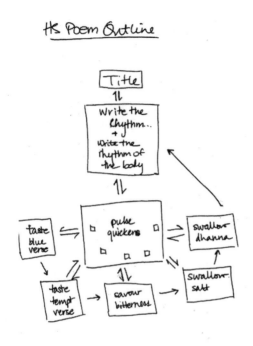

guides that move the reader along, but how the reader moves from one point to the next is left to the reader.

Embedding the transition of one poem within the work of group gives greater context to how the pieces emerged separately and together. There is a sense of many stories coming together, but in doing so the individual pieces weave together a greater story. How different responses move a piece of text along is captured in a group multimedia design. Responses may come in many different forms and link to other sites that will further develop and connect one piece of writing to another. The interconnections within an individual piece and amongst the group as a whole are illustrated below.

Moving the "Pulse of the Poem" from a text that was hiding behind words to an exploration of the body that hid beneath those layers to an interconnected existence, I realized a depth and richness to poetry that I had not previously imagined. Writing as part of a back and forth process, as something experienced and shared, gave my writing more

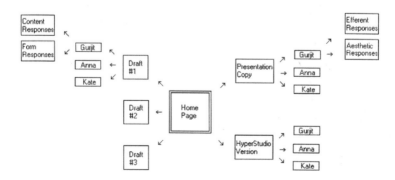

fluidity and possibility. Other voices took me back to my voice and taught me to listen to the voice that needed to speak through the poem. I began to question the "I" and ownership I felt for my writing. Writing became a dialogue and place of collaborative work. It not only involved me as author, but it was an art that begged the interaction and response of others. HyperStudio is such a place where writing stands on its own, but the poem exists only through the inactions and interconnections the reader chooses to make.

TEACHING POETRY IN A DIGITAL SPACE

Our work with poetry in a digital space led us to realize that such an experience can be inviting and playful for students and one that engages them in understanding the genre in concrete ways. The intimidation factor of poetry was greatly reduced by offering other forms for its creation. The opportunity to explore and understand the melapoeia, the logopeia and the phanopoeia of poetry is enhanced through a digital space, as are the contributions of other writers and texts. What follows are some suggestions for teachers to consider when planning to try poetry in hypertext.

1. Choose a hypertext program that is accessible and easy to learn. HyperStudio is one that very young children to adults can use easily, but equally effective are web page programs such as Netscape Composer, which is free on the Internet. Create time to learn how to use the program. Although they are readily learned, one needs to have time to play and experiment to discover the range of possibilities before beginning to work on a specific assignment. We did not leave enough time for this phase.

2. Begin with existing poems. While our students used poems of their own, for less experienced writers, choose published poems that they enjoy. Ask students to use the existing lines and choose how to work with the text. What images or sounds might they add? How might they choose to divide the poem? Where will they create their own writing and link it to places in the poem?

3. Talk about Pound's aspects of poetry and have the students identify how they have exemplified these particular characteristics.

4. Once the students have developed their own interpretation of a poem, ask them to develop links with each other's work. This activity is particularly useful if everyone is working on the same poem.

5. Invite them to create their own poems and create interconnections and links to their own and others' work.

6. A measure of the insight they have gained is to return to "paper" poems and see what details they notice about the melapoeia, logopeia and phanopoeia.

Spending more time with poetry will benefit much of the writing that students do. Poetry teaches attentiveness to language and to detail. Students develop a stronger sense of the rhythms of language and economy of expression. Even if one never becomes a poet, the discipline of such writing enhances the enjoyment and skill one brings to reading and writing in all genres.

Jane Hirshfield notes how everyday speech tends to hide the rich history of words' creation, but "a good poem draws on the originality hidden at language-making's core and also replenishes that originality. It flenses the dulling familiarity from words, allowing them to gleam as they did when first made" (p. 35). Through poetry, we can offer our students the joy and creativity of language.

REFERENCES

Brandt, D. (1996). *Dancing naked: Narrative strategies for writing across centuries*. Stratford, Canada: The Mercury Press.

Davis, B., Sumara, D. & Luce-Kapler, R. (2000). *Engaging minds: Learning and teaching in a complex world*. Mahwah, NJ: Lawrence Erlbaum.

Foucault, M. (1984). What is an author? In P. Rabinow (Ed). *The Foucault reader*. New York: Pantheon Books.

Guillén, C. (1993). *The challenge of comparative literature* (C. Franzen, Trans.), Cambridge, MA: Harvard University Press.

Glück, L. (1994). *Proofs and theories: Essays on poetry*. Hopewell, NJ: The Ecco Press.

Hirshfield, J. (1997). *Nine gates: Entering the mind of poetry*. New York: HarperCollins.

McHugh, H. (1993). *Broken English: Poetry and partiality*. Hanover: University of New England Press.

Moulthrop, S. (1995). Traveling in the breakdown lane: A principle of resistance for hypertext. *Mosaic, 28,* 4: 55-77.

Rosenblatt, L. (1978). *The reader, the text, the poem: The transactional theory of the literary work.* Carbondale: Southern Illinois University Press.

END NOTES

[1] For more about this writing group, please see Luce-Kapler, R., Chin, J., O'Donnell, E. & Stoch, S. (March, 2001). The design of writing: Unfolding systems of meaning. *Changing English, 8* (1): 43-52. This group was one of eleven formed over three years in Rebecca's research project, The Form of Writing and the Expression of Meaning, sponsored by Social Sciences and Humanities Research Council.

[2] HyperStudio is a multimedia authoring program that creates a series of cards that can be linked in various ways. The cards support text, imagery, sound, animation, movie clips, etc. It was created by Knowledge Adventure Inc. We chose this program because it is licensed for use in schools in Ontario and thus readily available to teachers.

[3] Pseudonyms.

[4] There were second and third drafts, each receiving additional responses. For this paper, only the first draft and two subsequent responses are included for illustrative purposes.

[5] Pseudonyms.

ASSESSMENT IN
MEDIA EDUCATION
CHRIS M. WORSNOP

(This chapter is based on an article which first appeared in *Reading On Line*, International Reading Association, 2000, http://www.reading online.org/newliteracies/)

OVERVIEW

This chapter discusses some issues in media education assessment in a context of a definition of media education and its pedagogy. Assessment in media education is compared to assessment in English language arts. Samples of assessment instruments illustrate the possibilities for good assessment in areas such as: personal response to media texts, analytical/critical response to media texts, assessing student media productions and assessing sensitive issues in media texts. The chapter ends with some suggestions for future work that needs to be done in media education assessment.

MEDIA EDUCATION:
PITFALLS AND A DEFINITION

Media education seeks to make students knowledgeable about and skilled with the media. It is a study of the media themselves and of their importance in our culture. Students of media learn how to "read" and "write" media texts in a way roughly analogous to the way they learn in English/Language Arts to read and write printed texts. In my earlier work (Worsnop, 1994), I listed a number of basic misunderstandings about media education:

Orthodoxy #1: Media Education as Civil Defense

The media are seen as wicked influences on human behavior. The course of study consists of teaching students how to discard their misbegotten tastes and media habits in favor of a set of more appropriate ones, like those of the adults in the community. Media education is seen as a cure or a form of prevention.

Orthodoxy #2: Media Education as Ideological Means Test

Everything is subjected to a political scrutiny to see if it conforms to the *correct* or *accepted* or *dominant* ideologies. Media that strays away from the accepted ideology of the course – to the left or to the right – is condemned. Media education is seen as a course in convergent thinking.

Orthodoxy #3: Media Education as Multiplication Tables

The student does little more than learning a set of definitions, rules and names of equipment parts and technique, sometimes mistakenly called "knowledge and skills." There is little place for creativity, critical thinking or divergence of any kind. Media education is seen as memory work.

Orthodoxy #4: Media Criticism 301

The course is a carbon copy of advanced university literary criticism courses. The media are seen as the (usually inferior) equivalents of books. Media education is seen as a course in theories of criticism.

A DEFINITION

In *Media Literacy through Critical Thinking* (Washington State Office of the Superintendent of Public Instruction – Commission of Student Learning, 2000), I listed the five key concepts I consider central to any good course in media education:

– Media texts are carefully wrapped packages (In media ed. talk: "Media are constructions").

– Media construct versions of reality (In Media ed. talk: the same).

– Media are interpreted though individual lenses (In Media ed. talk: "The audience plays an important role in media").

– Media are about money (In Media ed. talk: "Media have important commercial implications").

– Media promote an agenda (In Media ed. talk: "media contain values and ideological messages").

I make no claim of originality for these key concepts. All can be easily traced back as far as 1985 (and perhaps earlier) in *Teaching the Media* (Masterman, 1985). There are other versions of the key concepts in the *Media Literacy Resource Guide* (Ontario Ministry of Education and Training, 1989), in the British Film Institute curriculum documents

(Bowker, 1991) and in other places. While the concepts may vary in wording and number from one source to another, they are more remarkable for their commonalities than for their differences. Most important of all, they all proclaim the importance of starting from a conceptual framework. These five key concepts should, I believe, be incorporated into and should drive every good media education course. In teaching the course, the teacher will occasionally take a stance in the "civil defense" mode, will take ideology into account on a regular basis, will find several occasions when it will be necessary to instruct some terminology, and will find it necessary to teach some critical skills. But these forays into the orthodoxies will be in the context of a well-rounded media education course, rather than a doctrinaire exercise.

To this definition I would add some educational conditions that I consider vital to a good media education classroom. First, the pedagogy should be learning-oriented rather than instruction-oriented, student-centered rather than teacher-centered. Second, the classroom process should encourage exploration, inquiry, investigation and discovery approaches to learning. Third, cooperative and collaborative styles of learning should be favored and encouraged. Fourth, co-learning should be a practice often pursued. Last, assessment practices and instruments should be open and public, authentic, valid, reliable and fair.

WHY IS MEDIA EDUCATION IMPORTANT?

This is the same question that faced 19th century education reformers wanting to revolutionize the British secondary school curriculum to include the study of English literature. Until then, cultural studies for secondary students consisted largely of the memorizing of the ancient Roman and Greek classics. The reformers argued that contemporary culture should form an important part of contemporary school curriculum. We need again to apply this logic to today's educational system to bring it up to date with the dominant forms of cultural expression. We need to insist that culture is not the exclusive domain of literature or even of books. Culture is now carried largely in moving images on screens in cinemas, televisions and computers, in sound waves from music and radio, or in a thousand other new ways of cultural expression varying from T-shirt messages to display ads projected on the sides of buildings. Print is not dead, but it has a lot more competitors.

Media education is not merely a campaign to incorporate more technology into schools. What is important about classroom information delivery is not so much the technology itself as the quality of the information, and the ways that technology and the processes of transmission and reception influence information. Media education is a plea to legitimize the study of the culture and cultural engines of modern society. The media are now so much a part of our cultural, political and economic environment that not to study them in detail and depth in schools would compel students to bury their collective heads in the sand and rubble of an out-of-date curriculum.

Why is Assessment Important?

Good assessment information - assessment information is very different from evaluation scores, which do not contain any *information* at all - will help teachers know:

How well they are teaching

If students all achieve well in a program, it is likely the program is being successfully taught. It could also be the case that the material is too easy for the students, or that the students are remarkably capable and are learning the material despite poor teaching. If some students do well and others do not, the teacher knows which group in the class needs extra help, or which topics were less well taught than others. If all students perform poorly in a class, at least three things need to be examined: the curriculum, the teaching and the students.

How well the students are learning

Assessment information gives teachers a profile of each student's learning. (If the assessment is authentic, that is.) This information is valuable in forming groups for remediation, further instruction or acceleration.

Whether they are teaching the right material at the right time

Some material is harder to learn if it is not approached in the right manner or at the right time, or in the right sequence. Assessment information helps teachers keep check on their pedagogy, timing and sequencing. Sequential teaching is important, but should not be adopted as orthodoxy.

What they should teach next

When students have achieved one expectation in a program, a well-informed teacher knows what those students are ready to learn next. It is a good teacher who recognizes which students need to progress in one direction while others move in another.

What they should teach again

When students fail to learn something in a program, the teacher can investigate a number of possible causes, including:

— the program is at fault in that the material is not accessible to these students;

— the teaching is at fault in that the presentation did not connect with these students;

— the students are at fault in one way or another.

What they do not need to teach at all

Sometimes students show they are already competent in a skill, knowledge, understanding, experience, task or concept that has not yet been taught. In that case, there is no need to teach the topic, or the topic can be covered only lightly.

Whether or not they are covering the expectedcurriculum satisfactorily

Teachers can use assessment information to tell them if all the expected skills, knowledge, concepts, etc., are being covered and achieved by the students.

What to report to parents and administrators

Assessment information is exactly what teachers need to fill out reports for parents, outlining students' learning.

Whether or not they should worry about accountability

Teachers who willingly embrace good assessment as an important part of their program are making it clear to their community of parents, administrators and politicians that they are happy to be held accountable for their programs.

MY ASSESSMENT WORK
IN MEDIA EDUCATION

I came to assessment work in media education through my earlier work in language arts and English during 25 years of work as a curriculum coordinator in the Ontario public school system. This work involved me in curriculum development, implementation and assessment – the classical cycle of curriculum work. I did original work in assessment in both reading and writing (Worsnop, 1980, 1996b; Peel District School Board, 1995). After my retirement in September, 1995, I decided to write *Assessing Media Work: Authentic Assessment in Media Education* (Worsnop, 1996a) to combine all I had learned about assessment into one work addressing a subject area that has always been my passion. The previous year I had published the first edition of *Screening Images: Ideas for Media Education* (Worsnop, 1994), which covered the topics of media education theory and practice, but which did not thoroughly cover assessment. Furthermore, I believed that one reason teachers were shy of media education was that they were unsure about assessing work that students might produce in formats like video, audio, poster, story board, photo story, etc. I was convinced that a book on media education assessment would be a welcome boost to those teachers anxious to teach the media.

At the centre of *Assessing Media Work* (Worsnop, 1996a) is a scale (rubric) that derives largely from the work I had previously done in assessing writing and in creating scales for writing assessment. My "taken for granted" was that all human expression shares the same components with writing:

- Ideas and content,

- Organization,

- Effective use of language (rhetoric of the medium),

- Voice/audience,

- Technical competence.

Also from my experience with writing assessment, I imported my preference for analytical, detailed scales over holistic scales, believing that detail would serve teachers and students in guiding them towards better practice and performance, and would also enhance the reliability of the scale. I developed the scale on five levels – despite the fact that my own province had switched to a four level scale – because of my conviction that an odd number of levels is preferable to an even number, since it has a centre; and also because five is the most common number of levels used in assessment scales. I applied all that I had learned about carefully separating the descriptions in the different levels with language that clearly differentiated one level from another while attempting to make the "gaps" between the levels linguistically even. I made every effort to limit the scale to the description of the actual work itself, avoiding attempts to assess process or any internal state (intention, motivation, etc.) of the "writer" that an assessor might be tempted to believe they can perceive through the work. I insisted that teachers using the scale should be able to share the scale with their own students as part of the process of "making the rules clear." I developed separate assessment instruments for purposes that fell outside the realm of the major scale – for assessing "personal response to a media text," for instance. I developed a number of assessment forms for record keeping, diagnostic, self-, peer- and formative assessment uses. Above all, I wanted my work to be an example of authenticity in assessment: I rejected any kind of assessment that did not support and encourage the very best classroom practice. I avoided any kind of assessment that would be compromised if teachers indulged in "teaching to the test." It was important for me to demonstrate that the best kinds of assessment are the kinds that are open to scrutiny by students, where the rules for performance and assessment are perfectly clear in advance of the task, and in which teaching to the test reinforces the curriculum rather than interrupting it.

From the beginning I was aware that *Assessing Media Work: Authentic Assessment in Media Education* (Worsnop, 1996a) would be incomplete in one important way: it would not offer the anchor pieces that teachers would prefer to have as models for assessment. The development of anchors would be an enormous task. First, there would need to be anchors in every imaginable media format that students might use. Then there would need to be anchor samples for students at every age/grade in their first media education course, then their second, etc. There is an enormous difference between this, and providing anchors for writing, where you need a single set of papers at each grade level, with perhaps some flexibility incorporated for different genres of writing. (See: http://www.media-awareness.ca/eng/med/class/Worsnop/intropg-p.htm.)

WHY IS ASSESSMENT IMPORTANT IN MEDIA EDUCATION?

Assessment is important in all programs, not just in media education. But new programs like media education come under special scrutiny when it comes to assessment. Media education is frequently accused of being a "soft" course because it deals with material that is already part of students' everyday knowledge and experience. Some critics ask, ignoring the irony in their question, "Why would we set up a course to teach kids how to watch TV? They already know how to do that." One way of disarming this criticism is to show that the assessment in the course will be rigorous and demanding. New program areas often have great difficulty getting established as mainstream subjects. There are many reasons for this, often connected to budget, time availability in a crowded curriculum, internecine jealousies among teachers in different departments, board politics, etc. See the introductory section of my Web page for a comprehensive list of reasons people give for not implementing media education.

New subject initiatives can have a good chance of success if a number of criteria are met. Among these are:

– Official support is provided in terms of provincial or state curriculum legislation, but the initiative to set up the course must be local.

– The building and district administrators support the grassroots curriculum initiative.

– Teachers who are not connected directly with media education support other teachers who want to implement it.

– Parents are informed and supportive.

– Budget is provided for a new program (budget means time, space, training and personnel, as well as money and equipment).

– The school has a well-prepared and -articulated program outline.

– There is a clear plan for assessing student progress and program effectiveness.

It is often folly to try to implement any program without first making sure that most if not all of these items are in place. Yet many new programs are implemented without the last of these conditions in place.

The existence of good assessment can be used as a lever to bring politicians, administrators, parents and other teachers on side.

WHAT DOES GOOD MEDIA EDUCATION ASSESSMENT LOOK LIKE?

Screening Images: Ideas for Media Education (Worsnop, 1994, 1999a) states that media education has to have three components. These components can be aligned with three components of language Arts:

Screening Images Component	Language Arts Equivalent	Assessment Needed
Experiencing media	Broad reading; reading for enjoyment	Journals, logs, observation records, personal response
Interpreting media	Studying texts	Criticism, critical response
Making media	Writing	Assessment rubrics

The way I interpret this similarity with language arts in assessment terms is to look to the theory and practice of assessment in writing to inform the way I would assess *making media*; to look to the theory and practice of literary (cultural) criticism to inform the way I would assess *interpreting media*; and to look to reading assessment theory and response (audience) theory to inform the way I would recommend assessing *experiencing media*.

The analytical scale at the centre of *Assessing Media Work: Authentic Assessment in Media Education* (Worsnop, 1996a) is the equivalent of a writing assessment scale or rubric. It operates in precisely the same way, except that it is offered as a way of assessing not only one kind of expression (writing) but many (e.g., video, audio, poster, photograph, website). The scale (or rubric) assesses five traits of media work (ideas and content, organization, effective use of media language, voice/audience, technical competence) on a scale of five levels (plus a level 0). Each of the five traits is assessed and reported separately to give a sample piece of student work five descriptive assessments rather than one arithmetical conglomerate. On the next page is the scale for Ideas and Content as a sample.

Ideas and Content	
Level 5 Consistently exceeds expectations	The controlling idea is perceptive and insightful.
	Details (evidence, anecdotes, examples, descriptions, etc.) are exact and add power to the controlling idea.
	The development of the controlling idea is perfectly clear, complete, coherent and strongly focused.
Level 4 Consistently meets and may occasionally exceed expectations	The controlling idea is thoughtful.
	Details (see examples Level 5) are relevant and reinforce the controlling idea.
	The development of the controlling idea is clear, coherent and well focused.
Level 3 Usually meets expectations	The controlling idea is clear but may be conventional.
	Details are relevant and help expand the controlling idea.
	The development of the controlling idea is fairly clear, focused and generally coherent.
Level 2 Inconsistently meets expectations	The controlling idea is apparent but may be simple or derivative.
	Details are generally relevant and help clarify the controlling idea to some extent.
	The development, focus and coherence of the controlling idea are clear in parts.
Level 1 Does not meet expectations	The controlling idea is indiscernible, sketchy (or plagiarized).
	Details are few, and weakly connected to the controlling idea.
	The development of the controlling idea, where it can be discerned, is weak.
Level 0 Not present	The controlling idea is absent or must be inferred.
	Details are sparse, disconnected or irrelevant.
	NA.

The holistic scale (next page, Worsnop, 1996a) for assessing personal response to a media text is an instrument that draws from the research and practice of "response to literature," well known to language arts educators.

ASSESSMENT SCALE FOR PERSONAL
RESPONSE TO MEDIA TEXTS

LEVEL 5

The student integrates personal feelings, experiences, hopes fears, reflections or beliefs with the text. The personal response is rooted in the text and a clear understanding of the whole text, and its subtext(s), and makes connections to other texts.

LEVEL 4

The student connects personal feelings, experiences, hopes, fears, reflections or beliefs with the text. The personal response refers to the text, conveys a sense of understanding of the text and partial understanding of its subtext.

LEVEL 3

The student explores personal feelings, experiences, hopes, fears, reflections or beliefs and makes a superficial or concrete connection to the text.

LEVEL 2

The student retells or paraphrases the text or identifies devices in isolation, making only a superficial reference to personal feelings or experiences. Or the student writes about personal feelings, etc., without connecting to or referring to the text.

LEVEL 1

The student response shows little or no interaction with or understanding of the text.

LEVEL 0

The student response is irrelevant or incomprehensible.

Media Literacy through Critical Thinking (Washington State Office of the Superintendent, 1999) provides an instrument for assessing *analytical* response to a media text, which is more akin to traditional critical approaches to analyzing literary texts.

I have recently been engaged with media educators from a number of countries in a project designed to develop an assessment instrument for determining the level of "critical awareness" in students' insight into a text such as a feature film. This project is based on the research of Alexander Fedorov of the Taganrog Pedagogical Institute in Russia. (http://www.mediaeducation.org.ru/) Briefly, it uses an assessment scale to analyze how students talk about a text. It uses leveled descriptions of

SCALE FOR ASSESSING LEVELS OF CRITICAL INSIGHT IN FEATURE FILMS			
Plot (fabula)	Character (persona)	Author (creator)	Synthesis (adjudicator)
High Level Sees the story as one component of the author's, actor's & other artist's work. Expands comprehension by connecting story to universal mythological patterns & other works.	Understands the complexity of performance & psychology of characterization. Comprehends how performances complement other components of the work. Expands comprehension by connecting characters and performances to models in other works.	Identifies with/ points out the concrete & conceptual work of the media author(s). Editing, script, lighting, sound, camera placement/movement, composition, ideology. Expands comprehension by perceiving the interaction of the various artistic components of the work & by connecting to other works by this & other authors.	Views the work as a united and integrated whole. Is aware of & can articulate excellences, gaps, excesses & deficiencies. Cites sources to substantiate conclusions. Makes predictions based on multiple & integrated insights of the oeuvre.
Middle Level Understands the story, its development & syntax.	Identifies with character(s) – their psychology, motives, actions – as heroic figures.	Understands (some) separate components of the authoring arts & may make occasional connections among them.	Can state & support personal preferences informally. Can make judgements based on knowledge of genre and/or the body of work of an actor or an individual artist (e.g., Steven Spielberg). Predicts outcomes based on insights/ patterns of plot & character.
Low Level May not follow the entire narrative thread, but naively focus on fragments or episodes as the principal focus/purpose of the work. Makes little distinction between representation and reality.	Sees (one or a small selection of) characters in two-dimensional terms.	Is very marginally aware of some aspects of the author's art (e.g., special effects, sound).	May refer to other works in simple comparison. Makes predictions based on simple plot conventions.

discourse to make assessments on depth of insight. Here is the scale used in that project. The scale has been validated in use with classes of 16+ students in both Russia and Ontario. The next stage I would like to pursue is to incorporate an overlay of assessment language that would include references to the five key concepts of media education (see page at left).

ASSESSING SENSITIVE ISSUES
IN MEDIA TEXTS

In one chapter of *Screening Images* (Worsnop, 1999a), I attempted to create a system for approaching so-called "sensitive issues" in media texts without promoting censorship. Language arts teachers are familiar with the notion of "sensitive issues in literature." Think only of book titles like *Huckleberry Finn, The Merchant of Venice* and *The Catcher in the Rye*, to illustrate what is meant by the expression. The basic question is this: "How can schools include the study of recognizably worthwhile cultural expressions when they include topics or treatments of subjects to which some people are sensitive, or to which they outright object?"

The chapter was prompted by the experiences I had as a curriculum coordinator in refereeing objections to books, and by the perpetual discussion among media educators about the "effects" of media texts on human behavior. (Does violence in TV lead to violence in society? Is sexual content in films and TV having a direct effect on sexual behavior in society? See Orthodoxy #1, Media Education as Civil Defence, above.) I wanted some sort of instrument to focus discussion not so much on forceful expressions of personal feelings (biases) about a text, as on the understanding that there were different sets of feelings about individual texts, all deserving consideration, if not agreement. I am not so naïve as to believe that many people will alter their own feelings as a result of this. I have found, though, that some people are able to broaden their point of view sufficiently to acknowledge the existence (and perhaps the validity) of alternative, competing interpretations of cultural products. This is much preferable to a situation where individuals bludgeon one another with their own opinions until one of them gives in or walks away.

I have found that the "effects" debate in media education is made more polite when there is an agreed basis for the discussion, a basis I have tried to provide in a scale that helps media consumers/observers to rate a text's sensitive issues frankly against their personal tolerance. The top level is described as "better than generally expected in my personal value system." The middle level is described as: "consistent with my personal value system." The lowest level is described as: "not acceptable in my personal value system". This establishes a three-level scale for discussion, and makes it clear that it is differences in *personal* values systems that account for differences in assessment.

The content of the scale is different from other rating scales for sensitive issues in that it tries not to rely on arithmetic as the prime arbiter. Other scales, used to rate movies or TV programs, for example, employ a system of counting instances of violence, enumerating the frequency and kind of nudity or sexual behavior, tallying up the representations of drug use, etc.

My contention is that a simple counting mechanism does not do justice to the complexity of the issues. Do we want to compare *On the Waterfront* to a TV cop show based simply on the number of violent depictions? Do we want to compare the nudity in *Schindler's List* to that in the Playboy Channel by merely counting which one has the least footage of nakedness? Obviously, to me at any rate, there has to be some other gauge.

What I propose is to rate the *qualities* of the manner in which the sensitive issue is used in the text, instead of the *frequency*. The qualities I selected are:

Integrity: how important (or integral) to the overall purpose of the text is the use of the sensitive issue?

Restraint: how much is the sensitive issue pushed to the front of our attention, and how much does the author hold back or restrain?

Challenge: to what extent does the inclusion of the sensitive issue in the text truly serve a serious and challenging (to the audience) purpose?

Consequences: to what extent does the depiction of the sensitive issue include a depiction of its realistic consequences?

Glamorizing: to what extent is the depiction of a sensitive issue made falsely or unrealistically attractive?

Bundling: to what degree does the text combine sensitive issues (such as sex, violence, racism) to each other?

These six qualities of sensitive issue use are each described at the three levels of acceptability to create a chart that can be used in many settings and situations.

The complete chart can be found in *Screening Images: Ideas for Media Education* (Worsnop, 1999a, pp. 130-133). Here is a sample, the scale for INTEGRITY:

INTEGRITY	
References to sensitive issues in the text are:	
Level 1	integral and important to other parts of the text.
Level 2	generally connected to other parts of the text.
Level 3	gratuitous and/or unrelated to other parts of the text.

THE "ROTE-MAP" OF STANDARDS, PROGRESSIVE EDUCATION AND PERFORMANCE TASKS

The recent fashion of defining curriculum in terms of "standards" has created an impression among some teachers that meeting the standards is their only job. The effect that such an interpretation can have upon classrooms is stultifying. Students are in danger in some areas of encountering nothing more stimulating than a stream of work sheets keyed to specific standards. Creative, investigative, collaborative work is relegated to the pedagogical backseat.

Teachers tend to look at the "standards movement" with skepticism. They have seen a number of other curriculum initiatives come and go (e.g., behavioral objectives, mastery learning, minimum-competency testing, outcomes-based learning). Some expect standards to come and go in like fashion, and feel inclined to do nothing in the meantime. Others are overwhelmed by the amount of detail contained in some of the lists of standards and despair of ever being able to do justice to each minute item in turn. Others, believing the standards are picayune for the reason of completeness, provide their own conceptual framework for the subject to make up for the frequent absence of such theoretical underpinnings in the "standards" system, and continue to teach in a holistic rather than atomistic fashion.

I believe the promoters of standards endorse this last teacher reaction (Worsnop, 2003, in press). I believe they want to see progressive teaching and learning in classrooms, as much as they want to see thorough teaching and learning. It is not their intention to bring the classroom down to the methodological level of the parade ground, and that is certainly not the intention of media education. However, whatever the intentions of the standards-makers, they often belie their good intentions by connecting the standards to assessment and testing practices that encourage teachers to adopt the worst kind of rote teaching techniques.

In *Media Connections in Ontario* (Worsnop, 1999b, 2000b) I analyze and comment upon the expectations (objectives/outcomes/standards) for media education in official Ontario curriculum documents grades 1-10 (Worsnop, 1999b) and 1-12 (Worsnop, 2000b). The curriculum standards for various North American jurisdictions are readily found on the Internet (e.g., Ontario standards at http://www.edu.gov .on.ca/eng, the Eastern consortium (Canada) and Western Consortium (Canada) standards available at http://www.media-awareness.ca/eng/ med/bigpict/meinca.htm site; and Province of Quebec standards at http://www.qesn.meg.gouv.qc.ca.ela and standards for US States are listed in Frank Baker's excellent site, *The Media Literacy Clearinghouse*, http://www.med.sc.edu:81/medialit. Readers might be particularly interested in examining the standards for the State of Texas, in all their multiplicity).

THE IMPORTANCE OF PERFORMANCE TASKS IN TEACHING AND ASSESSMENT

If you scratch a media educator, you will often reveal a progressive educator who has been attracted to the subject by the likelihood that progressive pedagogy will be a perfect fit to the content. Media classrooms often display the following characteristics, which are typical of progressive education:

– Group and collaborative work is encouraged and rewarded.

– Independent and project work are encouraged and rewarded.

– Self and peer assessment are practiced and acknowledged in final grades.

- Abstractions like creativity, originality and experimentation are encouraged and rewarded.
- It is not a problem when student knows more than a teacher.
- The process of work is valued, sometimes as much as and more than the product.
- Sometimes exploratory work is undertaken without a clear vision of the expected outcome.
- Risk-taking, experimentation, investigation, discovery are all acknowledged as powerful learning tools.

Some jurisdictions are trying to make it clear that their delineation of standards is meant as a clarification of expectations rather than as a strict "rote-map," by including performance tasks in their large-scale assessments. Performance tasks are not just tests; they are activities deliberately designed to give students the chance to show their very best performance. They are designed to assess not only knowledge and skill – both low-level kinds of learning – but also understanding, application, conceptual thinking, ability to extrapolate into other areas of learning: the synthesis and evaluation levels in Bloom's taxonomy (Bloom et al., 1956).

In my personal view, learning begins with application. Therefore, my vision of good classroom practice is more focused on broad performance tasks than on drill activities. The qualities I would look for in an ideal teacher or classroom are these:

- seeks to provide the best possible conditions for learning in classrooms.
- considers learning to be a lifelong, integrated activity.
- recognizes that classroom relationships revolve around power, and seeks to share power with students.
- believes that learning should have motivation and be enjoyable.
- provides for individual differences in learners and teachers.
- tries to make the learning of knowledge and skills a natural part of the more important learning of concepts, applications, understandings, competencies, abilities.
- practices active learning and teaching at least as much as passive learning and teaching.

- considers the classroom as an important but not the only site for learning.
- acknowledges that students can be teachers and teachers can be learners without any conflict of role or power.
- values and stresses co-learning, cooperative learning and collaborative learning as much direct instruction.
- sees assessment as a learning opportunity as well as an occasion to make judgments.

Performance tasks, if they are made important in provincial or state testing programs, remind teachers that there is a lot more to good education than just covering a list of skills and knowledge. Here is a list of the qualities of good performance tasks, compiled by Judith Fine (2000). You will notice more than a passing similarity between this list and the description of an ideal classroom above.

- Present engaging, "real-world," meaningful, substantive issues or problems – the "big ideas."
- Are directly related to important curriculum expectations.
- Focus on what students can do, how they apply and extend their knowledge.
- Require students to utilize and integrate a variety of essential skills, knowledge, concepts, procedures.
- Emphasize the *processes* students use to achieve solutions, rather than only the "right" answers.
- Present students with complex, loosely structured problems that allow for a wide range of products – this makes the task accessible to all students.
- Require students to justify, defend, explain the conclusions they reach.
- Involve the use of complex thinking skills, and the extension of knowledge, skills, abilities – the task should help students make connections and generalizations that increase their understanding of important concepts and processes.
- Often encourage a team effort, collaboration, group discussions, brainstorming.

- Require students to demonstrate, create, explain, perform, produce, present something – i.e., generate solutions, not select answers from a list.

- Are often inter-disciplinary in nature.

- Make available to students assessment criteria (e.g., rubrics), and also models examples of high-level products – this encourages students to self-assess and contributes to their becoming independent learners.

- Focus on learning that cannot easily (if at all) be assessed with tests.

- Are usually longer term, rather than one-shot, efforts.

- Are designed to emphasize depth more than breadth.

- Give teachers rich data on how well students understand a topic, use the tools of the discipline, and support a point of view.

I believe that classroom and assessment activities should always display at least some of these same qualities. But that should not be a surprise. I am, after all, an inveterate and irreconcilable progressive, as well as a passionate media educator.

MEDIA EDUCATION ASSESSMENT ISSUES STILL OUTSTANDING

There is plenty work to do to improve assessment in general and to address some of important issues in media education assessment. These include the four main issues I describe in this section.

ISSUE 1: WRITING BECOMES THE ASSESSOR

One of the biggest bugaboos of assessment is the tendency to rely on writing as the medium of reporting, and on the essay as the dominant format or genre for that writing. Both *Screening Images* (Worsnop, 1994, 1999a) and *Assessing Media Work* (Worsnop, 1996a) contain a list of 186 ways a student could report on learning other than the essay. Even when it is sensible and necessary to assess some part of media education learning through writing, the essay is only occasionally the best format to use. Of course, the op ed piece and the editorial are both variants of the essay, but they are also superior to the "school" essay in my estimation as measures of media learning because they are both common media formats – perhaps the dominant versions of the essay among writers today. The school or academic essay is an "in-house" format intended to measure not only how well students can report about having learned something, but also how well they have mastered the dominant academic rhetorical form. Not being able to write an essay under pressure is sometimes the reason students fail in subjects where they are otherwise perfectly competent. Insistence that students would restrict themselves to essay writing in the assessment of their media learning is sometimes found in conjunction with Orthodoxy #4: Media Criticism 301 (see above). It is an approach to media education that can be called "print snobbery."

A little analysis ought to make it clear that a student-made video as a report of learning is capable of telling the teacher information that is not available at all in an essay. The capability of video to carry images, sound, rhythm and pace, not to mention color, distance, time and point-of-view can all be considered as "value-added" to the pseudo-essay of the voice-over. What's more, a successful video is a demonstration of skills – including several forms of language and writing – many of which need to be practiced collaboratively rather than in isolation. The ability to bring all the skills of video-making together in a group project is an indication of a number of social and synthetic skills that would warm the hearts of both Piaget and Bloom. I do not want to argue that students should not learn how to write academic essays. I want to argue that their success or failure in a subject like media education ought not to depend on their facility in a kind of rhetoric that is not part of the subject under study. However, many teachers honestly assert that they do not feel comfortable or qualified in assessing work that comes to them in other formats than the tried-and-true essay.

The serious media education teacher needs to ask if it should be possible for students to do well in this course if they are good at media education but weak at writing? Clearly, my own answer to this question is a resounding "Yes!"

Studies are needed to test whether students learn as well in courses where essay writing is not a major component of their assessment. These studies should be conducted not only in media education classes, but in other subject areas as well, as an investigation of whether writing requirements might actually serve as a deterrent to learning (or to the demonstration of learning) in some subject areas, or for some learners. Teachers could conduct their own action research projects in which they teach a unit or a class in different ways, requiring students to report on their learning in various formats, or in a format of their own choice. The control assessment measure in all instances could be a common performance task or an oral interview at the end of the course/unit in which students are allowed to demonstrate their understanding of course concepts orally, using any other supports they choose.

ISSUE 2: MEASURING STUDENT MEDIA PRODUCT AGAINST A STANDARD OF PROFESSIONAL PRODUCTION

In my workshops I often show samples of student-made media collected from colleagues in many countries. I have sometimes been shocked to find that some teachers assessed the student work against a yardstick of professionally produced materials. I have seen student documentaries criticized (and thus assessed at a lower level) because they were not up to the standard of editing and pacing of the best available on TV. I have seen student dramas criticized because their script or music was not up to Hollywood standards, as if, to get the highest assessment, that was the standard to achieve. This approach to assessment, sometimes described as "waiting for Steven Spielberg," effectively places a false ceiling on the highest assessment available in a course at some point lower than the maximum of 100%.

My personal belief on this point is that all student materials should be assessed against a standard of what it is possible for the best student materials to achieve under the same circumstances as the piece being assessed. By this I mean that a student piece that is made with a domestic quality camera, and without sophisticated sound or editing facilities, should be judged in terms of how well it was made given the equipment and facilities available. I have seen plenty of poor work that was completed with very sophisticated equipment, but I have also seen some outstanding work achieved with rudimentary facilities. Furthermore, I want to stress that the technical component of a student project is only one component of many, and should not be allowed to over-ride the others which should carry at least the same weight in assessment. Those others are: ideas and content, organization, use of media language (rhetoric) and voice/audience (Worsnop, 1996a). I believe in giving 100% when the work fulfills or surpasses all the requirements of the

108 ASSESSMENT IN MEDIA EDUCATION

assignment. If Steven Spielberg – or the equivalent – ever showed up in my course, I would happily award a mark of 110%.

The chief resource to be developed is the set of exemplars referred to above. Teachers assessing writing have access to banks of writing samples that exemplify performance at different ages and levels of achievement. Teachers need access to the same sort of resource for other kinds of media. Video and audio are the logical places to begin this huge task. Modern technology will soon make it feasible for such a bank of samples to be available world wide through the Internet, and so the samples should be international as much as possible.

I have already made a very modest beginning by collecting samples of student-made video from teachers in a few countries, and would welcome contacts from teachers interested in providing further samples. The project, however, will remain informal and of limited use unless it can find more energy and resources than my own. In an ideal situation it would be funded long term by a university and/or corporate partner. There is already an initiative to develop an International Media Literacy Project (McMahon, Quin et al., 2002) and it might be appropriate to add the anchor task into that mandate.

ISSUE 3: IF YOU CAN LIST IT – IT EXISTS AND IT IS IMPORTANT

The fact that we can make a list of characteristics, skills, requirements or standards sometimes implies that the list has an authority greater than it deserves. It is important in all assessment – not just in media education – to make allowances for thinking and performing "outside the box," for fear of squelching the extraordinary, disadvantaging the different and disempowering the unfamiliar. The very best evidence of learning sometimes comes in a form and fashion that we cannot possibly anticipate in even the most comprehensive provincial, state or national plan. We must avoid the hubris of believing our plans and schemes are all-encompassing, finished or perfect.

I have noted above how important it is for classrooms to incorporate good performance tasks into the work that students are required to do. Researchers should study the impact of such practices on the overall performance of all students. It would be interesting to see if such classrooms not only improve academic learning, but also encourage better attendance, have fewer discipline problems, create improved teacher-student relationships, suffer less thievery and vandalism.

ISSUE 4: INTERNATIONAL STUDIES

We need to avoid parochialism and pay respectful attention to what is happening in other countries. In the UK, for instance, there is a tremendous store of experience in examining "media studies" as a high school graduation subject. Also there are numerous international researchers who have published works using case study methodology, "discourse analysis" and demographic and action research approaches as tools of investigating how people experience media (e.g., David Buckingham, 1996; Martin Barker, 1998; Andrew Hart, 1998; Jeanne Prinsloo and Costas Criticos, 1991; Ulla Carlsson and Cecilia von Feilitzen, 1998 and 1999).

In some countries media education is seen as a defense against a return to authoritarian government – literally a bulwark of democracy. Assessment in those countries – countries like Spain, South Africa, Argentina, Russia and Brazil – takes on different priorities than it does for those of us who take democratic systems for granted. Understanding how those countries stress the empowerment of the individual and the understanding of the political system through media education is not something we can afford to ignore, but something we can use to expand our vision of media education and assessment.

CONCLUSION

Media education is positioned to become an important part of the accepted curriculum in North America. Without good and authentic assessment it runs the risk of becoming just another dreary list of stuff that students are expected to "learn" so they can be tested on it. Such visions of learning and testing are, at best, disappointing, and potentially debilitating. Media teachers have the opportunity now to demand and embrace authentic and valid assessment as an integral part of their subject area. This is particularly true in North America, where large-scale assessment in media education is not yet established. Media teachers and their professional organizations in Canada and the USA can seize the moment and collaborate to set up a system of assessment that is superior to those provided by governments.

REFERENCES

Barker, M. & Brooks, K. (1998). *Knowing audiences: Judge Dredd, its friends, fans and foes.* London: University of Luton Press.

Bloom, B. S., Krathwohl, D. R. & Masia, B. B. (Eds.) (1956). *Taxonomy of educational objectives: Handbook I, cognitive domain,* New York: D. McKay.

Bowker, J. (1991). *A curriculum statement.* London: The British Film Institute.

Buckingham, D. (1996). *Moving images: Understanding children's emotional responses to television.* Manchester: Manchester University Press.

Carlsson, U. & von Felitzen, C. (Eds.). (1998). *Children and media violence,* UNESCO, Goteborg University, Sweden.

Carlsson, U. & von Felitzen, C. (Eds.) (1999). *Children and media image education participation,* UNESCO, Goteborg University, Sweden.

Fine, J. (1999). Quality Performance Tasks. Unpublished.

Hart, A. (Ed.). (1998). *Teaching the media: International perspectives.* Mahweh, NJ: Lawrence Erlbaum Associates.

McMahon, Q. et al., (2002). International Media Literacy Proposal. Available at: http://www.geocities.com/jseddon_2000/RQweb/media_literature_website/index.html

Masterman, L. (1985). *Teaching the media.* London: Comedia.

Peel District School Board, (1995, 1998). *Peel writing scales.* Mississauga, ON: Author.

Prinsloo, J. & Criticos, C. (Eds.) (1991). *Media matters in South Africa,* Durbam: University of Natal (Media Resource Centre).

Washington State Office of Superintendent of Public Instruction – Commission on Student Learning (2000). *Media literacy through critical thinking,* Washington State Office of Superintendent of Public Instruction (authored by Worsnop, C. M.). Available at http://www.k12.wa.us/toolkits/AC258.pdf

Worsnop, C. M. (1980). A Procedure for Using the Reading Miscue Inventory as a Remedial Teaching Tool with Adolescents. Masters of Education thesis (unpublished), Queen's University, Kingston, Ontario.

Worsnop, C. M. (1994). *Screening images: Ideas for media education,* Mississauga, ON: Wright Communications.

Worsnop, C. M. (1996a). *Assessing media work: Authentic assessment in media education.* Mississauga, ON: Wright Communications.

Worsnop, C. M. (1996b). The beginnings of retrospective miscue analysis. In Goodman, Y. M. & Marek, A. M. (Eds.). *Retrospective miscue analysis: Revaluing readers and reading.* Katonah, NY: Richard C. Owen Publishers.

Worsnop C. M. (1999a). *Screening images: Ideas for media education* (2nd edition). Mississauga, ON: Wright Communications.

Worsnop, C. M. (1999b). *Media connections in Ontario.* Mississauga, ON: Wright Communications.

Worsnop, C. M. (2000a). A research proposal for comparative view response. *Telemedium: The Journal of Media Literacy, 46*(1).

Worsnop, C. M. (2000b). *Media connections in Ontario* (2nd edition). Mississauga, ON: Wright Communications.

Worsnop, C. M. (2000c). Assessment in media education. *Reading On Line,* Available: http://www.readingonline.org/newliteracies/

Worsnop, C. M. (2003-in press). Issues and opportunities in media education assessment. In Muffoletto, R. (Ed.). *Breaking the classroom wall: Resistance and the quest for learning with technology.* Mount Waverly, AU: Hampton Press.

POPULAR MEDIA CULTURE, ICTS AND THE ENGLISH LANGUAGE ARTS CURRICULUM

HELEN NIXON

INTRODUCTION

Within the field of English language arts education it is now commonly agreed that literacy practices are changing as people engage with new forms of representation and communication associated with computers and the new media. In Canada, the UK and Australia, educators are grappling with shifts in meaning-making practices associated with information and communications technologies (ICTs) that have profound implications for English/literacy curriculum policy and pedagogical practice. Similar issues face educators across the globe at the level of national policy development, in education departments and district boards, and in schools and classrooms.

In many countries the previous cornerstones of English language arts curriculum – reading, writing, listening and speaking – have come under challenge because of the multiple and hybrid forms of literacy practice required to use and produce electronic and multimedia forms of communication. The range of presentational as well as representational tools now at students' disposal has created new emphases and new dynamics for "readers" and "writers" (Goodwyn, 2000). In the new media and ICT-saturated learning environments, what it means to be "literate" is emergent and changing. It is now clear that in order to develop and teach an appropriate English language arts curriculum for the future, educators need to think differently about how children communicate and make meaning in a world no longer centered on the page and the printed book (Kress, 2000).

But how can English and literacy educators be assisted to understand and meet these challenges? What theoretical and practical resources can they draw on? This book is designed to grapple with these issues. In this chapter I use examples from the popular teen TV drama *Dawson's Creek* to illustrate how concepts from cultural studies might supplement concepts from English language arts and literacy education to assist educators to address some of these issues in everyday classroom practice.

YOUNG PEOPLE AND GLOBAL MEDIA CULTURE

Cultural theorists have argued that many people across the world today operate within a globalized, high-tech media culture. This is an important phenomenon for educators to consider because the media "contribute to educating us how to behave and what to think, feel, believe, fear, and desire – and what not to" (Kellner, 1995, p. 2). From this perspective, the media can be understood as sources of stories and other symbolic forms that educate people about how to buy, consume, negotiate and value commodities and services within everyday life. In this respect, the media produce forms of "cultural pedagogy" (Kellner, 1995), and function alongside school-based pedagogy as one of the "pedagogies of everyday life" (Luke, 1996). The "educative" function of the contemporary media in this regard is quite complex. As Morgan (1993) points out:

> It is no longer possible "to talk about education as though it takes place exclusively in schools and classrooms;" the media "transform our living rooms into learning rooms," constituting in effect new sites of education and potent resources for meaning construction. (p. 39)

Hence the media are more than "influences" on behavior or significant "backgrounds" to daily life. Rather, they are the new "environments we live in" (Morgan, 1993, p. 36). Understood from this perspective, the media provide the very materials out of which people forge their identities, and make decisions and take social actions that have material consequences.

Research conducted within cultural studies has shown that global media culture is increasingly central to the lives of today's children and youth. It has become integrally bound up with their affiliations, identities and pleasures (Buckingham, 2000; Howard, 1998; Kenway & Bullen, 2001; Sefton-Green, 1998). Because these affiliations and pleasures are key to learning, it is necessary for educators to understand how these affiliations are constructed by the global cultural economy and made available to and experienced by young people. However, traditional approaches to English and literacy education are unable to provide these understandings. Rather, it has become necessary for educators to look to cross-disciplinary theory to explain the evolving contexts of consumer-media culture in order to explore what it might mean for curriculum and pedagogical practice.

School curriculum has by and large failed to capitalize on young people's engagement with and knowledge about the media and ICTs. Some researchers in the field of English language arts argue that this neglect has been to the detriment of many young people of school age from early childhood through to adolescence (e.g., Bean, 1998, Dyson, 1997, Marsh, 2000, O'Brien, 1998). They argue that for some children there is a large gap between home literacies and school literacies that might be bridged by the integration of popular culture into the curriculum. Other researchers point out that the advent of ICTs and the commodification and marketization of education have blurred the boundaries between home and school and between informal and formal learning (Sefton-Green, 2000). According to this latter argument, the home and the school are becoming less distinct from each other as "locations" for the development of new or changing literacies associated with ICTs and new media. No matter whether popular media culture is envisaged as a bridge to the valued curriculum, or is valued in its own right as an informal site for learning, many challenges for teachers and pedagogical practice present themselves.

If English language arts teachers are to take into account the centrality of popular culture and global media culture to their students' lives, then they are faced with the following questions. What are the implications of global consumer-media culture for young people's literacy and communication practices? How might teachers best engage with the popular pedagogies of consumer-media culture in their classrooms? How might consumer-media culture be approached from a "critical" perspective and in ways that are generally recognized as educationally worthwhile?

COMMUNICATIONAL WEBS AND
GLOBAL MEDIA CULTURE

As they participate in global media culture, young people operate within "new communicational webs" (Kress, 2000) as depicted in the following scenario.

The 12-year-old boy who spends much of his leisure time either by himself or with friends in front of a video game terminal, lives in a communicational web structured by a variety of media of communication and of modes of communication. In that, the "screen" may be becoming dominant, whether that of the TV or of the PC, and may be coming to restructure the "page." The visual mode may be coming to have priority over the written, while language-as-speech has newer functions in relation to all of these. The media in this web would be TV, PC, video game, magazine, book, talk and Internet websites. The modes of communication would be, probably dominantly, image, then writing, then talk. In contrast, the 12-year-old's 10-year-old sister is likely to live in a quite differently structured communicational web; yes TV and PC figure, but quite differently. Instead of the books on science fiction (derived from video games) or books on games themselves, there might be much more conventional narratives, and the magazines might be absent. Talk would figure more prominently, as would play of a self-initiated kind (Kress, 2000, p. 143).

Children and teenagers – who constitute key target audiences for products and services associated with global media culture – operate within communicational webs centered on the world of popular media culture and digital technologies. From the point of view of English language arts, a key feature of communicational webs is that they simultaneously include a number of different media and modes of meaning making or communication. But what might these communicational webs and these media and modes of communication actually look like in the life of a middle or secondary school student? What tensions might arise for English language arts teachers who try to respond to students' engagements with global media culture within the parameters of institutionalized schooling? In the following section I explore these questions by focusing on communicational webs constructed by global media culture around the popular US-produced teen TV drama *Dawson's Creek* (1998-2002).

COMMUNICATIONAL WEBS AND THE
TEEN TV DRAMA *DAWSON'S CREEK*

One reason for beginning an exploration of communicational webs by focusing on a television program is that surveys of young people show that television remains central to their leisure time even though they now also spend time engaged with newer media such as the internet and mobile phone. Moreover, today's teens use the television and computer-based media simultaneously and tend to "multi-task" as they use media devices (Center for Media Education, 2001).

The television series *Dawson's Creek* focuses on the everyday lives and angst of a group of teenagers (originally aged 15-16 years of age) living in Capeside, a small fictional harbor town in Massachusetts, USA. From creator and executive producer Kevin Williamson, the program was first broadcast in the USA in 1998 and in Australia in 1999 and quickly established a high level of popularity among young audiences worldwide.[1] A sixth series of *Dawson's Creek* is being produced for screening in the USA late in 2002.

During the first four series of the program, audiences followed the main character Dawson Leery and his childhood friends Joey Potter and Pacey Witter as they tried to find ways to establish and maintain friendships, establish autonomy from parents and peers, and come to terms with sex and sexuality. In the fourth series the characters were in their senior year of high school, while in the fifth series they begin to live their post-school lives in college or at work. The following extract from the "official website" (www.dawsonscreek.com, accessed July 26, 2002) summarizes "information about the show":

A startlingly fresh and realistic portrayal of this passage from adolescence to young adulthood, "Dawson's Creek" takes a dramatic turn in its fifth season as the teens embark on their post-high school lives. At this crossroads, expectations are turned on their head as the friends surprise each other with the people they grow into being, how well they thrive in this new world and who steals their hearts.

Last season culminated with the bittersweet graduation of Dawson (James Van Der Beek, "Varsity Blues"), Joey (Katie Holmes, "Wonder Boys"), Pacey (Joshua Jackson, "The Skulls"), Jen (Michelle Williams, "Dick") and Jack (Kerr Smith, "Final Destination"). Lifelong friends and confidantes, Joey and Dawson shared one last kiss as they faced being on separate coasts with Dawson following his Hollywood dream at USC film school and Joey fulfilling her academic destiny at Worthington College in Boston.

The third side of last spring's romantic triangle, Pacey, begins the fall entering the working world. He left Capeside after graduating from high school and headed for the high seas. At the end of the summer, he reluctantly returns to Boston and faces his future. While his friends are all in college classes and co-ed dorms, Pacey gets a job in a restaurant and gains confidence that he actually might find something he's good at doing.

Even this short snippet about its content suggests that the program "teaches" its young audience lessons about the possible educational and life trajectories they might follow in their own lives. The program offers cultural stories about being young and growing up, about establishing and maintaining friendships, and about making one's way in the world. It makes available to young people cultural scripts which they can appropriate or reject as part of their quest to establish an identity and to become "somebody."

However, the promotional 'information about the show' reproduced above also provides some insight into the ways that global media culture has structured a web of different media and modes of communication around *Dawson's Creek*. Firstly, there is an official website for fans that is copyrighted to Sony Pictures Digital Entertainment Inc, producers of the TV series. Secondly, information about the series published on the website couples the names of actors from the television series with motion pictures in which they have also appeared:

Dawson (James Van Der Beek, "Varsity Blues"), Joey (Katie Holmes, "Wonder Boys"), Pacey (Joshua Jackson, "The Skulls"), Jen (Michelle Williams, "Dick") and Jack (Kerr Smith, "Final Destination").

Thus for fans of *Dawson's Creek*, global media culture explicitly interconnects the different media of television, film and internet website.

The website home page points to other media and modes of communication made available to site visitors and to the connections between them constructed by global media culture. This in turn is

Dawson's Creek *home page (www.dawsonscreek.com)*

indicative of the kinds of communicational webs fans of the TV series are likely to operate within in their daily lives.

On the home page interconnections are established between the *media* of television, film, photography, radio, music, newsletter, PC (screensaver, e-cards, desktop), mobile telephone, digital video and personal digital assistant (pda). The *modes of communication* the home page

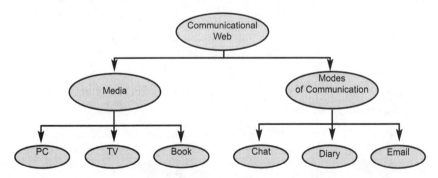

Figure 2: A communicational web constructed by the Dawson's Creek *website*

illustrates or enables through hyperlinks include writing (script, diary, e-mail), talk (chat, interview), and still and moving image. A communicational web constructed by this website could be represented by building on the diagram in Figure 2.

The *Dawson's Creek* TV program continues to receive extensive cross-media exposure and has created multiple media spin-offs. As has been noted, all of the young actors from the central group of characters have appeared in at least one feature film. Their cross-over from television to film has been facilitated by creator Williamson's career as a scriptwriter of high-grossing "teen" horror films *Scream* (1996), *Scream 2* (1997) and *I Know What You Did Last Summer* (1997). In addition, Columbia Tri Star Interactive/Sony also produces films that feature roles created for the series' characters (e.g., the film *Go* in 1999 for Katie Holmes). Such crossovers are indicative of the opportunities for global media culture's capital investment in the *Dawson's Creek* "brand." In addition, two successful "official" music CDs, *Songs From Dawson's Creek*, have been produced from the series soundtracks by Sony TriStar, makers of the TV series.

One purpose of this media strategy is to create products that can be sold on fan websites using what the industry calls "viral marketing" techniques (Center for Media Education, 2001), whereby many different products and services provided by the same media conglomerate can be promoted and sold by hot linking. However, another effect of such media strategies is to construct repertoires of products and practices that become associated with being a "fan" of a particular program. These in turn become associated with certain identifying characteristics such as particular ways of speaking, dressing and behaving; or appreciating particular kinds of music or film. Thus what is essentially a commercial media strategy becomes linked to the cultural scripts made available to and taken up by some of the young people who watch the TV program or who want to be associated with those who do. The media therefore are sources of cultural materials in which young people have significant affective investments and out of which they shape identities for themselves.

The fact that popular cultural forms constitute significant new sites for learning as well as resources for meaning making and identity construction in the lives of children and young people is a compelling reason for their purposeful introduction into the classroom. However, we should not underestimate the potential hazards of working with material that some young people may consider their own domain, and that some adults may consider inappropriate because it raises value-laden issues of an aesthetic, ethical and moral nature (see Giroux, 1994; Misson, 1998; Nixon, 2002). Nonetheless, I agree with Alvermann (2000) that:

> *Drawing lines of demarcation between topics that adolescents find appealing to read, write and talk about in our classes and those that adults find worthy of taking up in school time is a counterproductive pedagogical practice (p. 437). This is particularly so at a time when the media – and increasingly digital media – dominate leisure and culture.*

A 3D FRAMEWORK FOR CONSTRUCTING ENGLISH LANGUAGE ARTS CURRICULUM

The above exploration of communicational webs constructed around a popular teen TV drama uses concepts from communication and cultural studies to demonstrate how global media culture works to construct significant interconnections for young people between one popular medium and another, and one mode of communication and another. These connections in turn make available repertoires of cultural practices on which young people can draw to shape their social identities. Research into media use shows that the communicational webs in which today's young people actually operate parallel the interconnections of media and modes of communication discussed in relation to *Dawson's Creek*. For young people aged between 9 and 18, internet use is primarily associated with popular media culture. Many of the websites and chat rooms they visit relate to their interests in other media such as music, film, television and video and computer games (Burton, 1999; Center for Media Education, 2001). Fan websites of all kinds are particularly popular with young web users and website and other media production plays a key role in many of their cultural lives.[2]

In this section of the chapter I turn to the potential significance of popular media culture for the teaching of "reading" or "viewing" within the English language arts curriculum. My point is that as young people operate within communicational webs like the one described in the previous section, they not only construct social identities, they also construct other kinds of meaning as they engage with a broad repertoire of literate practices. However, many of these evolving literacy practices are not yet generally made central to school-based English language arts curriculum. So how might teachers begin to make coherent curriculum and pedagogical responses that take into account such phenomena as popular culture fandom (see Alvermann, 2000)? Moreover, how might teachers begin to work not only with concepts from *cultural studies*, but also with theoretical models of *literacy* learning, in order to inform their teaching about new media and communication? I have found the 3D model of literacy learning developed by Australian educator Bill Green to be extremely helpful when considering such challenging questions. In what follows I briefly describe the model and then outline how it might be applied to curriculum based on a popular teen TV program like *Dawson's Creek*.

Since the 1980s Bill Green has been developing a three-dimensional model of literacy that has been extended to embrace ICTs. Beginning from a socio-cultural perspective of literacy, Green's 3D model was originally developed in relation to subject-specific literacy (Green, 1988). His argument was that literacy must be seen in "3D," as having three interlocking aspects or dimensions of learning and practice: the operational, the cultural and the critical. The *operational* dimension involves technical competence and "how-to" knowledge. The *cultural* dimension stresses that language and literacy are not stand-alone skills or proficiencies but are used in specific contexts with particular social goals. The *critical* dimension recognizes that stories, histories, school subjects, text books and so on are always written from particular points of view that imply certain relationships between language, knowledge and power. These are open to challenge using certain deconstructive analytic strategies.

In his subsequent theoretical work (Durrant & Green, 2000; Lankshear & Snyder with Green, 2000) Green stages a dialogue between established work in literacy studies and the socio-cultural paradigm, and the "constructionist" work in computer culture and learning as developed in the work of Seymour Papert. He uses the shorthand device of emphasizing the IT in the word l(IT)eracy to symbolize the bringing together theoretically of literacy and IT within his 3D model. The following applies to the 3D model when ICTs are taken into account:

- the *operational* dimension of l(IT)eracy learning includes how to make the computer work from the basics of turning on to searching databases or operating a CD ROM.

- the *cultural* dimension of l(IT)eracy learning includes understanding that we use texts and technologies in particular contexts to make meaning and to do things in the world. In schools, this means using technologies within the "culture" or real world applications associated with learning areas or disciplines. It also implies giving priority to the use of texts and technologies in the service of authentic meaning making and meaningful effective practice in the worlds inside and outside school.

- the *critical* dimension of l(IT)eracy learning includes being able to assess and critique software and other resources, and to appropriate or re-design them where appropriate.

The emphasis on re-designing in the critical dimension highlights the importance of production or "making" for learning through, with and about the new media and ICTs. In this chapter I do not focus on how production might be integrated into the English language arts curriculum. However, Hammett (see this volume) describes in some detail how this might be done in ways that address the cultural and critical dimensions of l(IT)eracy learning and learning about the media.

USING THE 3D MODEL OF L(IT)ERACY
TO DESIGN CURRICULUM BASED
ON *DAWSON'S CREEK*

I begin from the assumption that teachers who use the 3D model of literacy/l(IT)eracy to design curriculum would make the model explicit to students. This would be part of their educative goal to assist students to develop a meta-language with which to describe their learning in English language arts at a time when developing competence with the media and ICTs is an increasingly important part of becoming literate. The *Dawson's Creek* television program could itself easily provide the starting point for curriculum work of the kind I am advocating (see Nixon, 2001). However, in this section I once again take the official *Dawson's Creek* website as my starting point. My discussion is not intended as an uncritical promotion of commercially produced websites. Rather, the website has been chosen as a potentially useful starting point for an exploration of the changing and hybrid literate practices associated with new media and modes of communication that constitute the communicational webs in which young people operate within global media culture. What follows is a set of hypothetical assignments that draw on Green's 3D model and use the *Dawson's Creek* website as focus material. Each of three sets of questions equates to one dimension of the 3D model. Each set of questions is supplemented by discussion about the potential value of asking such questions and the kinds of responses students could be expected to make.

Green (Durrant & Green, 2000) is insistent that none of the dimensions of the 3D model has any necessary priority over the others. All dimensions need to be addressed simultaneously, in an integrated view of literate practice and literacy pedagogy. The model can be depicted as follows (Durrant & Green, 2000, p. 98):

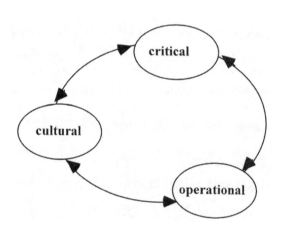

In order to assist students to explore the 3D model in practice, teachers could provide students with an enlarged version of Figure 3 that includes plenty of blank space under the three words. Students could use this to record their preliminary explorations of the website based on the following three sets of questions. They could then be invited to provide expanded responses to a self-selected or teacher-selected sub-set of questions from each of the three sets listed below.

EXPLORING THE OPERATIONAL DIMENSIONS OF LITERACY PRACTICES MADE AVAILABLE ON THE WEBSITE

1. What technical competence or "how-to" knowledge about "reading" or navigating the website is assumed by this site? Explain your

answer with reference to at least one full page of the site that you print off and annotate or annotate electronically.

2. What "how-to" knowledge about computing and other media does this website "teach" or provide for its users? Provide at least three examples.

3. What "old" literacy practices are users encouraged to engage in as they navigate this website (e.g., reading, writing, listening, speaking)? Discuss with reference to at least two pages of the website.

4. What "new" literacy practices – e.g., use of new media and modes of communication – are users encouraged to engage in as they navigate this website? Discuss with reference to at least two pages of the website that you have not yet discussed.

5. Using pencil and paper or sticky labels, on a large sheet of paper map one reading pathway that you are interested in following through this site. Map your choices as you move through at least six pages of hypertext and explain the basis on which you made your navigation choices. Illustrate the map with pages printed off from the site if this is helpful.

6. These questions might assist students to articulate that websites like this offer opportunities to experience "older" or more familiar forms of communication such as reading spin-off books and writing diaries and film scripts. However, it will soon become clear to students that the site also offers opportunities to participate in newer multi-modal forms of literacy and modes of communication that incorporate word, image, movement and music. These modes of communication on the *Dawson's Creek* website include email, internet chat, web casting and online game playing. The final activity should alert students to fact that, unlike reading a book, "reading" a website requires non- or multi-linear and associative reading (Thurstun, 2000) and forms of meaning making that do not rely on language alone.

EXPLORING THE CULTURAL DIMENSIONS OF PARTICIPATION IN THIS WEBSITE

In Green's 3D model, the cultural dimension of literacy practice is not completely separate from the operational or critical dimensions.

However, the cultural dimension refers specifically to learning how to make meaning that is "authentic" or meaningful in a particular discourse or cultural practice and context. In relation to the Dawson's Creek website, the context is popular media culture. The site has been produced within global media culture to target a particular group – young fans of the TV program. As young people engage with the website, they participate in discourses and cultural practices that are shared among and valued by other fans of the program. Within the curriculum students can be encouraged to explore this cultural dimension and to articulate the kinds of cultural activities and social identities that global media culture invites them to take up and value.

Questions that might assist students to explore the cultural dimensions of fan website texts and practices include:

1. What are the assumed leisure interests of users of this website? Explain with reference to at least five web pages. How do these fit with the leisure interests of you and your friends?

2. What opportunities are provided for users to register their own interests, provide feedback, "talk back" to the website or become involved in the creation of content? Explain with reference to at least three web pages. Which of these opportunities for interaction with the site might be taken up by you or some of your friends, and which might be rejected and why?

3. What kinds of "personalized" services are offered on the site? How do they connect with either young people's leisure activities or the *Dawson's Creek* website or TV program?

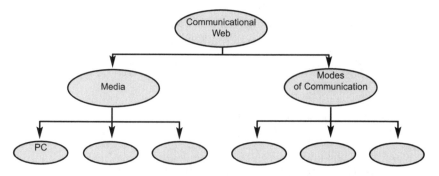

*Figure 4: Mapping a communicational web
constructed by the website*

4. Use a blank graphic like the one provided (see figure 4) or the soft-ware Inspiration (Inspiration Software, 1998-1999) to map the range of media (e.g., TV, PC, website) and modes of communication (e.g., chat, image, writing, mobile phone) that fans of *Dawson's Creek* are assumed to participate in or to want to know about. (You may have discussed some of these in your answer to the previous question.) Once you have done this you have created a representation of a communicational web that is constructed by the *Dawson's Creek* website and made available for young people's participation.

5. Use another blank copy of a graphic like figure 4, draw a second communicational web that more accurately reflects the range of media and modes of communication that you actually operate within in your leisure time. Point out and discuss the differences between the two communicational webs you have drawn.

6. What features of the website are designed to tell you more about your favorite *Dawson's Creek* characters? Which of these features are familiar from other media such as magazines? Which features are unique to the digital medium?

7. Explore the "characters' desktop" feature of the *Dawson's Creek* site. What do the desktops tell you about one or more of the characters and how do they do this?

8. Which character's desktop is either most like your own, or most like the desktop you would like to have, and why?

The following questions might assist students to reflect on and make sense of their responses to the above:

1. What kinds of cultural activities and social identities are *Dawson's Creek* website users invited to "try on" or take up? Explain with reference to annotated examples of at least three web pages.

2. Which aspects of the activities and identities on offer on the website do you find appealing and why? Discuss and debate your choices with others in your class.

Popular culture and media culture provide material against which young people test their identities and with which they connect socially with liked-minded peers. Audience research into the reading and viewing patterns of children and young adolescents suggests that they use popular culture as one way to "learn" about and identify with people who are several years older than they are (Buckingham, 2000). Pre-teens' film and television viewing choices, for example, are informed by a broad sense of a "teen" lifestyle to which many of them aspire, even when they don't yet see themselves as teenagers. Popular media culture can be attractive to pre and young teens precisely because it enables the pleasures of "trying on" a range of range of identities, attitudes and values associated with teen lifestyles. In this regard, there are many similarities between the "old" media of teen magazines and the "new" media of fan websites. A close examination of the *Dawson's Creek* website uncovers features like personality tests and "star" and viewer diaries that are very familiar from teen and fan magazines.

However there is an obvious difference between teen magazines and the *Dawson's Creek* website in that the latter makes integral to this identity work the "trying on" of new media and the "trying out" of new forms of literacy associated with electronic media and communication. On the website, the online year book can be signed and short films can be made and emailed to friends. Thus the website continues to offer users the kinds of subject positions for teens that are offered in other popular cultural forms such as magazines. At the same time, however, it also provides the tools by which this "identification" can be taken to further levels of involvement.

The "characters' desktop" feature of the *Dawson's Creek* site provides an interesting example of this practice. It functions as a form of induction for young fans into the whole gamut of activities now possible on desktop computers. Moreover, it is a clear example of the pedagogical function performed by such websites and the links between this function and commercial objectives.

WHAT ARE THE DESKTOPS ALL ABOUT?

Ever wish you could see inside someone's computer? Someone like one of your favorite characters on *Dawson's Creek*? Well, here's your chance! Each week one of four different desktops appears here – Dawson's, Joey's, Pacey's or Jen's! Between the episodes, you can delve into their journals, e-mails, Instant Message chats – even their trash cans! Just click "Go" to enter. Once you're on the "desktop" you can click on any of the icons, or just click "Begin." Like on your own desktop, there are many ways to navigate. And since Dawson and his friends are often online, there's something new every day! (www.dawsonscreek/desktop/)

During 2000 and 2001 the Movie-Pro Mixer Shockwave software located on "Dawson's desktop" allowed users to edit and play pre-selected clips from the series, to combine music clips with selected images, and to write their own text as closing credits. In 2002, the inclusion on the desktop of "Dawson's Creek MovieCreator on Screenblast" allowed users to "mix video clips and dialogue from their favorite characters, add music, and create new scenes over and over again" (*Dawson's Creek Scoop*, online newsletter edition 182, May 20 2002). The "films" produced on website users' own desktop are then available to be emailed to friends. These facilities offer the opportunity not only to try out movie editing software, but also to try on the role of amateur filmmaker that the main character Dawson Leery occupies in the TV program. The desktop feature of the *Dawson's Creek* website is a potentially powerful device. Not only does it enable a high level of interactivity with the website, it also provides opportunities for the psychological pleasures of identification. It enables fans to access and download the "personal" (albeit fictionalized) computer files of characters from the TV series, and to play with or take on some of the characters' attitudes and characteristics.

As Green has emphasized, the operational, cultural and critical dimensions of literacy practice and literacy learning have equal priority and are often practiced simultaneously. Hence it is possible to use many of the questions listed in this section in relation to the *cultural* dimension as a lead in to a more specifically *critical* literacy practice that will be discussed in more detail in the following section.

EXPLORING CRITICAL READINGS OF THE *DAWSON'S CREEK* WEBSITE

One goal of critical practice in English language arts is to assist students to be critical readers of texts. This involves considering how texts position readers and examining the political and cultural assumptions on which such positioning is based. One aspect of critical literacy practice is the analysis of texts as pedagogical sites where "lessons" are taught about social identities, social values and power relations and the exploration of how they might have been constructed differently. The theoretical and methodological foundations for such critical explorations in English/literacy education have their roots in the political projects of cultural studies and critical discourse analysis. So what might such critical *reading* look like in relation to the texts and practices of a popular website? (For a discussion of critical *writing* or production and digital media, see Hammett, this volume.)

Before I explore this question in relation to *Dawson's Creek,* I need to acknowledge that the rational imperative which informs the "critical" impulse may be at odds with the affective imperative that accompanies young people's engagement with popular culture. It is certainly a challenge for teachers of adolescents that, just at the age when young people are more inclined to respond affectively to their surroundings, the school curriculum requires them to engage in reading and writing for academic rather than affective purposes (Bean, 1998). How teachers might work productively with the pleasurable *and* the critical remains an open question in the research on critical media literacy (Alvermann & Hagood, 2000). As Janks (2002) persuasively argues, educators adopting critical approaches need to develop ways of working with popular texts that go "beyond reason" and acknowledge the pleasures of the taboo and that which cannot easily be spoken.

As I have already suggested, it is somewhat artificial to separate out the three dimensions of l(IT)eracy. It is therefore highly appropriate to build an exploration of the critical dimension on explorations of the operational and cultural dimensions or to find ways to explore all three dimensions at the same time. The main difference between activities focused on the critical and activities focused on the operational or cultural is that students are explicitly encouraged to explore questions of ideology and economics. Classroom activities might focus student attention on the ideological positions that accompany the uncritical take-up of social identities offered on the website and on the commercial imperatives that underpin the communicational webs constructed by the website. For example, the questions "What does this website allow you to do?" and "Where does it allow you to go?" might be used to assist students to examine the operational dimensions of what the website makes available. However, when combined with questions about ownership of the services and products that website users are directed towards, explorations of what the website "allows" take on a more critical inflection.

Depending on the age group, appropriate classroom activities and questions for students to consider when exploring the critical dimension of engagement with the website might include the following:

1. Read the sections of the website which describe the main characters in *Dawson's Creek*. Are these characters representative of American society as a whole? Why might this be the case?

2. What kinds of popular teenage activities are not represented in the TV series or on this website? Why might this be so? Draw a communicational web (see figure 4) that some young people you know operate within that paints an alternative picture than the one constructed by this website.

3. What kinds of "personalized" services are offered on this site? What links are there between these services and commercial activity? How and where can you find out more about this?

4. Make a list of all the products and services referred to or advertised on this site. Can they be grouped in categories? What kinds of products are they? Who makes up the target audience(s) for these products? How and where can you find figures and statistics about this? What other services do young people use that are not represented here, and what do you make of that?

5. Return to the map or communicational web you made in a previous activity that shows the range of media and modes of communication made available by this website. Layer on to this map any information you can glean about the commercial interests related to these media and modes of communication. Who provides, distributes and sells the products and services mentioned? Which companies own which media? How and where can you find figures and statistics about this?

6. Look again at the website and annotated map you have just created. What signs are there of cross-media promotion and cross-media ownership? How and where can you find figures and statistics about this?

7. Look again at the website and annotated map you have just created. How does content produced about the TV series *Dawson's Creek* seek to connect fans' use of old media with their use of new media like the desktop PC, hand-held computers and mobile phones? What other products and services are users of new media directed

towards? What new forms of literacy and meaning-making do these new products make available?

The sharing of students' responses to some of these critical questions could be expected to foreground for students the ways these texts construct different positions for them to take up. It could also highlight the different interpretations students make of the texts and provide them with a meta-language with which to discuss these differences.

CONCLUSION

In this chapter I have described two theoretical concepts drawn from cultural studies and literacy studies that might be used as a basis for the design of English language arts curriculum that addresses some of the changing literacy and communication practices associated with ICTs and new media. The concept of communicational webs has been used to consider how global media culture constructs the range of media and modes of communication within which many of today's young people operate. A three dimensional model of l(IT)eracy learning and practice has been used to suggest the new operational, cultural and critical dimensions of "reading" and media participation that might be foregrounded within the English language arts curriculum in order to assist students to critically examine a broad range of new media texts and practices. Taken together, these concepts can be used to foreground for students the textual and other meaning-making processes in which they participate as they play with and learn from the new media. They can facilitate the development in students of shared tools for critical reading and discussion. The objective of such curriculum work is not to denigrate students' leisure choices and affective investments. Rather, the objective is to provide students with forums in which to explore and discuss the new literacies as well as the enticements and pleasures they are offered by global media culture and to assist them to develop thoughtful and socially responsible attitudes to them.

REFERENCES

AC Nielsen (2001). *Australian TV Trends 2001*. [Online]. Available: www.acnielsen.com.au

Alvermann, D. (2000). Fandom and critical media literacy. *Journal of Adolescent and Adult Literacy, 43*(5), 436-446.

Alvermann, D., & Hagood, M. (2000). Critical media literacy: research, theory, and practice in 'New Times'. *The Journal of Educational Research, 93*(3), 193-205.

Bean, T. (1998). Teacher literacy histories and adolescent voices: changing content-area classrooms. In D. Alvermann, K. Hinchman, D. Moore, S. Phelps, & D. Waff (Eds.), *Reconceptualizing the literacies in adolescents' lives* (pp. 149-170). Mahwah, NJ: Lawrence Erlbaum Associates.

Buckingham, D. (2000). *After the death of childhood: Growing up in the age of electronic media.* Cambridge, UK: Cambridge University Press.

Burton, L. (1999) The options generation: a discussion of young Australians' media use. *Australian Screen Education*, 22, 54-63.

Center for Media Education. (2001). *Teen Sites.com. A field guide to the new digital landscape.* Available at: www.cme.org.

Durrant, C., & Green, B. (2000). Literacy and the new technologies in school education: meeting the l(IT)eracy challenge? *The Australian Journal of Language and Literacy, 23*(2), 89-108.

Dyson, A. H. (1997). *Writing superheroes: Contemporary childhood, popular culture, and classroom literacy.* New York: Teachers College Press.

Giroux, H. (1994). *Disturbing pleasures. Learning popular culture.* New York and London: Routledge.

Goodwyn, A. (2000). *English in the digital age: Information and communications technology (ICT) and the teaching of English.* London and New York: Cassell.

Green, B. (1988). Subject-specific literacy and school learning: a focus on writing. *Australian Journal of Education, 32*(2), 156-179.

Janks, H. (2002). Critical literacy: beyond reason. *The Australian Educational Researcher, 29*(1): 7-26.

Kellner, D. (1995). *Media culture: Cultural studies, identity and politics between the modern and the postmodern.* London and New York: Routledge.

Kenway, J. & Bullen, E. (2001). *Consuming children: Education-entertainment-advertising.* Milton Keynes, UK and Philadelphia, PA: Open University Press.

Kress, G. (2000). A curriculum for the future. *Cambridge Journal of Education, 30*(1), 133-145.

Lankshear, C., Snyder, I. & Green, B. (2000). *Teachers and techno-literacy: Managing literacy, technology and learning in schools.* Sydney: Allen and Unwin.

Luke, C. (Ed.). (1996). *Feminisms and pedagogies of everyday life.* Albany, NY: State University of New York Press.

Marsh, J. (2000). Teletubby tales: popular culture in the early years language and literacy curriculum. *Contemporary Issues in Early Childhood, 1*(2), 119-133.

Meredyth, D., Russell, N., Blackwood, L., Thomas, J. & Wise, P. (1999). *Real time: Computers, change and schooling. National Sample study of the information technology skills of Australian school students.* Canberra, AU: Australian Key Centre for Media and Policy.

Misson, R. (1998). Theory and spice, and things not nice: popular culture in the primary classroom. In M. Knobel & A. Healy (Eds.), *Critical literacy in the primary classroom* (pp. 53-62). Sydney: Primary English Teaching Association.

Morgan, R. (1993). Transitions from English to cultural studies. *New Education, 15*(1), 21- 48.

Nixon, H. (2001). Dawson's Creek: Sex and scheduling in a global phenomenon. *Screen Education,* (25), 82-89.

Nixon, H. (2002). South Park: not in front of the children. In D. Buckingham (Ed.), *Small screens: Television for children.* London: Continuum.

O'Brien, D. (1998). Multiple literacies in a high-school program for 'at-risk' adolescents. In D. Alvermann, K. Hinchman, D. Moore, S. Phelps & D. Waff (Eds.), *Reconceptualizing the literacies in adolescents' lives* (pp. 27-49). Mahwah, NJ: Lawrence Erlbaum Associates.

Sefton-Green, J. (Ed.). (1998). *Digital diversions: Youth culture in the age of multimedia.* London: UCL Press.

Sefton-Green, J. (2000). Beyond school: futures for English and media. *English in Australia, 127-128,* 14-23.

Sefton-Green, J. (2002). Cementing the virtual relationship: children's TV goes online. In D. Buckingham (Ed). *Small Screens: Television for Children.* London: Continuum Press.

Thurstun, J. (2000). Screenreading: the challenges of the new literacy. In D. Gibbs & K.-L. Krause (Eds.), *Cyberlines: Languages and Cultures of the Internet* (pp. 61-78). Albert Park, AU: James Nicholas Publishers.

END NOTES

[1] AC Nielsen (2001) research showed that in the year 2000 *Dawson's Creek* rated as the fourth most popular television series among Australian

viewers aged 13-17 years.

2 A national sample of students in 399 Australian schools found that 85% of all students used computers outside schools, more than half the students (65%) knew how to connect to the web, and 38% could make a website or home page (Meredyth et al., 1999). According to a recent American report (Center for Media Education 2001), nearly 75% of Americans aged 12-17 years operate online.

Reading, 'Riting, Representing, and Resisting Media Violence

Roberta F. Hammett

The "Rs" of English pedagogy – reading and 'riting – are being supplemented with new ones like "representation" and "resistance." These
terms point to different directions and challenges for English teachers as
media and cultural studies, combined with critical theory, squeeze into
secondary English language arts curricula. Societal pressures contribute
to the mix as media commentators, in the wake of violent incidents in
the schools, urge teachers to take up issues like violence in the media,
and cultural theorists advocate that "pedagogical interventions might be
made on this terrain [of popular culture]" (Giroux, 1994, p. xi).
Students' own interest in horror and violence adds to the challenge
issued to teachers to teach popular cultural texts along with canonical
ones. New technologies, which offer "other ways of representing"
(Atlantic Provinces Education Foundation, 1996; Western Canadian
Protocol, 1998) to writing as a means of expressing knowledge, further
extend English teachers' pedagogical responsibilities and opportunities.
In this chapter, I discuss this mixed bag of issues and challenges as I
demonstrate how high school English teachers might incorporate into
their curriculum Stephen King's novels and films (and any other media
texts that feature violence and horror). I'll use King as an example that
can be easily updated with the current popular writer of violent fiction.

The pedagogy I am proposing extends beyond reading and discussing any particular Stephen King novel or set of novels in conventional ways. What I am suggesting is a critical feminist reading of these
popular texts that would ask students to examine representations of violence which often intersect with constructions of gender in Stephen
King's or others' fictional works. This pedagogy would further require
students to think about their own identities and pleasures and about the
ways that "public texts of everyday life construct our understandings of
the world, and position persons to take up various social, political, and
cultural identities" (C. Luke, 1997, p. 21).

Inviting students to engage in a feminist or critical analysis of popular culture texts is risky business, even without the identifier "feminist," and often results in student resistance (another of the new "Rs" of English pedagogy). I think there are a number of explanations for such resistance, a phenomenon I experienced in my own high school teaching practice. I faced mixed results and not a few conflicts when I attempted to engage students in what are commonly described as critical literacy activities (or sometimes feminist or critical pedagogy). My asking students to study images of women for the purposes of exploring patriarchy and understanding the social constructions of gender is probably somewhat responsible for this, as has been pointed out by various researchers (Lather, 1988; Ellsworth, 1987). For example, such feminist work may examine advertising or television and film genres for portrayals and roles of various groups (males, females, Asians, Blacks). However, to move beyond the "so what" response predicted by Fiske (1989, p. 127) such feminist content analysis incorporates discussions of relations of power, and its intent is transformative and political (Shannon, 1993).

Asking students to critique popular culture texts in general may incite resistance, as students defend against potentially negative criticism of the texts that give them pleasure. The resistance I experienced in my classes took many forms, including explicit expressions that such analysis "ruins it" and questions like, "Why can't we just watch it for enjoyment?" Close viewing in the different context of school seems to undermine the pleasure, interrupt the social relations, and belittle and expose the desires which are all bound up in the out-of-school consumption of popular texts (C. Luke, 1997, p. 43). What the students wanted was to more closely simulate their own viewing habits: watching the entire program, once, without interruption, in physically-comfortable milieus. I experienced much less resistance when I asked the students to engage in traditional textual analysis of canonical texts – there being no pleasure to ruin with analyses of genre and other literary conventions and devices! And little challenge to the status quo of knowledge and power.

Still, I suggest, it is important for students to undertake analyses of media representations – expanded to include childhood, family life, race and ethnicity, as well as masculinity and femininity. These representations do help all of us to formulate our understandings of our world, and I believe it is important for English educators to foreground and examine them and the multiple perspectives implicit in them and in our interaction with them. When I, as a high school teacher, extended the focus of critique to include a wider range of representations for examination (beyond representations of gender) and associated the investigations with collaborative, inquiry-based textual work, and framed it in ways that shifted the intent from "making" students into critical and liberated viewers, my students were less resistant of the critiquing activities. For example, in one unit students investigated media representations of friendship, relating these to novels on the curriculum and supplementary young adult novels (and there are several often listed for novel study: *Lord of the Flies, Huckleberry Finn, The Joy Luck Club, Who Has Seen the Wind?* and many more). Exploring and analyzing these representations in explicit relation to one's own identity construction also met with more enthusiasm and less resistance. In this way, I took advantage of the possibilities of connecting curricular texts with those present in other media, including popular culture.

Similarly, what I am suggesting in this chapter is that students might be quite interested in exploring representations of violence in media texts and Stephen King in particular as they study curricular texts like *Macbeth, Lord of the Flies* and others that depict violence. I am also going to explain how computer technologies may assist this inquiry and extend it beyond a somewhat passive response.

STUDYING VIOLENCE

For many of us, fortunately, our notions and understandings of violence are formed in and from media culture, although current focus on bullying in schools and streets reminds us it is sometimes embodied knowledge, as well. Although some of us may not have experienced war, shootings or other forms of violence in our lived experience, we have a strong sense that we know what those events – those realities constructed outside of our own personal realities – are like. The popular media, especially television, mediate both our experience and its representation and even preclude the relating of words and images to their referents in the object world. As Baudrillard (1988) would suggest, simulacra (which is simulation of non-existent reality) and hyperreality (another term to suggest the exaggerated portrayals of reality in the media) so interfere with our ability to grasp reality that we define, interpret and understand it *only* through the lens of hyperreality. Thus we may not relate violence in the media to the familiar cruelty of the schoolyard. I would like to take up such issues of representation with students. With them, I want to explore the intersections of representations of violence, and of femininity, masculinity, class and ethnicity, and their own senses of reality.

Representations of violence come in all media. To begin this study, I might begin by examining a variety of those representations. Questions I might pose with students include:

– Are there differences from one medium to the next?

– What characterizes the representations of violence in Stephen King's novels?

– How are those representations different or similar from novel to novel?

– Are different or similar words and phrases used to describe the acts of violence? The results of violence? The victims? The perpetrators?

– What about other authors' novels? Are there similarities to and differences from Stephen King's style and content?

These are some of the questions students might want to investigate in print texts. Such questions challenge students to more closely examine the sources of their pleasure as well as understand how words, signs, symbols and other semantic devices are used to represent real and imagined events.

Other media might be similarly investigated by students and visual representations compared with the scenes in novels. Stephen King novels are often transmediated to film; students may be invited to discuss their differing reactions and emotional experiences when reading and viewing scenes of violence. Representations of violence in newspapers, magazines and television programs, examined by groups of students, may be compared as well.

From these inquiries, students may be ready to move on, without resistance, to examinations of other representations in King novels. Thus they might question:

– What are the roles of women in violent situations? Of men? How are each described?

– What words and phrases are important in the representations? Again, what sorts of patterns are discernible text to text?

Teachers or students wishing to situate horror fiction historically within its gothic and Greek roots can research such canonical texts for similar themes, phrases and representations as they find in more contemporary, popular texts. To follow through with representations of masculinity, for example, Shakespeare's *Macbeth* might be compared with a whole series of villains, including Stephen King's murderous husband in *Rose Madder* (1995), a novel discussed in *Reading Stephen King* (Albright & Hammett, 1997).

Let me emphasize here that I am not expecting or advocating monolithic interpretations of any text. Nor do I want to lead students toward pre-determined conclusions or to drum particular interpretations into their heads. I agree with Kellner (1995) that, in order to attract as large an audience as possible,

> *The texts of media culture incorporate a variety of discourses, ideological positions, narrative strategies, image construction, and effects (i.e., cinematic, televisual, musical, and so on) which rarely coalesce into a pure and coherent ideological position. (p. 93)*

And with Lather (1991), who adds:

> *Deconstructive pedagogy encourages a multiplicity of readings by demonstrating how we cannot exhaust the meaning of the text, how a text can participate in multiple meanings without being reduced to any one, and how our different positionalities affect our reading of it. (p. 145)*

Rather, I am advocating open-ended student determined investigations of themes and aspects of texts they decide are worthy of attention.

Examining media representations of violence and viewing violence as social constructions does not negate other explanations of violent behavior (physiological, psychological) or abrogate individual responsibility and accountability (MacCormack, 1996). Nonetheless, the prevalence of media representations of violence and its attendant role in media representations of masculinity and femininity are worth investigating, particularly as violence relates to the larger issues of power and control, whether socio-political, economic or physical. Although treading on sometimes dangerous ground with often anti-feminist teenagers (both male and female), a feminist critique that examines violence with-

142 READING, 'RITING, REPRESENTING & RESISTING

in a "patriarchal social context, unequal power distribution and culturally supported patterns of gender relations" (Tolman & Bennett, 1992,
p. 88) may be the ultimate, if unstated, goal of the inquiry from the
teacher's perspective. To this end, students may need to be supported
with scholarly readings about violence, carefully chosen by the teacher
for their accessibility and balance. The MacCormack article cited above
is one such resource that students might read. They may also be supported with other tools for investigation and critique, specifically computer technologies. Thus in the next section of this chapter I will focus
on such technologies and depart from the rather traditional methods
and activities that I have described thus far.

COMPUTERS TO FACILITATE CRITIQUE

Computer technologies may be used as "mindtools" (Jonassen,
1996) to augment thinking and intelligence (Englebart, 1963; Papert,
1999) and as tools for representing knowledge in different ways. One
technology which functions in both senses of "tools" is hypermedia.
Hypertext software like Storyspace, ToolBook, HyperStudio and
Netscape Composer allow students to link texts through hyperlinked
words or images. They also permit the intermixing of words, sounds
and songs, digitized video, still images and so on. Thus lexias or portions of text (broadly defined to include any medium) can be displayed
with or linked to any/many other texts. Picture, then, student
researchers selecting portions of text (songs, movies, novels) that illustrate the representations and constructions of violence and other concepts they are investigating as groups and linking these with other lexias to demonstrate connections they determine to be significant.
Storyspace, my favorite hypermedia software on Macintosh, allows two
or more text windows to remain open on the screen at one time so that
authors may create hyperlinks back and forth between them, selecting
words and phrases in one text that may echo or contradict or question
the other text. In print texts the selected words may be highlighted with
different color or style of font; video clips, song clips or images can be
linked to other texts in any medium, so that their juxtaposition conveys
the author's message. To facilitate the discussion of similarities and differences, to raise questions, and to suggest intertextual connections, the
teacher may display the students' selected texts side by side on the pro-
jection screen. Inviting students to analyze the texts to identify and dis-

cuss their similarities and differences may help them get at genre or ideological characteristics that may be less easy to see in other environments. Students can be challenged to identify and add links between their own and others' hypertexts, and to discuss the patterns they see emerging from the texts they are reading and studying individually or in groups. Education students in my and my colleagues' courses, who were working with "text sets" (Short, 1992), selected from multiple texts (novels, songs, videos, still images) to create powerful hypermedia about representations of women, Native Americans, spirituality, and identity in general (See Myers, Hammett, & McKillop, 1998; Hammett, 1999; Myers, Hammett, & McKillop, 2000; and Hammett, 2000).

In analyzing these hypermedia and reflecting on both our own and our students' accounts of the composition experience, we have concluded that the hypermedia technology facilitated the media critique as well as students' developing and expressing understandings of power, representation and a variety of media and cultural issues (Myers, Hammett & McKillop, 1998; Hammett, 1999; Myers, Hammett & McKillop, 2000).

Other technologies, too, can be used to juxtapose texts to express particular meanings or to open pedagogical possibilities for critical questioning. Still images or video clips can be assembled and sequenced in computer-generated movies with recorded commentary, sound tracks and song clips to communicate messages or demonstrate patterns identified in the research into and analysis of chosen texts. Digitized video can be examined frame by frame to counteract overwhelming special effects and filmic techniques that use quick cuts, high-tech images, and fast-paced action to overcome the viewer's critical perspective. Isolated from the context of the film, individual scenes and even frames can be examined closely. Thus students can deconstruct the film using the same computer tools (like Adobe Photoshop and Adobe Premiere, or similar sophisticated image and film-editing software) as the professionals may have used to construct it.

Using these computer technologies (Adobe Photoshop and Premiere) education students have also created computer-generated movies that explore and expose issues of representation (Hammett, 1999; Hammett, under review). For example, in one movie, images of Native Americans in the media were assembled so that they questioned one another and revealed the social constructions of Native Americans implicit in each representation (Myers, Hammett & McKillop, 1998; Hammett, 1999). Another movie created more recently by graduate students examines media representations of winning and losing in sports. In this movie, still images, songs, news clips and video clips were assembled to portray reactions to various sports events, raising questions about what we value as sports participants and spectators and why.

Computer technologies offer new possibilities for investigation, composition and dissemination. These tools are highly appropriate for the activities I am advocating in this chapter, and I assume students, assembling representations of violence and its intersections with race and gender, for example, will develop additional understandings of what they are reading and viewing. As Jonassen (1996) suggests, "a Mindtool is a way of using a computer application program to engage learners in constructive, higher-order, critical thinking about the subjects they are studying" (p. iv). Using Bloom's (1956) taxonomy as a definition of critical or higher-order thinking, it is relatively easy to recognize the cognitive activities of comprehension, application, analysis, synthesis and evaluation. Furthermore, these are engaged in social, cultural contexts in which identities as well as knowledge are constructed, as the next section of this chapter explains.

INVESTIGATING IDENTITIES

Student investigations should not end with what is in the texts themselves. "multiperspectival method" as Kellner (1995, p.99) calls the kind of inquiry I am advocating, attempts to examine a number of texts and uncover a variety of readings that modify and inform one another in a struggle to explore how cultural texts produce social identities and subject-positions (Kellner, 1995, p.101). Here Lather (1991, p. 145) may be helpful. She assembles a list of "critical" questions from several writers to facilitate readings that examine the ideologies of texts and readings and their inter-relationship with identities:

—Why am I reading this text?

—What kind of act was the writing of it?

—What question about it does it itself NOT raise?

—What am I participating in when I read it? (Johnson, 1987, p. 4)

—Why am I reading this way and what produces this reading? (Van

Maanen, 1988)

–What are the various positions a reading subject may occupy?

–How are these positions constructed?

–Are there possible distributions of subject-positions located in the text itself?

–Does the text construct the reading position or does the reading subject construct the text? (Fuss, 1989, p. 99)

–What intensities does the text produce? (Johnston, 1990, p. 91)

To this list I would add:

–   What desires and pleasures are being offered and constructed in texts like this?

These hard questions challenge students to construct knowledge in ways they may not previously have been permitted or required to do. They require students to take ownership of the pleasures and ideologies inherent in the books and movies they enjoy personally and share with their friends.

WHAT ABOUT PLEASURE?

Do such investigations as I have been advocating close down the pleasure that is such an important part of the horror genre and other popular and media texts, whether read or viewed? I suppose this is inevitable, just as "The Making of…" documentaries or the study of special effects replaces "pleasure from fear" with the different pleasure of "understanding how." Even the "knowing" that comes from multiple viewings of horror films to some extent shuts down pleasure, "the thrill of terror," as Buckingham (1997) reports from his extensive interviews with children. Perhaps, as Buckingham suggests, this is a necessary coping mechanism.

Students, as Vinz (1996) demonstrates, can articulate their pleasures in horror. As Kellner (1995) suggests, they can also investigate their constructedness and influence.

Pleasure itself is neither natural or innocent. Pleasure is learned and is thus intimately bound up with power and knowledge. [...] We learn what to enjoy and what we should avoid. We learn when to laugh and cheer. [...] Pleasures are often, therefore, a conditioned response [...] and should be problematized along with other forms of experience and behavior, and interrogated as to whether they contribute to a better life and society, or help trap us into modes of everyday life that ultimately oppress and degrade us. (p. 139)

Without forcing our viewpoints and politics upon students, we can use whatever tools are at our disposal to create and nurture spaces where they can come to see how texts work in identity construction, how alternative representations produce new and different identities, and how, ultimately, we can gain power over our culture. They and we can use media tools (various computer technologies) for constructing rather than passively receiving knowledge; for engaging and examining identities, experiences, and social practices; and for representing to as wide an audience as we wish our own representations of knowledge about violence in the media. Specifically, students can actively engage in cross-cultural, trans-national and inter-school discussions using various Internet technologies; can create and transmogrify images, videos, computer-generated movies and audio texts; can produce Web pages and sites individually and collaboratively; and can create a variety of multimedia texts using the huge tool chest of software being offered by a wide range of software providers.

As teachers we cannot fear but must deal with both student resistance and desire. We must aim at developing pedagogies that are intellectually challenging, that help young people to think critically about their lives and worlds, and that encourage them to envision and work towards different possibilities. In so doing, we may foster new "Rs" in the list of school activities: representing, resistance and responsibility – resistance that takes the form of active participation in democratic politics and projects of possibility that demonstrate responsibility for global social justice.

REFERENCES

Albright, J. & Hammett, R.F. (1997). Disrupting Stephen King: Examining alternative reading practices. In B. Power et al. (Eds.), *Reading Stephen King: Issues of censorship, student choice, and popular literature* (pp. 83-94). Urbana, IL: National Council of Teachers of English.

Atlantic Provinces Educational Foundation. (1996). *English language arts foundation*. Halifax: Nova Scotia Department of Education. Available at: http://doc-depot.ednet.ns.ca/

Baudrillard, J. (1988). *Jean Baudrillard: Selected writings*. M. Poster (Ed.). Stanford: Stanford University Press.

Bloom, B. (1956). *Taxonomy of Educational Objectives, Handbook I: Cognitive Domain*. New York: David McKay Inc.

Buckingham, D. (1997). *Moving images*. Manchester, UK: Manchester University Press.

Ellsworth, E. (1989). Why doesn't this feel empowering? Working through the repressive myths of critical pedagogy. *Harvard Educational Review, 59*(3), 297-324).

Englebart, D. (1963). A conceptual framework for augmentation of man's intellect. In P. W. Howerton and D. C. Weeks (Eds.), *Vistas in information handling: Volume 1. The augmentation of man's intellect by machine* (pp. 1-29). Washington: Spartan Books. Republished (1988) in I. Greif, *Computer supported cooperative work: A book of readings* (pp. 35-65). San Mateo, CA: Morgan Kauffman.

Fuss, D. (1989). Reading like a feminist. *Differences, 1*(2), 77-92.

Giroux, H. (1994). *Disturbing pleasures: Learning popular culture*. New York and London: Routledge.

Hammett, R. F. (1999). Intermediality, hypermedia, and critical media literacy. In L. Semali and A. Watts-Pailliotet (Eds.), *Intermediality: The teachers' handbook of critical media literacy* (pp. 207-221). Boulder, CO: Westview Press.

Hammett, R. F. (2000). Girlfriend in a coma: Responding to literature through hypermedia. In and A. Watts-Pailliotet & P. Mosenthal (Eds.), *Reconceptualizing literacy in the media age* (pp. 105-127). Stamford, CT: JAI Press Inc.

Hammett, R. F. (under review). Constructing computer-generated movies to represent media critique.

Johnson, B. (1987). *A world of difference*. Baltimore: Johns Hopkins University Press.

Johnston, J. (1990). Ideology, representation, schizophrenia: Toward a theory of the postmodern subject. In G. Shapiro (Ed.), *After the future: Postmodern times and places* (pp.). Albany: SUNY Press.

Jonassen, D. (1996). *Computers in the classroom: Mindtools for critical thinking*. Englewood Cliffs, NJ: Prentice Hall.

Kellner, D. (1995). *Media culture: Cultural studies, identity and politics between the modern and the postmodern*. New York and London: Routledge.

King, S. (1995). *Rose Madder.* New York: Viking.

Lather, P. (1991). *Getting smart: Feminist research and pedagogy with/in the postmodern.* New York and London: Routledge.

Luke, C. (1997). Media literacy and cultural studies. In S. Muspratt, A. Luke, & P. Freebody (Eds.), *Constructing critical literacies: Teaching and learning cultural practice* (pp. 19-49). Cresskill, NJ: Hampton Press.

MacCormack, T. (1996). Looking at male violence, *Canadian Journal of Counselling, 30*(1), 17-30.

Myers, J., Hammett, R. F. & McKillop, A. M. (1998). Opportunities for critical literacy/pedagogy in student-authored hypermedia. In Reinking, D., McKenna, C., Labbo, L. and Kieffer, D., (Eds.), *Handbook of literacy and technology: Transformations in a post-typographic world* (pp. 63-78). Mahweh, NJ: Lawrence Erlbaum Associates, Inc.

Myers, J., Hammett, R. F. & McKillop, A. M. (2000). Connecting, exploring, and exposing self in hypermedia projects. In Gallego, M. A. and Hollingsworth, S., (Eds.), *What Counts as Literacy: Challenging the School Standard* (pp. 85-105). New York: Teachers College Press.

Papert, S. (1999). *Mindstorms: Children, Computers, and Powerful Ideas* (2nd edition). New York: Basic Books.

Shannon, P. (Ed.). (1992). *Becoming political: Readings and writings in the politics of literacy education.* Portsmouth, NH: Heinemann.

Short, K. (1992). Making connections across literature and life. In K. Holland, R. Hungerford, and S. Ernst (Eds.), *Journeying: Children responding to literature* (pp. 284-301). Portsmouth, NH: Heinemann.

Tolman, R. M. & Bennett, L. W. (1992). A review of the quantitative literature on men who batter, *Journal of Interpersonal Violences, 5,* 87-118.

Van Maanen, J. (1988). *Tales of the field: On writing ethnography.* Chicago: University of Chicago Press.

Vinz, R. (1996). Horrorscapes (in)forming adolescent identity and desire. *Journal of Curriculum Theory, 12*(4), 14-26.

Western Canadian Protocol for Collaboration in Basic Education. (1998). *The common curriculum framework for English language arts, kindergarten to grade 12.* Edmonton: Alberta Education. Available at: http://www.wcp.ca/

COLLABORATIVE ENTANGLEMENTS

THE MALAISE OF MEDIA LITERACY IN THE CLASSROOM

VALERIE MULHOLLAND AND DOUGLAS ZOOK

The popular television program *Boston Public* (2002) is an attempt to depict the life of teachers and students in a typical urban high school. Mrs. Parks, a recurring character in the series, is a parent who expresses her concerns about school issues with the imperative "Smell this shoe! …This is the shoe of…" Her role parodies the opinionated conservative parent. While her claims are often investigated by the administrative team at Winslow High School, such investigation results in quite the opposite action than has been hoped for by Mrs. Parks.

The scenes with Mrs. Parks in *Boston Public* underscore attempts by teachers who wish to raise questions about the various ways students understand, act upon and react to issues surrounding media literacy and popular culture. The attention of popular culture upon school situations is not new, but its ubiquitous nature and overwhelming influence deserves intense consideration, especially among teachers.

In this chapter we describe our efforts to focus attention on the importance of critical media literacy. We wanted our students to learn ways to teach media literacy to high school students. We also understood that it was necessary to understand one's own subjectivity as a priori to subsequent work with students. We recognized the political nature of studying media texts. To this end we combined one English language arts and one social studies curriculum and instruction class over the course of one semester to create interdisciplinary, collaborative and critical projects that they in turn could use with their high school students.

Canadian culture is significantly formed and informed by the dominant media culture, which in turn is dominated by North American corporate entities. Canadians are voyeurs and consumers of media culture. We are a spectator society which derives pleasure from viewing, more commonly referred to in film theory as *scopophilia* (Stam, Burgoyne & Flitterman-Lewis, 1992, p. 160). Our postmodern society is one in which the printed text is being replaced by a visual screen. Lyon (1997) argues that there is an increasing movement from "logocentrism to iconocentrism" (p. 7). This movement is certainly evidenced with the proliferation of constantly changing Internet technologies. We not only derive pleasure from such viewing but we also interpret meaning from the visual texts we choose to view or are unwittingly exposed to. We decipher our multi-layered personal and corporate identities in large part from the popular culture within which we exist.

Douglas Kellner (1995) argues for a critical media literacy because, as he says,

> *media stories and images provide the symbols, myths, and resources which help constitute a common culture for the majority of individuals in many parts of the world. Media culture provides the materials for creating identities whereby individuals insert themselves into contemporary technocapitalist societies and which is producing a new form of global culture. (p. 1)*

Working at a critical media literacy has the potential to increase individual power over this cultural environment leading to possible newly created forms of culture. Developing critical media literacy among teachers increases their abilities to deal with and work towards new forms of culture necessary to counteract some of the issues within current media culture. It is additionally and *equally* important to explore the desires that underlie popular culture which teachers and students alike respond. Thus there is a two-fold purpose in our work: one ideological and the other personal.

We decided to learn about collaborative, interdisciplinary, transformative media literacy with our preservice English language arts and social studies teachers. The combination of these two groups of students was in large part due to their overlapping interests. While we recognized at the outset that we were novices in such a project, we engaged the possibilities with enthusiasm. Both of us had integrated aspects of media literacy into our curriculum courses, but we wanted to try something different. We hoped to do something more intentional, more collaborative more interdisciplinary and more critical with our students. We found the words of Peter McLaren (1995) to affirm our desires. He writes that there is a

desperate need within our schools for creating a media-literate citi-
zenry that can disrupt, contest, and transform media apparatuses so
that they no longer have the power to infantilize the population
and continue to create passive, fearful, paranoid, and apolitical
subjects. (p. 9)

We hoped that by providing students with a carefully selected theoretical orientation to the topic of media literacy and popular culture
that there might be some fissures created, resulting in a new way of seeing and thinking. We encouraged students to critically read the theory
across their own experiences. We anticipated, as Simon (1987)
describes, for a "pedagogy of possibility" to emerge with an increased
critical sensibility that might lead to transformative practices in their
own future classrooms. In short, we simply hoped that students would
begin to think differently and consequently to act differently – that is
to say that they would become more consciously critical of the popular
media representations they consume and distribute so readily. We find
that the interests of many of these students are not significantly different than the high school students they will soon teach.

The interrogation of media texts is necessary to understand their
constructed and ideological nature. Avner Segall (1997) raises important questions about the stories that are told through the media. These
questions focus upon the origins, choices, forms and benefits of the
shared stories. As he pointedly writes, "[a]s media texts are investigated,
students engage in examining what underlies the text – the subtext –
and consider who has the power to name the world..." (p. 239). Segall's
view of how students come to understand the ideological constructions
of media texts in terms of race, class, sexuality and gender is vital.

Graeme Turner (1988) delineates the discourse of ideology in films,
but with applications to other visual texts. He explains ideology as an
evolving and contestable term, but one which posits a "theory of reality" (p. 131). At its base, writes Turner, a "culture's ideological system is
not monolithic but is composed of competing and conflicting classes
and interest, all fighting for dominance" (p. 131). The complicitous
nature of teaching is evidenced in Turner's accurate analysis that one
cannot examine ideology from a non-ideological stance or without a
discourse entangled with ideological language. It is incumbent upon
teachers to recognize the ideological frames they bring to the examination of media literacy and to assist students in recognizing their ideo-

logical positioning. Readings of a text are subject to competing and sometimes contradictory positions, and are often covered over by dominant cultural readings. Turner suggests, nonetheless, that despite this hegemonic reality, "cracks or divisions through which we can see the consensualizing work of ideology expose" new readings of the text which challenge dominant readings (p. 147). Teaching students about alternative readings of texts holds promise as hegemonic constructions are not permanent.

Joe Kincheloe, Patrick Slattery and Shirley Steinberg (2000) unpack the neologism "kinderculture" – referring to the explicit and implicit influences upon children and youth in the North American cultural context. In arguing for a serious consideration of kinderculture, they emphasize the further consideration of "cultural pedagogy" (p. 381). This "cultural pedagogy" recognizes the economic factors that affect the lives of children and youth. They contend that teachers need to become aware of cultural pedagogy because it in turn produces "kinderculture." Kincheloe, Slattery and Steinberg advocate for an interdiction between popular culture and cultural pedagogy to mediate the problematics of such cultures. The challenge they raise, and one with which we concur, is that

> [k]inderculture is primarily a pedagogy of pleasure and, as such, cannot be defeated merely by removing our children from it. We must, instead, devise strategies of resistance proceeding from an understanding of the relationship between pedagogy, knowledge production, identity formation, desire and, of course, the contextualization of teaching. (p. 381)

The subjectivity of the viewer is something important to explore. How do students position themselves as consumers of the culture? Do they recognize what brings pleasure to them? Can they articulate their complicit positions? How do they read the visual texts they consume? Such questions intrigued us and propelled us forward as we worked with teachers. In response to some of these questions, the work of John Fiske (1987) served to frame some of our discussions. Fiske provided a variety of useful approaches for understanding and exploring responses to visual texts, especially television. In particular his notions of preferred and oppositional and discursive and realistic readings of the media were used with our students. These approaches assisted us in our attempts to examine media texts for viewer's readings of them.

Valerie Walkerdine's (1986) work also proved helpful. She argues that interrogating the media for its problematic aspects often results in the denigrating the viewers of such media. The task is complex and even uncomfortable when affective responses to such texts are considered. The polymorphous nature of desire is such that its mapping is not only difficult and complex, but it is also mostly elusive. As Walkerdine notes "different readers will 'read' films, not in terms of a preexisting set of relations of signification or through a pathology of scopophilia, but what those relations *mean to them*" (p. 190). How the readers of film – or any text, visual or otherwise, for that matter – interpret meaning is related to the formation of pleasure in the historical context of the moment.

Kincheloe, Slattery and Steinberg (2000) also take up the subjectivity of the viewer, in their case, children and youth in the school systems. Popular culture, they note, provides powerful influences through a kaleidoscope of acute emotional experiences. They write that "power mixed with desire produces an explosive cocktail; the colonization of desire, however, is not the end of the story. Power permeates both the conscious and the subconscious in a way that evokes desire – to be sure – but also of guilt and anxiety" (p. 384). While they are not explicit about a theory of desire, psychoanalytic theory takes up notions of desire from a variety of approaches. Stam, Burgoyne and Flitterman-Lewis (1992) emphasize the economy of desire that circulates between a viewer and a filmic text that is not limited to the material context but necessarily re-enacts (unconscious) dynamics. A psychoanalytical approach to the examination of films is one way to read viewer response(s). Such an approach can be a useful means by which further possibilities emerge in an examination of media literacy especially concerning viewer identificatory practices.

Judith Mayne (1995) provides a useful critique of unexamined appropriations of psychoanalytic film theory to the classroom. Mayne takes care to unpack the sometimes-unmitigated claims for negotiated readings of texts as in and of themselves liberatory. The attention to difference can be understood through the discourses intersecting within a single film as well as through the cultural and psychic aspects of film attendance. She emphasizes that the task of examining the dualities and ambiguities of desires for and responses to filmic representations is complex. She calls for a continued inquiry into spectatorship, which moves from the "passive, manipulated (and inevitably white and heterosexual) spectator" to the "contradictory, divided, and fragmented subject"(p. 179). The challenges to psychoanalytic film theory that Mayne explicates revolve around understandings of subjects and viewers as they interact with film texts and invite all kinds of new initiatives.

The epistemological basis for work with teachers regarding the prolific nature of popular cultural influences is enhanced by psychoanalytic theory. It is only when we can begin to grasp what it is that attracts or repels us in a text that possibilities for transformative practices emerge – practices which we seek to facilitate. As we enunciate our desires, we come to own what it is that nourishes our fantasies about ourselves as good teachers, and in this case, how it is that we can become good teachers of media literacy.

We would like to take up some of the questions that emerged from our attempts to incorporate media literacy in the courses we teach. These questions will shadow us beyond this chapter as we wrestle with their implications for our future teaching. We believe that we are grappling with significant questions regarding media literacy that cascade from post-secondary to secondary classrooms. In the interests of space we have chosen to reflect, re-examine and respond to selected questions – the others we continue to live with. Some of our questions relate to the lack of interrogative practices followed by our students, and perhaps inadvertently, perpetuated by our practices.

It needs to be underscored that some students are astute at unpacking multiple meanings circulating through and among print, visual and online texts. Other students, however, are less skillful at – and more uncomfortable with – deconstructing the complex social, economic, political discourses surrounding these same texts. The students may have a vernacular, according to Thomas McLaughlin (1997), to discuss media portrayals, but they do not acknowledge their own collusion with these discourses. This lack of skill and comfort was demonstrated in their completed projects. The missing embodiment of these vernaculars was most apparent in the projects submitted where all but a few of them took an arms-length approach to the topic under study. Thus our students prepared projects about racism, sexism, anti-Semitism and other social issues, but did not consider how their own subjectivities positioned them in their exploration of these topics.

The students' projects were consistent with our established objectives for the assignment, and either met or exceeded our expectations. The inherent ideology and values in the student projects cause us to consider specific questions which are applicable to high school contexts: How is it that students separate their public selves from their private selves in the process of investigating media literacy? What contribution do teachers make to promote disembodied learning? How do teachers promote a self-censoring practice among students? We need to stress that these questions are interrelated and their separation is merely an attempt to structure our analysis because they collapse and resurface as we engage with them.

How is it that students separate their public selves from their private selves in the process of investigating media literacy? To become media literate, a teacher needs to consider how viewers, their students and themselves, are created in the dynamics of historically particular practices and relations of power and oppression. Walkerdine (1986) writes that the "fantasies, anxieties and psychical states" (p. 190) of viewers must be understood within that history. Despite the hegemonic nature of most popular visual texts, Dixon (1995) advocates learning about the "countertransgressive discourses" (p. 200) as a means to go against the grain of dominant discourses. The resistances that can and are offered by viewers are indicative of assumed spectator positions. In our media literacy work students resisted their own complicity in practices and relations of power and oppression. Most groups remained faithful to common targets: Disney animated films, television commercials and newspaper stories. They avoided media forms their potential high school students were more likely to be engaged with or invested in, such as music videos, 'zines, teen films or computer games. We were left with a lingering sense that the students knew teaching media literacy was important, but they were more interested in presenting themselves as good teachers conveying a standard message than in seriously disrupting established codes and conventions. Mayne's (1995) point that the multiple and ambiguous nature of desire is complex and as such, requires instruction and practice in bringing together an informed and informing media literacy practice where the public becomes personal. For high school teaching much more focused and intentional work is needed to aid students in the conflation of the public and the personal within the larger dynamic of the popular culture.

Assisting students to develop an awareness of culture as a compli-cated whole, as Stephen Greenblatt (1995) advocates, can provide enhanced ways to read texts. Through an examination of a set of cul-tural questions about the text, boundaries of the text become more porous and links between the text and values, institutions and practices are elucidated. We resonate with the caution Susan Bordo (1997) raises about student television viewing and extend it to the viewing of all media texts: "As educators, we need to…help students develop an abil-ity to 'see through' the mystifications of cultural appearances – to the complex historical and social realities" (p. 95). We need to explore fur-ther how it is that we can assist students in developing these abilities beyond cursory examinations.

What contribution do teachers make to promote disembodied learning? Our intention was to meld theory and practice, but it is an exercise in frustration to play the DVD of media literacy for students with our fingers continually pushing pause – having to repeatedly face the temporal, spatial and relational limitations with any pedagogical sit-uation. We provided a tangible, concrete and integrated process that resulted in a practical product. We became caught by an unself-reflex-ive pragmatism that propelled us forward without taking the time to consider where such pragmatism might lead. This point needs to be reiterated for the high school classroom where opportunities for such reflection are even more restricted.

If we want to work towards a transformative practice, pragmatism is not the course. If we want to name and examine concepts such as resistance, for example, we need to move beyond the merely pragmatic in our work. In our presentations to our students we inadvertently mod-eled a disembodied project, that of our own imbrication with the media we consume, with the ideological discourses that shape us and with the desires motivating our behaviors. Kelly (1997) reminds us that, for sub-stantive and enduring changes to occur within the classroom, students and teachers need to come to know their own subjectivities especially and specifically as connected to knowledge, desire and pedagogy.

In our media literacy work, most students chose to present conven-tional units using lecture, overheads and handouts, supplemented by clips from films or excerpts from newspapers. The majority of groups examined sexism and racism in popular culture, and suggested that teachers "combat these social problems by raising awareness using media." Most groups repeated the message, with varying levels of skill, in a remarkably similar fashion. Each group collected examples of racist, sexist or stereotypical images to show the class, but implications of what to do with this awareness were unclear. Our impression was that students had heard of the message of "stereotyping in media" many times before, and as new teachers, were comfortable with repeating the message to their students. The explosive nature of the topics was neutralized; important issues became safe and trite.

During the group presentations of their projects, one group deviated from the preferred model of transmission and prepared an elaborate drama. A dialogue, not a lecture, was developed in class. The group using drama without technological enhancement sustained the interest of the group most effectively. It was apparent that the use of technology is not a substitute for media literacy. Simply having the technological apparatus did not reflect meaningful learning about media literacy. Many of our students did not appear to engage with media as text that is intentionally constructed for multiple responses. For example, they understood that commercials have economic intentions and rely on stereotypical depictions to convey their messages. The surplus of meaning of these texts which spilled over and cannot be contained in a text – indicating the larger constructions of subjectivity inherent in a text – were not read well. It is incumbent upon teachers to consider commercial media.

High school students' sense of identity as deciphered from media requires specific attention in the classroom. The affective responses to such texts require a consideration of the fantasies underlying popular texts, as Judith Robertson (1997) describes, to illuminate pedagogical practices. Utilizing Greenblatt's (1995) approach to cultural criticism may serve high school teachers in this regard. Questions of identification, comfort, cultural setting and representation need to be introduced and investigated with students as they read media texts.

How do teachers encourage self-censoring practice among students? Beginning teachers are often engrossed by the question of what a good teacher does, says and teaches about media – to the exclusion of developing a risky, critical approach of it. They may want to examine media literacy in a way that would not be sanctioned – which of course subverts the process of being critical. In our media literacy work, teachers constructed and reinforced images of the good teacher. In our classes we viewed segments from two films most of our students were familiar with: *Renaissance Man* (1994) and *Election* (1999). Those who had not seen the films were at the very least familiar with the stereotypes illustrated: the outsider who saves the students by being relevant and the earnest teacher who tries to function in a corrupt system. In our context the good teacher is the one who would study media to fight racism, sexism, anti-Semitism and other social ills. Often the justification provided for the inclusion of media courses in K-12 schools is that in them the perceived *evils* of the larger culture can be named and attacked. These texts, which are associated with pleasure and leisure, are unmasked as promoting injustice, and a rhetoric neutralizing their potency develops. While we concur with McLaughlin (1996) that "no postmodern kid forgets his or her gender, race, class, sexual orientation and other group affiliations" (p. 156), high school students can, and do, learn very well to repress and represent these identities dependent upon the context created for their expression.

Teachers re-presentations of themselves partly reflect a uni-dimensional position which is often mirrored by their students. In this media literacy work we discovered things we already knew that are applicable to the high school context: many students will seek to please teachers and achieve success; students have different satisfaction rates with their work and levels of success; many students are reticent to take risks; critical thinking is developed, not inherent in or the result of instruction. Teachers are often as eager to satisfy students as students are to satisfy teachers. We *look* to them, in Dixon's (1995) fantasmatic longing sense, as much as they *look* back to locate their desires in our responses. We are as willing as they to police and censor ourselves, to promote our own sense of being a good teacher, to minimize our investment and capitalize upon the knowledge we are deemed to possess. The caution of Turner (1988) that one cannot escape from an ideological position needs to be coupled with the psychoanalytical sense of desire circulating within the pedagogical exchange and in the reading of popular texts. As the ideological and identificatory practices are named, greater freedom from restrictive practices in classrooms are made possible.

The spectacle of Mrs. Parks in *Boston Public* offers an image not unlike many teachers' investigations of media literacy. She creates an empathetic response in this extreme (melo)drama by representing a voice calling for a re-examination of emerging practices within a school.

Throughout numerous episodes of *Boston Public*, Mrs. Park's character is used to establish an oppositional voice, albeit done in mimicry, to the liberal notions preferred in the television program's diegesis of social tolerance.

Mrs. Parks draws attention to issues that other characters then consider differently, and often, result in a new awareness for them, which causes them to act differently. In *Boston Public*, liberal notions are reified while conservative notions are caricatured and then dismissed. In our work with media literacy we feel it is imperative to provoke strong responses from our students with the intention of engendering personal investment in the work. As Mrs. Parks offers a metaphorical object to incite change, we offered examples, activities and theory to encourage innovative instructional practice. Unlike Mrs. Parks, who is thwarted in her efforts to reform unacceptable behavior, teachers in classrooms are continually faced with challenges of how to advance an agenda of inclusion and respect for diverse responses to complex issues.

Certainly, we are aware that work with media and popular culture requires in-depth, intensive and long-term effort – it is not a "one-shot" process. It is an exercise in frustration, and perhaps futility, to play with media literacy without acquiring skill at reading media texts and recognizing the enormity of the task of media literacy exploration. We reject the tendency to believe that the naming of a distasteful practice will result in changed behavior; that awareness alone results in some kind of transformative practice. Teachers need to spend time working at basic interrogation of texts – material, social and economic – as well as affective response. Agreeing with Bordo (1997), we would "much prefer that they learn to analyze, interpret, critique and evaluate **one** thing...in all its complexity – including issues of race, gender, history and power – than that they be taken on a sightseeing tour of the globe" (p. 81). As a result of our collaborative efforts, we suggest that media literacy learning in high school classrooms focus on a personalized approach to developing a critical stance. Otherwise, we are committing the equivalent of channel surfing in our teaching practice.

REFERENCES

Abbott, E., Colleton, S., Feitshans, B., Greenhut, R. & Vajna, A. G. (Producers), & Marshall, P. (1994). *Renaissance man* [Motion picture].

United States: Buena Vista.

Berger, A., Gale, D., Samples, K. & Yerxa, R. (Producers) & Payne, A. (Screenwriter/Director). (1999). *Election* [Motion picture]. United States: Paramount Pictures.

Bordo, S. (1997). *Twilight zones: The hidden life of cultural images from Plato to O. J.* Berkley, CA: University of California.

Bracher, M. (1993). *Lacan, discourse and social change: A psychoanalytic cultural criticism.* Ithaca, NY: Routledge.

Dixon, W. W. (1995). *It looks at you: The returned gaze of cinema.* Albany, NY: State University of New York Press.

Felman, S. (1987). *Jacques Lacan and the adventure of insight: Psychoanalysis in contemporary culture.* Cambridge, MA: Harvard University Press.

Fiske, J. (1987). *Television culture.* New York, NY: Routledge.

Greenblatt, S. (1995). Culture. In F. Lentricchia & T. McLaughlin (Eds.), *Critical terms for literary study.* (2nd ed., pp. 225-232). Chicago: University of Chicago Press.

Kellner, D. (1997). *Media culture: Cultural studies, identity and politics between the modern and the postmodern.* New York and London: Routledge.

Kelly, U. (1997). *Schooling desire: Literacy, cultural politics and pedagogy.* New York and London: Routledge.

Kincheloe, J., Slattery, P. & Steinberg, S. (2000). *Contextualizing Teaching: Introduction to Education and Educational Foundations.* New York: Addison Wesley Longman Publishers, Inc.

Lyon, D. (1994). *Postmodernity.* Minneapolis, MN: University of Minnesota Press.

Mayne J. (1995). Paradoxes of specatorship. In L. Williams (Ed.), *Viewing positions: Ways of seeing films* (pp. 155-183). New Brunswick, NJ: Rutgers University Press.

McLare, P. (1995). *Critical pedagogy and predatory culture: Oppositional politics in a postmodern era.* New York and London: Routledge.

McLaughlin, T. (1996). *Street smarts and critical theory: Listening to the vernacular.* Madison, WI: The University of Wisconsin Press.

Robertson, J. P. (1997). Fantasy's confines: Popular culture and the education of the female primary-school teacher. In S. Todd (Ed.). *Learning desire: Perspectives on pedagogy, culture and the unsaid* (pp. 75-95). New York and London: Routledge.

Segall, A. (1997). De-transparent-izing media texts in the social studies classroom: Media education as historical/social inquiry. In I. Wright, & A. Sears (Eds.), *Trends and issues in Canadian social studies* (pp. 228-249). Vancouver, BC: Pacific Educational Press.

Simon, R. (1987). Empowerment as a pedagogy of possibility. *Language Arts, 64,* (4), (n.p.). As cited in W. F. Pinar, W. Reynolds, P. Slattery, & P. Taubman (1995). *Understanding curriculum: An introduction to the study of historical and contemporary curriculum discourses.* New York: Peter Lang Publishing, Inc., p. 263.

Stam, R., Burgoyne, R., & Flitterman-Lewis, S. (1992). *New vocabularies in film semiotics: Structuralism, post-structuralism and beyond.* New York and London: Routledge.

Steinberg, D., Sakmar, J. J. & Lenhard, K. (Writers) & Schultz, M. (Director). Chapter thirty [Television series episode]. In D. E. Kelly, & J. Pontell (Executive Producers), *Boston Public.* United States: Fox Broadcasting Company.

Turner, G. (1988). *Film as social practice.* New York and London: Routledge.

Todd, S. (1997). Desiring desire in rethinking pedagogy. In S. Todd (Ed.), *Learning desire: Perspectives on pedagogy, culture, and the unsaid* (pp. 1-13). New York: NY: Routledge.

Walkerdine, V. (1986). Video replay: Families, films and fantasy. In V. Burgin, J. Donald, & C. Kaplan (Eds.), *Formations of fantasy* (pp. 167-199). New York: Metheun.

Zizek, S. (1991). *Looking awry: An introduction to Jacques Lacan through popular culture.* Cambridge, MA: Massachusetts Institute of Technology.

Zizek, S. (1992). *Enjoy your symptom: Jacques Lacan in Hollywood and out.* New York and London: Routledge.

Viewing Television with Critical Eyes

Interrogation, Identity, Ideology

Carl Leggo

A Curriculum of Epistemological Curiosity

The Canadian Broadcasting Corporation (CBC) is celebrating its 50th anniversary, and since I am almost 50 years old, too, I am reminded that I am part of the first generation that has grown up with television. I have known television all my life. The CBC celebration is my celebration, too. I have been shaped by encounters with Wojeck the Coroner, the Friendly Giant, Mr. Dress-up, Juliette, Quentin Durgens, M.P., the King of Kensington, Wayne and Shuster, the Beachcombers, Gordon Sinclair, Betty Kennedy, Fred Davis, Pierre Berton, Howard the Turtle, Don Messer, Knowlton Nash, Anne Murray and the Forest Rangers. Nevertheless, considering the number of hours (really years) I have spent viewing television, I still confess that I know little about television – its history, technology, craft, aesthetics, economics, ethics, production, ideology, pedagogy, psychology, erotics, administration, politics. Yet, I suspect that the only social institutions that have had more influence in shaping and informing my cultural understanding of identity (Williams, 1975, p. 119) are home and school.

In a lecture about television presented on television, Pierre Bourdieu (1998) observed, "in general, I think that you can't say much on television, particularly not about television" (p. 13), and I think that most teachers feel the same way about saying much about television, particularly in the classroom. Because children and adolescents are steeped in TV, then, to teach television is to intervene in the common cultural experience of students with a pedagogical and curricular mandate to construct TV as an object of study. Needless to say, television presents significant challenges for the classroom.

School curricula typically valorize a few educational experiences at the expense of many others. In effect, school curricula frequently exclude the kinds of discursive experiences that students know as integral in their lives outside the classroom. John Fiske (1989) describes popular culture as democratic, open-ended and organic: "Popular culture is made by the people, not imposed upon them; it stems from within, from below, not from above" (p. 25). Fiske also adds that "culture is a living, active process" (p. 23). Why is popular culture not more popular in schools? I do not want to recommend popular culture as second-rate, as tolerable, as the rather disreputable aunt or uncle who must, a few times a year, be humoured and entertained. Popular culture deserves our attention in schools because ignoring popular culture is tantamount to erecting a high wall of exclusion around our schools, a wall that only helps to convince students that school is not a place where they can exercise freedom of choice, a place where the interests and experiences of their lives are regarded as important. School is perceived as a place separate and isolated from the world outside school. A pedagogical commitment to critical viewing will be promoted when the popular culture of students is not barred from the classroom, when experiences of the popular culture, such as television, are invited into the classroom for investigation and discussion.

Neil Postman is an indefatigable critic of television. In *Amusing Ourselves to Death: Public Discourse in the Age of Show Business*, Postman observes: "We are by now well into a second generation of children for whom television has been their first and most accessible teacher and, for many, their most reliable companion and friend. To put it plainly, television is the command centre of the new epistemology" (1985, p. 78). Postman claims that "the major educational enterprise now being undertaken in the United States [and I contend for Canada as well] is not happening in its classrooms but in the home, in front of the television set, and under the jurisdiction not of school administrators and teachers but of network executives and entertainers" (p. 145). Postman also refers to television as "our *culture*" (p. 79) and as "a curriculum" (p. 145), but I am particularly intrigued with the claim that "television is the command centre of the new epistemology" because in this observation Postman is emphasizing how we know what we know. By focusing on television as inextricably connected to epistemology, Postman opens the door to an ongoing critical engagement with television as technology and text. While Postman is an inveterate critic of television with his claim that "television does not extend or amplify literate culture" but

instead "attacks it" (p, 84), he does not quixotically promote the elimi-
nation of TV. His hope resides in promoting critical viewing literacy:
"The problem...does not reside in what people watch. The problem is
in that we watch. The solution must be found in how we watch" (p.
160). For Postman, "the asking of the questions is sufficient. To ask is
to break the spell" (p. 161). While I have many questions for Postman
(and particularly his sometimes alarmist, even strident, claims that TV
involves an attack on literacy),[1] I agree with his contention that school
classrooms need to be places where a constant pedagogical practice of
questioning can lead to the kind of critical engagement that is needed
in viewing television. Postman writes:

> *In any case, the point I am trying to make is that only through a
> deep and unfailing awareness of the structure and effects of infor-
> mation, through a demystification of media, is there any hope of
> our gaining some measure of control over television, or the comput-
> er, or any other medium. (p. 161)*

Postman recommends the same kind of pedagogical enterprise that
Paulo Freire promotes in *Pedagogy of the Heart* where he writes about
"facilitating the exercise of epistemological curiosity. Without that, the
progressive educational practice deteriorates" (1997, p. 97). According
to Freire, "knowledge has historicity. It never is, it is always in the
process of being" (p. 31). Freire writes: "In order to know better what I
already know implies, sometimes, to know what before was not possible to know. Thus, the important thing is to educate the curiosity
through which knowledge is constituted as it grows and refines itself
through the very exercise of knowing" (p. 31). For Freire, "only an education of question can trigger, motivate, and reinforce curiosity" (p. 31).
I especially admire Freire's conception of human beings as people of will
and conscience who create their ways in the world:

> *I am not a being in the life support but a being in the world, with
> the world, and with others; I am a being who makes things, knows
> and ignores, speaks, fears and takes risks, dreams and loves, becomes
> angry and is enchanted. I am a being who rejects the condition of
> a mere object. I am a being who does not bow before the indis-
> putable power accumulated by technology because, in knowing that
> it is a human production, I do not accept that it is, in and of itself,
> bad. I am a being who rejects a view of technology as a demon's
> deed designed to throw out God's work. (p. 35)*

In eloquent language, Freire expresses an inspiring conviction of pedagogical hope: "We are transformative beings and not beings for accommodation" (p. 36). Freire champions a pedagogy of interrogation and possibility: "We are conditioned beings but not determined beings. It is impossible to understand history as possibility if we do not recognize human beings as beings who make free decisions" (p. 37).

CRITICAL ENGAGEMENT:
FOUR APPROACHES

Motivated by Freire's pedagogical hope, I recommend four approaches for teaching a critical engagement with television. The first approach is **viewer response**. Akin to reader response, this approach to viewing television encourages personal responses to TV. This is a useful starting place, to begin with viewers' experiences of TV, to invite their subjective reactions. Second, I promote an approach informed by **semiotics** which focuses on television as a network of signs and codes. In a semiotics approach, the TV episode is interrogated for its rhetorical or textual devices. Third, **deconstruction** reminds viewers that every text can be interpreted with multiple meanings. Finally, **cultural criticism** encourages viewers to pay attention to the ever-changing political, social, cultural, and historical contexts in which TV is produced, viewed, reviewed and discussed. By approaching TV from the perspectives of viewer response, semiotics, deconstruction and cultural criticism, students can understand that viewing is never a simple or innocent act. Instead, viewing television is a complex critical activity that includes viewers, producers (or creators), texts and cultural contexts in intricate networks of relationship.[2]

VIEWER RESPONSE

I borrow the notion of viewer response from theorists of reader response. In particular, I am indebted to Louise Rosenblatt, a pioneer in the debate about the role of the reader. Rosenblatt (1978) explains: "The reading of a text is an event occurring at a particular time in a particular environment at a particular moment in the life history of the reader. The transaction will involve not only the past experience but also the present state and present interests or preoccupations of the reader" (p. 20). For Rosenblatt, the "text" is only "a set or series of signs interpretable as linguistic symbols" (p. 12). The "poem," on the other hand, is "the experience shaped by the reader under the guidance of the text" (p. 12). In other words, the poem is produced through the transaction between the reader and the text. I especially like Rosenblatt's suggestion that the reader is a performer impressing his or her own individuality upon a unique production or evocation of the poem (p. 28).

In a viewer response approach the viewer is active. There are no couch potatoes. Instead the viewer attends to the TV episode in productive ways. Viewing is an active process of literate engagement between viewers and TV texts. Therefore, I recommend that students engage in several kinds of personal responses to television. For example, students can ask questions about the television texts they are viewing. Needed are viewing strategies that defer closure and promote openness in the encounter with texts. Therefore, I recommend that a useful initial strategy for encouraging a critical response to TV is to ask questions. Too often students are motivated by the sense that they need to answer questions. I prefer to ask questions, and leave them dangling, open and tantalizing. So, viewers can be invited to pose their initial responses in the form of questions which do not need to be answered. Instead of expressing their interaction with a TV text in expository prose that declares and concludes, viewers can record a long list of questions that generate a space for critical attending. In addition to recording questions, viewers can record their subjective responses to television in a viewer-response journal. They can be invited to write down impressions, connections, emotions, and anecdotes that are evoked and provoked during the experience of viewing the television text. In turn, the viewer response journal can provide a useful starting place for small group and large group discussion as students and teachers engage in a collaborative and critical inquiry of their diverse viewing experiences.

While learning to articulate personal responses to a television text is significant, even more important is assisting students to learn the skills and develop the confidence to articulate responses to TV texts that acknowledge the complex balance between viewer and text. Always, the viewer's personality, experiences, emotions and worldviews interact with the TV text as a system of signs generated in complex contexts. So, both the subjective and objective dynamics of the viewing process need to be attended to. The viewer response orientation recognizes the daily experience of many students regarding TV, and invites them to express their personal and subjective responses as a valuable engagement with TV.

But students need more than an invitation to respond personally to TV; they also need skills and understanding to instruct and guide their critical responses to TV, to produce complex emotional and intellectual responses that attend to the many dynamics at work in TV. Viewers need to know the conventions, codes and rules of TV. To guide them, the theoretical perspective of semiotics is useful.

SEMIOTICS

In *Messages and Meanings: An Introduction to Semiotics*, Marcel Danesi (1994) explains that "semiotics teaches us to read or interpret the meaning inherent in any human-made message or artifact. It is the 'science of messages and meanings' and of the signs and codes we use to produce and understand them" (p. 2). According to semiotics, a TV text is a network of signs that can be interpreted as meaningful because the signs are part of specific contexts and codes that viewers understand as conventionally characteristic of television. Semiotics facilitates viewers' experiences of a TV text by making viewers more aware of the conventions of TV texts so that their viewing will be more receptive and perceptive. Semiotics promotes active and interpretive engagement in the viewing process. A semiotics approach begins with close attention to the text, to the way that the parts of the text relate to one another and to the larger contexts of generic expectations and conventions. A TV text is a network of signs that relate to one another in order to create meaningful effects. Every TV text invites multiple responses, and students need to be reminded that a text never has a single interpretation.

Fundamentally, a semiotics approach to viewing television is based on two principles. First, anything in a TV text can signify, including atmosphere, beauty, character, design, emotion, frames, games, horror, imagery, jumps, knowledge, language, mothers, novelty, operations, plot, questions, rhythm, setting, time, uniformity, violence, war, Xmas, youth and zigzags. The basic questions that teachers and students need to ask themselves in regard to a TV text are, "What can this mean?" and "What does this do?" Second, the working tools for viewing TV can be developed during the viewing process. So, a semiotics approach invites viewers to attend to how the effects of TV are created by interrogating the signs that compose and shape the experiences of TV. Viewers can interrogate the craft of television by attending to the techniques of camera angles, editing, costumes, laugh tracks, and studio sets. And viewers can question the recurrence of familiar genres, like the domestic drama, and dramas about detectives and doctors. Always, viewers ought to interrogate the pervasive presence of advertising, which is the engine that drives most of the television enterprise. Semiotics reminds viewers to investigate the ways that different programs vie for the viewers' attention. A whole semester could be spent questioning the current popularity of reality TV, including the hugely successful *Survivor* phenomenon, or the ways that a successful program often leads to spin-offs, or the longevity of soaps.

Guided by a semiotics approach, viewers can attend to a television text as a construct, a technically and aesthetically composed and crafted artefact. The possibilities for a semiotic interrogation of TV are as endless as TV is endless. About any program – narrative, documentary, news, talk, comedy, information, cartoon, education, music, interview, infomercial – the viewer can ask what are the signs that compose this text, what are the defining characteristics of this kind of text, how is this kind of text shaped and crafted, how is this kind of text revised and transformed?

In addition to viewing TV informed by a semiotic understanding of how a TV program works as a text, as a system of signs, students can also attend to the plural meanings that a TV text generates. The theoretical perspective of deconstruction provides useful tools for viewing TV with imaginative insight.

DECONSTRUCTION

Deconstruction is founded in the contemporary philosophical view that the world, as perceived, experienced and known, is constructed and disclosed in language practice. Reading (or viewing) texts with the philosophical approach of careful and rigorous critique, deconstruction demonstrates that language use constructs plural meanings. As an approach to responding to texts, deconstruction always seeks to go beyond the apparently clear and manifest meanings in order to reveal how texts can be interpreted in many different ways because language is always slipping and sliding as it works, and is worked, rhetorically to create meanings. Instead of looking for a harmonious meaning of a text, the reader (or viewer) brings a sceptical and questioning approach to the text, and pays attention to elements in the text that contradict one another or fail to cohere. By attending to the gaps in the text, the reader (or viewer) keeps the text open.

Deconstruction objects to interpretive closure. There can be no univocal, authoritative response to a text. There is always something more. Deconstruction encourages a multiplicity of responses. Therefore, any television text is a site where the viewer's imagination, experience, understanding and emotions come into play in unique and imaginative performances. Deconstructive viewing is self-conscious viewing; nothing is taken for granted. Viewers are motivated and influenced in their viewing by their personalities, values, experiences, education, and command of conventional strategies for viewing. Their practices of viewing are informed by both personal and communal matrices of expectations and assumptions. By being aware of these personal and communal matrices, viewers can adopt different perspectives in relation to the text as a site for the production of multiple meanings.

Brenda Marshall (1992) addresses the fundamental pedagogical issue of diverse responses to a text. She holds that "as thinkers we need to hold in our minds a space for interpretations that are other than ours" (p. 188). Marshall stresses the need for readers, and I add viewers, to "acknowledge our own agendas, our own histories, our own subject positions as we interpret texts, and simultaneously acknowledge the potential for the logic of other interpretations" (p. 188). She optimistically predicts that plural responses can open up a space that "may become the space for dialogue" (p. 188).

Based on this understanding of deconstruction as a critical and literate and creative practice, I invite viewers to consider the following four strategies informed by deconstruction. These strategies provide a useful heuristic for guiding viewers in asking questions that they might otherwise not consider.

First, deconstruction reminds the viewer to attend to *self-referentiality*. In one of my favorite Norman Rockwell illustrations titled "Triple Self-Portrait," Norman Rockwell is drawing an illustration of Norman Rockwell while watching Norman Rockwell drawing in a mirror. Of course, even this "Triple Self-Portrait" can only imply the presence of the real Norman Rockwell who remains invisible outside the frame of his "Triple Self-Portrait." This illustration reminds me to interrogate the complex dynamics of perspective and perception in a television text. What is the relationship between the world of the text and the empirical world? A deconstructive approach to viewing a TV text precludes simplistic identifications between the world of the TV text and the

world of the viewer. Instead the viewer acknowledges the textual construction or rhetoric of the TV text, the ways that various strategies and
tropes and conventions work together to create particular effects. Paying
attention to the self-referentiality of a TV text is a way of not forgetting
that the TV text is a textual construct. Deconstructive viewing seeks out
the ways that all texts are constructed and available for deconstructing
and reconstructing.

Second, deconstructive viewing attends to *viewing from different
positions*. Deconstruction promotes multiple ways of viewing a TV text,
especially by inviting viewers to interrogate their own responses to the
text as a text. Deconstruction reminds viewers to ask questions about
the perspectives from which the text can be viewed. The viewer is
encouraged to view from different perspectives, and to acknowledge the
ways that the text invites, not closure, but a dissemination of plural
responses. Students need to consider what perspectives are available for
them as viewers. When I view television, I sometimes focus attention on
characters other than the character who is speaking. What do events
look like from their perspectives? I ask how a male viewer might
respond and how a female viewer might respond. I question my
responses. What positions does the text invite me to occupy or what
positions are available for me as a viewer? What is the connection
between truth and fiction?

Third, deconstruction pays close attention to *binary oppositions* such
as light/dark, good/evil, love/hate, strength/weakness. Such binary oppositions involve a value-laden hierarchy with one element given priority
over the other. Deconstructive viewing contests this order of priority. By
calling into question the typical attitude towards the hierarchical ordering
of the elements in a binary opposition, viewers can open up spaces for
innovative perspectives and new insights. There is a poignant demonstration of this interrogative approach in the film *Malcolm X* when the camera focuses on the dictionary entries that define "black" and "white." One
color is extolled while the other is vilified. *Malcolm X* seeks to open up the
possibilities of understanding the words in new ways. Viewers need to be
continually alert to the ways that language is used.

Fourth, deconstruction acknowledges how all textual practices are
connected intertextually. Every text is related to other texts.
Intertextuality refers to the ways a text overlaps with other texts, and
cites other texts, and assumes a knowledge of other texts, the ways a text

intersects with other texts and incorporates references to other texts. How are viewers' responses influenced by their knowledge or lack of knowledge of other texts? Every text bears traces of other texts: citations, references, structural codes, allusions, phrases, images, generic conventions, themes. The concept of intertextuality will not be unfamiliar to most viewers because popular television shows like *Seinfeld* and *Friends* make many intertextual connections to other television and cinematic texts, as well as the events of current affairs and popular culture. A deconstructive approach to viewing emphasizes the ways that texts are intertwined and related to one another. To view a TV text with attention to its intertextual relationships is to be constantly reminded that every text comprises an inexhaustible convergence of influences, a braid of connections.

Finally, in addition to viewing TV informed by viewer response, semiotics and deconstruction, viewers can attend to the cultural, social, political, historical and ideological contexts in which television texts are generated and given attention. The perspective of cultural criticism is useful for guiding this kind of viewing.

CULTURAL CRITICISM

Cultural criticism proposes that television is a cultural production, and that the relationships between texts, producers, writers and viewers are informed and constituted by the cultures in which texts, producers, writers and viewers circulate. While I promote a viewer response approach to responding to TV in which viewers respond personally to TV texts out of their experiences, emotions and convictions, I do not want to promote the limiting expectation that all that is important in the relationship of the text and viewer is the viewer's personal and idiosyncratic identification with the TV texts. By interacting with TV texts in personal ways only, viewers will likely perpetuate their views of the world, instead of interrogating those views. Viewers need to attend to the ways social, economic, political, ethical and cultural realities are constructed and sustained. A cultural criticism orientation to viewing TV focuses on issues of gender, class, ethnicity, religion, economic status, sexual orientation, nationality, political conviction, race, age and ability, and helps students recognize that they always read and view from particular ideological orientations.

Ideology is more than a world view. Catherine Belsey (1980) defines ideology as "a way of thinking, speaking, experiencing" (p. 5). Through social and cultural and political institutions such as the church, the school, the media, the family, the legal system, people are introduced into powerfully determined ways of seeing and believing. While the term "cultural criticism" refers generically to a wide range of perspectives that are focussed on the ideological dynamics of culture, history, politics and society, the five following perspectives informed by cultural criticism will provide opportunities for teachers and students to interrogate their lived experiences, their values and beliefs, and to resist narrow parameters that promote ideological homogeneity by excluding diversity.

First, *historicism* addresses issues of historical context, and demonstrates how history is a story written by people, a crafted and interpreted version of events, always open for further retelling and interpretation. A TV text is the product of history. Composed in a particular place and time, it is motivated and constrained by the historical conditions of the place and time in which it was initially produced and viewed, as well as all subsequent places and times, including the present conditions of the viewing.

Second, *Marxism* focuses on how institutions, like school, church, government and business, shape the ways that people live, think, believe and relate in the world. A Marxist perspective asks questions, such as: How is class represented on television? What are the features that mark or distinguish one class from another? How do cultural artefacts like clothing, food, cars and music help to define the class identities of people? What are the images of the workplace and the home represented in TV?

Third, *feminism* addresses issues of the cultural production of gender identities, and interrogates inequities constructed around gender differences. Feminism reminds teachers and students to investigate the ways that identities and relationships have been gendered, to interrogate the stereotypes of women's roles and men's roles, to question inequities of power, and to promote possibilities for enhancing women's and men's lived experiences.

Fourth, *post-colonialism* addresses and revisits relationships between nations of the world where some nations have been colonizers and others have been colonized. Post-colonial theory and practice revisits and revisions the historical and contemporary relationships between the peoples of colonizer nations and the peoples of colonized nations. A significant question raised by post-colonialism is the question of who has the authority of authorship. By way of example, what are the images and stories of aboriginal peoples presented in TV? Viewers can examine the representations of native men and women in television, and compare the representations of native women and men in early television with representations in current television, as a way of beginning to ask questions like, Who constructs these images? Why are these images constructed? Who benefits from these images? Who does not benefit from these images? How do these images relate to the lived experiences of native men and women?

Fifth, *race* focuses attention on the ways that political and economic power have been divided up inequitably among different races, and how these inequities are propagated and perpetuated. A cultural criticism orientation does not privilege or sanction a particular interpretation; instead every television text opens up spaces for rethinking how culture, history, politics and commerce delineate, propagate and sustain the identities and roles of people by separating them into categories of race.

Fiske (1987) claims that television works "ideologically to promote and prefer certain meanings of the world, to circulate some meanings rather than others, and to serve some social interests better than others" (p. 20). And while I do not disagree, at least not entirely, with Fiske, I prefer to emphasize that TV presents a multiplicity of messages. I am not convinced that TV constructs a dominant ideology, a prevailing way of experiencing the world. Instead I prefer to understand TV as a site for contesting ideologies, for plural ideologies, for ideological messages that are contradictory and conflicting. Television invites our responses, our interactive viewing. Consider the perspectives and practices of Bill Cosby, who for decades has been one of the major players in North American television.

BILL COSBY VS. BART SIMPSON: ROLE MODELS?

One of the generic staples of television from its inception has been, and continues to be, the family drama. By way of illustrating my contention that TV is lined with complex ideological messages, I will share a little of my responses to two popular family-oriented TV programs, one that continues to be broadcast, and one that has ceased production.

The creators of *The Simpsons* and *The Cosby Show* are diametrically opposed in their philosophies concerning the effects of TV in shaping people's attitudes and actions. *The Cosby Show* presents an upper middle-class family, an Afro-American version of the Cleavers, where all problems are handled successfully, including poor grades, missing a curfew, violating a diet and the choice of unacceptable partners. The show is built around the patriarch, Dr. Heathcliff Huxtable, the source of wisdom and authority and humor. David Bianculli in *Teleliteracy: Taking Television Seriously* comments on how committed Cosby is to using his television show to make positive statements: "Cosby has been singularly sensitive to the messages *The Cosby Show* sends out each week, and runs them past psychologists and other experts to ensure that his programs present positive themes and role models" (p. 175).

Yet while I acknowledge the popularity of *The Cosby Show*, and while I have enjoyed watching some episodes, I frequently find offensive the saccharine, bucolic, idyllic world of the Huxtable clan. I find especially offensive the role of Claire Huxtable – perfect mother and perfect homemaker and perfect wife and perfect lover, always laughing at her husband's jokes, always sensitive to her children's needs, always glamorous in a pristine kitchen and even more pristine living room. And because homemaking and parenting and acting the straight woman in a comic team occupy so little of her time, she is a cracker-jack lawyer, too, though she is almost never seen actually practising law. And I find deeply offensive the episode in which a Huxtable daughter, Sondra, gives birth to twins, a boy and a girl. Cliff Huxtable has always opposed the daughter's marriage, partly because son-in-law Alvin dropped out of medical school to open a wilderness supplies shop. After the twins are born, Alvin, near the end of the episode and near the end of the production of the series, announces that he has made a decision. He will return to medical school. There is much joy among the Huxtables in the hospital. Alvin has seen the light. The only worthy occupations, for the Huxtables at least, are white collar. And in the midst of the celebration the happy parents of the twins announce that the son and the daughter will be named Nelson and Winnie. What else would you call black twins in 1989 with Nelson Mandela coming out of prison after decades?

My interrogation of *The Cosby Show* is not intended to critically dismiss the show, which enjoyed such consistently high ratings, and will continue to enjoy popularity in syndication for many years to come. My concern is that Cosby, with his doctorate in education, is a teacher full of didactic zeal. He is driven by the desire to use television to present positive messages. He says, "If you treat old people in a negative fashion, and have them always seen as people who can't remember, and are knocked back by the younger ones, and see kids who are putting the parents down just for a joke, you're giving kids the wrong picture" (quoted in Bianculli, p. 175). Cosby is concerned about giving viewers the wrong picture. But that suggests that there is a right picture, and I question what that right picture is, and who will be in charge of creating and perpetuating that right picture.

When *The Cosby Show* was still in production and showing regularly at eight o'clock on Thursday nights, its stiffest competition came from another show about another family, *The Simpsons*. Where the Cosbys celebrated unity and harmony and authority, the Simpsons celebrated anarchy and conflict and insubordination. Bart Simpson's motto is "Underachiever…and proud of it." According to Cosby, *The Simpsons* is "a show with an antisocial character" (quoted in Bianculli, p. 176). But I appreciate the comments of James L. Brooks, the executive producer of *The Simpsons*: "I think it's very dangerous to focus on television characters as role models. You know, it's so nakedly anti-art and pro-propaganda. My role model may not be somebody else's role model, so to say I'm doing a series to create role models for the society that will witness it is, to me, very dangerous terrain" (quoted in Bianculli, 1992, p. 178). I have watched *The Simpsons* many times, and I have been moved by the program over and over. For one thing the show is about working class people, the kind of people that are often ignored on TV. As a teacher I have met many children like Bart Simpson. I have heard colleagues refer to Bart Simpson-type students as "garbage." The Bart Simpsons of the world are often dismissed as "garbage," but Bart Simpson, for all his violation of authority and failure in school and madcap pranks, is a noble character, filled with desires, hopes, conflicting emotions, seeds of goodness. In one episode Bart studies for a history test. He has failed history tests many times. He doesn't want to study, but finally begins and studies all night. He writes the test, and waits eagerly for the result. His teacher tells him, "It's a 59; that's another F." Bart bursts into tears. His teacher comments, "I'd think you'd be used to failing by now." Bart replies, "You don't understand. I really tried. It's as good as I can do, and I still failed." He adds, "Now I know how George Washington felt when he surrendered Fort

Necessity to the French in 1754." The teacher is surprised with Bart's tearful reaction, and she is impressed with his knowledge of Washington and his ability to apply the knowledge to his own experience. She adds one more point to his grade, and he passes with a D. The episode invites the viewer's sympathy for Bart and for all the students that are short-changed by the school system, all the students that are dismissed as failures.

I understand Cosby's concern about the influence of television on viewers. I recall that as a kid I heard swearing on TV and figured that swearing was, therefore, now acceptable. But this is the kind of naive response to television that I challenge. It is possible for people to view television and be influenced to pursue destructive, criminal, unethical, immoral attitudes and actions. But surely this fear of the corrupting influence of TV is generated by a conception of TV that is too simplistic. Television provides multiple versions of reality, and multiple viewers respond to those multiple versions in multiple ways. Television is the purveyor of a plurality of points of view and vision, celebrating diversity and multi-vision.

REVIEW AND PREVIEW

Television is a significant pedagogical and ideological influence in our lives, and therefore television ought to be invited into our schools so that we can grow more television literate, and become more responsive and responsible viewers, filled with questions and challenges as we engage with television in a curriculum of epistemological curiosity. Television literacy promotes purposeful viewing. Every school ought to be committed to television literacy, and, therefore, an urgent goal for educators ought to be the development of opportunities for promoting television literacy in all schools at all grade levels. Informed by perspectives of viewer response, semiotics, deconstruction and cultural criticism, all viewers can attend to television with critical eyes, interrogating the ways that identity and ideology are constructed and deconstructed in the multiple practices of television as a popular and pervasive cultural dynamic.

REFERENCES

Belsey, C. (1980). *Critical practice*. London: Methuen.

Bianculli, D. (1992). *Teleliteracy: Taking television seriously*. New York:

Continuum.

Bourdieu, P. (1998). *On television*. New York: New Press.

Danesi, M. (1994). *Messages and meanings: An introduction to semiotics*. Toronto: Canadian Scholars' Press.

Fiske, J. (1987). *Television culture*. London: Routledge.

Fiske, J. (1989). *Understanding popular culture*. Boston: Unwin Hyman.

Freire, P. (1997). *Pedagogy of the heart*. (D. Macedo & A. Oliveira, Trans.). New York: Continuum.

Leggo, C. (2000). In defence of television: (Re)viewing the curriculum of literacy. In B. Barrell & R. Hammett (Eds.), *Advocating change: Contemporary issues in subject English* (pp. 162-176). Toronto: Irwin Publishing.

Leggo, C. (1997). *Teaching to wonder: Responding to poetry in the secondary classroom*. Vancouver, BC: Pacific Educational Press.

Marshall, B. K. (1992). *Teaching the postmodern: Fiction and theory*. New York: Routledge.

Postman, N. (1995). *Amusing ourselves to death: Public discourse in the age of show business*. New York: Viking Penguin.

Rosenblatt, L. (1978). *The reader, the text, the poem*. Carbondale: Southern Illinois UP.

Williams, R. (1975). *Television: Technology and cultural form*. New York: Schocken Books.

END NOTES

[1] I address Postman's criticisms in a chapter, "In Defence of Television: (Re)Viewing the Curriculum of Literacy," in *Advocating Change: Contemporary Issues in Subject English*, edited by Barrie R. C. Barrell and Roberta F. Hammett, published in 2000 by Irwin Publishing, Toronto, pp. 162-176.

[2] A more comprehensive examination of these four approaches focused on reading and teaching poetry is presented in my book, *Teaching to Wonder: Responding to Poetry in the Secondary Classroom*, published in 1997 by Pacific Educational Press, Vancouver.

PICTURE THIS

THREE INSTRUCTIONAL FRAMEWORKS FOR VIEWING AND REPRESENTING

KAREN E. SMITH

INTRODUCTION

The focus of this chapter is to describe how three instructional frameworks that employ the metaphors of a road map, a circle and a card game can be applied as starting points for pre-service teachers wanting to integrate viewing and representing into their teaching of the new English Language Arts curriculum. The senior years pre-service teachers that I teach have, on occasion, expressed how overwhelmed they are by the sheer amount of material to be taught and the myriad of connections that have to be made as they begin the process of learning how to teach English language arts. In particular, fears are raised when they must move from the vision of their own high school experience and apply something entirely new – viewing and representing. To calm their fears and to present them with a plan for integrating viewing and representing, I will say, "Picture this. If you began with only three things: what students will say, how they will say it, and how they will apply it, wouldn't that simplify matters?" Then we go on to learn about how a map, a circle and a card game can help them do this. This starting point helps to initiate dialogue about constructing knowledge through viewing and representing.

Another concern from my pre-service teachers is how transferable their newly-learned skills may be to other parts of the country and world where they may eventually attain a job. They wonder if the social construction of their knowledge, situated as it is in Manitoba, will translate to other jurisdictions. The repeated use of strategies from this chapter have helped to demonstrate that knowledge building is situated, but the instructional frameworks used to initiate dialogue and develop meaning-making are transferable. The important piece is to use instructional frameworks that are engaging, purposeful and dynamically structured to deepen meaning, no matter what the context or content.

Like many other provinces in Canada and other educational jurisdictions throughout the English speaking world (e.g., Western
Provinces, Atlantic Provinces, Australia), viewing and representing are
recent additions to the English language arts curriculum in my province
of Manitoba. In the past six years, since the adoption of the new curriculum in Manitoba, I have, out of necessity in my teacher education
classes, modified three language arts activities that connect viewing and
representing to the other four modes of listening, speaking, reading and
writing as outlined in the *Manitoba Curriculum Framework of Outcomes*
documents, Senior 1 through Senior 4 (grades 9-12). These instructional frameworks have helped to make a transition to including viewing and representing as a natural part of strategy instruction used in language arts. Additionally, they have provided an opportunity for using
inquiry, dialogue and application as a vital part of viewing and representing. The three instructional frameworks presented in this chapter
are: (1) a Deep Viewing Road Map, (2) a Conceptual Frame-work for
Viewing Circles and (3) an Electronic Writing/Representing Portfolio
Organizer.

Strategies that support specific outcomes frame practice in classrooms. The strategies outlined in this chapter are conceptual, strategic
to social construction of learning and differentiation, and aimed at self-
monitoring, as students and teachers explore new directions and technologies in language and literacy. The three instructional frameworks
can also be adopted for use in language across the content areas.

The following background is a description of the general framework
of curricular documents that were used to shape the description of, and
need for, the three strategies outlined in this chapter.

BACKGROUND

As elsewhere in the English-speaking world, a framework for curriculum delivery is based on outcomes that target specific English language arts skills and connect language skills to other concepts. For
example, connection to the specific outcomes of the *Manitoba English
Language Arts Common Curriculum Framework* is a vital part of instruction in Manitoba schools. Also, directions for Manitoba's English language arts are shaped by a redefinition of language arts (Manitoba
Education and Training, 1998) and an emphasis on connections to two

other curricular resource documents, *Success for All Learners* (1996a) and *Technology as a Foundation Skill Area: A Journey Toward Information Technology Literacy* (1998b). The shift in English language arts has been from reading, writing and the study of literary text to acquiring language and literacy skills through listening, speaking, viewing and representing, as well as reading and writing (Manitoba Education and Training, 1998a). Viewing and representing have extended English language arts study beyond reading, writing, listening and speaking to six modes that carry a relative equity in value for informing and meaning-making. Second, two resource documents support all Manitoba curricula and connect them to differentiated instruction and information and communication technology (ICT). The differentiated instruction connection in the document *Success for All Learners* (Manitoba Education and Training, 1996b) includes instructional frameworks and practical suggestions for implementing instruction in the diverse classrooms of today. The technology connection in the document *Technology as a Foundation Skill Area: A Journey Toward Information Technology Literacy* (Manitoba Education and Training, 1998b) supports information and communication technology as a skill area in classroom teaching, learning and assessment. Together, the new directions for ELA and the mandated connections to differentiation and technology provide an interesting challenge for developing viewing and representing, instructional frameworks. These same curricular principles are mandated by changes in other parts of Canada, Australia, the United States, the United Kingdom and New Zealand.

Viewing and representing in the Manitoba Frameworks document are described as follows:

> *Viewing and representing are integral parts of contemporary life. They allow students to understand the ways in which images and language can be used to convey ideas, value, and beliefs.*
>
> *Viewing is an active process of attending to and comprehending visual media such as television, advertising images, films, diagrams, symbols, photographs, videos, drama, drawing, sculpture, and painting. Viewing enables students to acquire information and to appreciate the ideas and experiences of others. Many of the comprehension processes involved in reading (such as previewing, predicting, and making inferences) are also used in viewing.*
>
> *Representing enables students to communicate information and*

*ideas through a variety of media, video presentation, posters, dia-
grams, charts, symbols, visual art, drama, mime, and models.
(Manitoba Education and Training, 1998a, pp. 5-6)*

Five general outcomes frame a series of specific outcomes, directly
tied to individual grade levels. The five general outcomes specify that
students will listen, speak, read, write, view, and represent in response
to these outcomes. The five general outcomes are:

*1) Students will listen, speak, read, write, view and represent to
explore thoughts, ideas, feelings, and experiences, 2) Students will
listen, speak, read, write, view, and represent to comprehend and
respond personally and critically to oral, print, and other media
texts, 3) Students will listen, speak, read, write, view, and represent
to manage ideas and information, 4) Students will listen, speak,
read, write, view, and represent to enhance the clarity and artistry
of communication, 5) Students will listen, speak, read, write, view,
and represent to celebrate and build community. (Manitoba
Education and Training, 1998a, p. 9)*

Fifty-six, specific-to-grade-level outcomes are tied to the five general
outcomes that are used in Senior 1 through Senior 4.

Another document provides support for the ELA Frameworks.
Success for All Learners (Manitoba Education and Training, 1996b),
Manitoba's differentiated instruction document, is an important
resource that emphasizes ideas and strategies that complement classroom diversity, different ways of learning and flexible classroom management. Teachers are urged to use active participation in learning and
to arrange activities that encourage interactive participation for all types
of learners working at many levels of ability. Suggestions for flexible
grouping, learning styles and multiple intelligences are provided. The
use of portfolios and technology are suggested as means to potentially
benefit the individual in today's diverse classroom.

A third document, *Technology as a Foundation Skill Area,* identifies
the connection between technology, society and the environment. The
growing importance of information and communication technology
(ICT) in society is emphasized. A continuum for information technology literacy, including steps for exploratory skill development and application and extension using ICT, is outlined. Five general outcomes

frame the continuum from the lowest level of engagement to the highest. Students will:

1) Develop knowledge, ability, and responsibility in the use of information technology, 2) Acquire , organize, analyze, evaluate, and present information using appropriate information technology, 3) Use information technology to expand their range and effectiveness of communication, 4) Solve problems, accomplish tasks, and express creativity, both individually and collaboratively, using information technology, and 5) Understand the role and impact of information technology and apply ethical, responsible, and legal standards in its use. (Manitoba Education and Training, 1998b, pp. 20-24)

The three documents together may appear to be overwhelming for new and practicing teachers alike. "Too many expectations for a limited amount of time," some would say. Yet, using a strategy-based instructional framework, the outcomes and conceptual frameworks of the documents can be achieved. They may even save time. If teachers give value to visuals as texts of their own type, with their own meanings and their own language, it follows that translating that language into instructional frameworks that are already a regular part of instruction in reading, writing, listening and speaking is merely a part of creating active learning activities that engage students in the process of reading and writing those texts, or in this case, viewing and representing those texts.

The act of being literate in those texts that can be "read" by viewing and representing, raises other questions about the focus taken in the classroom. Should the focus be on information literacy, media literacy, computer literacy, technology literacy, visual literacy or network literacy? All of these, and there are more, carry their own set of definitions, roots and importance; and it may not be obvious to the neophyte viewer that these competing literacies are even available for discussion or that these literacies compete for dominance in the groundswell of literacy types (Tyner, 1998). Kathleen Tyner in her book, *Literacy in a Digital World*, provides a solution for this, backed up by recommendations made by The New London Group (1996). Educators should recognize these multiple realities and present a more postmodern notion of literacies to provide a more realistic view of the literacy world. Inquiry and a critical eye can engage and help the student discern between literacies and shape their usefulness in creating meaning (Eisner, 1991).

Together, the three instructional frameworks in this chapter, support inquiry, critical viewing, social construction of knowledge and the application of learning to meaningful texts.

Although viewing and representing have been accepted as necessary modes for understanding and meaning making, many teachers find that there are few resources that make this connection explicit. The following instructional framework uses inquiry and critique to help students acquire an ever-deepening view of visual texts.

AN INQUIRY-BASED DEEP VIEWING ROAD MAP

DESCRIPTION AND BACKGROUND

Inquiry into visual texts can begin by introducing students to a method of viewing coined by the late Ann Watts Pailliotet (1995), called "deep viewing." Pailliotet derived her model from Margaret Himley's process of deep talk in Himley's book *Shared Territory* (1991). This model is placed in an instructional framework borrowed from Richard and Jo Anne Vacca (2002, p. 346) called a Reading Road Map. The Road Map provides a structure for responding to progressively more difficult questions and concepts at various "rates of reading" as students progress through their visual texts. Rates vary as students pause to discuss, respond to, question and view in real time. Used as an inquiry framework, students can ask progressively more challenging questions and explore progressively more challenging concepts as they advance through the framework. The Road Map can also be used when viewing a variety of visual texts, from still images such as paintings to moving images such as movies.

APPLICATION

Using this model, students can view visual texts individually or in jigsaw groups. A viewing sample is first selected. To begin viewing and responding, either individuals or groups must be assigned one of the six codes from the top right-hand side of the page. Watts Pailliotet's deep viewing method was adapted and used to separate visual codes (See Watts Pailliotet, 1995, for an in-depth description of deep viewing). Deep viewing includes six codes or stances for viewing: (a) action/sequence, (b) semes/forms, (c) actor/discourse, (d) proximity/

INQUIRY-BASED, DEEP VIEWING ROAD MAP

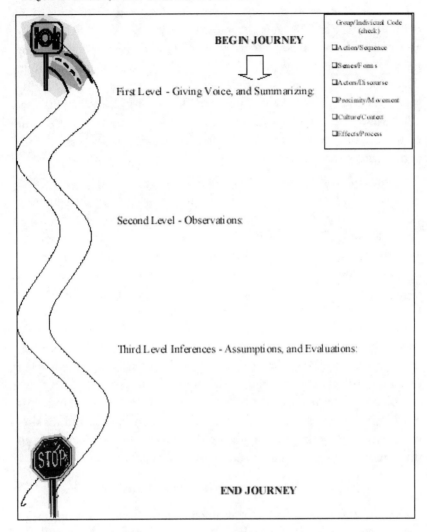

BEGIN JOURNEY

Group/Individual Code
(check)

☐ Action/Sequence

☐ Semes/Forms

☐ Actors/Discourse

☐ Proximity/Movement

☐ Culture/Context

☐ Effects/Process

First Level - Giving Voice, and Summarizing:

Second Level - Observations:

Third Level Inferences - Assumptions, and Evaluations:

STOP

END JOURNEY

movement, (e) culture/context and (f) effect/process. The action and sequence code refers to events in the visual text and can be represented by storyboards or described as a chain of events. Semes and forms are identifiable units of visual text such as color, movement or shape and can be represented by icons or described through relationships with other forms. Actors' discourse is separated from the other codes to assist in the analysis of the dialogue and can be described through a summary of noteworthy dialogue. Proximity/movement is a code used to describe the significance of visual elements such as actors or objects and their significant relationships to one another for emphasis and innuen-do. Visual symbols or descriptive words can represent this code. The culture/context code locates elements of the visual text in their socially and culturally significant territory. This code can be represented by naming the noteworthy element together with its contextual referent. The effect/process code is complex in that it is meant for scrutinizing artistic devices such as light, camera angle, and musical elements that affect viewers' perceptions of the visual text. All codes can be represent-ed both visually and/or through written notes right on the instruction-al framework sheet.

Next, the code groups or individuals proceed through three stages of viewing and stopping to respond. The first stage is about gathering code information and summarizing it in order to share with other stu-dents. This stage begins by viewing with a purpose of deciphering one's assigned code, selecting significant elements, and recording the results as closely as possible to how the viewer(s) feel about the visual text. This stage emphasizes literal observations. The second stage, called *Making Observations*, is geared toward the interpretive. The teacher prompts dis-cussion of interferences and connections within and between codes, encouraging students to think between the visual elements (as in read-ing between the lines). The third and final stage is when the teacher prompts students to formulate conclusions about the visual text. This can be done by reflecting on the text, drawing conclusions about con-nections to other texts and codes, formulating conclusions and making judgments. The journey through the three stages prompts students to think more deeply and have richer dialogue about the visual texts.

ASSESSMENT AND EVALUATION

In the course of informal assessment, teachers can prompt deeper viewing and dialogue through inquiry questions, as their students progress through the three stages of the instructional framework. Formally, teachers can collect the Road Map sheets to evaluate the clar-ity of descriptions and depth of responses. Students experience a pattern that demonstrates a deepening of viewing concepts rather than just a series of questions with varied depth of response. The Road Map increases depth of response with repeated use and taking a journey through a variety of visual texts. The added value of using the Road Map is that it can be used as guided practice before students begin a more student-directed process of viewing and representing called Viewing Circles.

VIEWING CIRCLES: LITERATURE CIRCLES WITH A TWIST

DESCRIPTION AND BACKGROUND

Viewing Circles is a visual/media literacy strategy borrowed from language arts literature circles. Viewing Circles is a structured viewing activity that permits powerful, high-ordered discussion and thinking to go on around good illustrations and other visual representations. In Viewing Circles, students critically respond to visual representations (e.g., children's literature illustration, advertisements, film). This strategy supports students through independent dialogue in the language of viewing and representing (Close, 1992; Daniels, 1994; Scott, 1994). Viewing Circles can be approached through a variety of critical viewing methodologies, including deep viewing; however, in this example Ontario's eight provincial standards (Anderson & Pungente, 1997) and five questions to promote critical thinking about media messages (Thoman, 1997) provide a framework for thinking about media. The Viewing Circles exercise in this example allows students to choose their topics freely and to openly discuss visual, and in particular, media text.

APPLICATION

This instructional framework can also be used with photo journals, political cartoons and other still visuals. In one class, pre-service teachers used the logo on one of their credit cards as the visual text. The initial decision for the teacher is to provide an opportunity for students to select their own visual texts. Rich discussion can come from the teacher providing a variety of visual text selections that have a common thread. For example, the teacher could have students select an appealing photograph of artwork from a collection of old art journals such as the *Canadian Art* journal. Students will then find other students that have what they think are similar or related selections. This self selection exercise will provide choice and motivation. To maintain consistency, no group may be smaller than three students or larger than six students. The teacher's role is to keep all the groups functioning by briefly par-

CONCEPTUAL FRAMEWORK
FOR VIEWING CIRCLES

Team Member Directory: Director:_____ Word Wizard(s):_____ _____ Visual Wizard(s):_____ _____ Summarizer:_____ Finale Organizer:_____ _____		Assessment Questions:
Individual Summaries:		Group Summary:
Story Board for Culminating Activity		
Title:_____ _____	Frame 1	Frame 2
Frame 3	Frame 4	Frame 5

ticipating in and circulating among the groups, stimulating activity through strategic questioning, reinforcing group goals, offering ideas and providing encouragement. Like Literature Circles, Viewing Circles should take place at regularly scheduled intervals, over a period of time to establish student independence and self-monitoring.

First, if students have little reference for choosing materials or selecting groups, then introduce the following lists to help guide their selections and discussions:

ONTARIO'S 8 PROVINCIAL STANDARDS

1. *All media messages are constructions.*
2. *The media construct versions of reality.*
3. *Audiences negotiate meaning in media messages.*
4. *Media messages contain commercial implications.*

5. *Media messages contain ideological and value messages.*

6. *Media messages contain social and political implication.*

7. *Form and content are closely related in media messages.*

8. *Each medium has a unique aesthetic form (Anderson & Pungente, 1997).*

FIVE QUESTIONS TO PROMOTE CRITICAL THINKING ABOUT MEDIA MESSAGES:

1. *Who created this message and why?*

2. *What techniques are used to attract my attention?*

3. *What lifestyles, values and points of view are represented?*

4. *How might different people understand this message differently?*

5. *What is omitted from this message? (Thoman, 1999)*

Students will then choose their own visual text materials. Providing students with the opportunity to make their own choices motivates them by engaging them in self-selection. A variation of this is when teachers introduce a selection of titles or groupings and then allow students to independently choose from that list. Examples of choices include: (a) choosing from a collection of multiple copies of visual texts such as political cartoons, (b) choosing from collections of visuals with a common theme, (c) choosing from a series of commercials on the same topic and (d) choosing from a group of books where several common forms of illustration can be detected, based on the cover, for example.

Students are then told to form groups based on common choices/interests, not abilities. Groups will range from 3 to 6 persons depending on selections. The teacher may assist in forming these groups until students are accustomed to the procedures for initiating Viewing Circles.

Next, group members must find and develop their own topics of discussion. This is a type of inquiry into viewing responses, including discussion about meaning, function and personal experience. Students will need to be equipped with language that describes the elements of visuals. The Inquiry-Based Viewing Road Map may be a good prior knowledge introduction to the language of visuals, although guided practice in developing powerful language in response to visual representation is essential. Students can use role-playing to begin developing expertise at discussions.

STUDENT ROLES WITHIN GROUPS

Cooperative learning models have shown us that students perform better through contribution roles. Their role helps them to engage in successful discussion. Keegan and Shrake (1991) suggest using roles during Literature Circles to help students contribute to discussion and provide direction for group conversations. Keegan and Shrake's roles have been adjusted to suit Viewing Circles as follows:

Discussion Director/ix – Ensures that all members of the group have contributed and all tasks are completed. The director also uses open-ended questions such as, how did this work for you? The director releases the group from the notion that it is necessary to obtain the same meaning and the same ideas and feelings from the visuals.

Visual Wizard(s) – Focuses on interesting and powerful use of elements (e.g., shape, line, form, movement and color), illustrator's or film maker's interpretation of the text and visual response.

Word Wizard(s) – Focuses on the interesting and powerful use of language that can be used to share the experience of viewing.

Summarizer – Provides a brief overview of the visuals and viewing circle discussion. The Summarizer highlights key points. Sticky notes can be used by the summarizer to write down key points on each note, then later the greatest number of notes committed to one particular idea will determine the main point generated by the group.

Finale Organizer – Organizes a dramatic, visual or textual representation that will be a presentation to the whole class regarding the group's selection(s).

Since there are only five separate roles, groups are permitted to have two visual or word wizards to support discussion. Students assume their roles within the group and the teacher facilitates the use of the critical questions to direct students toward a group consensus on the meaning of the works that the group has individually selected and then brought together collectively. It is important to have students move toward a summary so that they can all participate in a culminating activity that represents their group's discussion.

ASSESSMENT AND EVALUATION

Viewing Circles conclude with a culminating activity or visual presentation to the other groups. To conclude Visual Circles, the culminating activity is used to summarize, for the rest of the class, what the group has seen and learned. A drama tableau that is afterwards explained to the rest of the class, a quick sketch "poster" using markers and large poster paper, or a minimalist dramatic presentation are excellent conclusions to this activity. Having students use maximum time to discuss and develop depth in their discussion and minimal amount of time to prepare the culminating activity seems to work best. Students should be encouraged to be as creative as possible in their culminating activity presentations. I have seen students create a Reader's Theatre production, a mime, a dance, a fashion show and an improvisational opera in response to their Viewing Circles. The culminating activities can be evaluated both informally, by just reacting to the presentation through clapping, or formally, on a rubric, evaluating the quality of the presentation. Viewing Circles can then be used to launch related presentation projects such as book making, play writing, movie making or electronic portfolios. A movie of the culminating activity could be included in a student's personal writing/representing portfolio.

AN ELECTRONIC WRITING/REPRESENTING PORTFOLIO ORGANIZER

DESCRIPTION AND BACKGROUND

A growing number of reading researchers recommend exploration of new texts (Giles, Macaul & Rodenberg, 2000; Leu, 2000; Luke & Elkins, 1998). Students feel connected to their culture through the exploration of new literacies available in media and electronic texts. As language arts has expanded through new literacies in electronic forms, there is greater opportunity to use viewing and representing in these texts. Even simple forms of electronic texts such as e-mail encourage writers to utilize icons and visuals by their very nature. Commands such as "insert picture" are as commonplace as "change font" in electronic writing environments. Furthermore, electronic texts have a flexibility that allows readers and writers to think of the writing as a network of ideas that they negotiate as they read. This has implications for the reading and writing of the electronic text and implications for the way the writer conceives of the text before writing.

Electronic portfolio preparation is not just a simple matter of transferring word processed texts and corresponding visuals to an electronic environment such as a website. Although that is one way of doing it, the conceptualization often lacks the advantages that electronic writing environments offer. A more sophisticated process is to outline the electronic text utilizing the non-linear and multi-linear aspects of that text. Landow (1997) claims electronic text is a form of text composed of pieces of text and images joined by links that permit multi-linear reading, neither non-linear reading nor non-sequential, but multi-sequential reading.

It helps students to think of the "representing" from a viewer's multiple points of view. Since the text should be written in such a way that the viewer can choose how they wish to read the text, the writer/representer needs to provide opportunities within the writing of the text for the reader to make choices. The opportunities provide a reading environment that is supported for purpose/clarity of meaning and efficiency of use. Rada (1984), a computer scientist, describes this process of thinking through choice-oriented writing. He explains that writers of electronic texts need to think of the reader as their mirror image, on the other side of the looking glass. As writers write, so they must imagine the many paths readers might take in reading. To aspire to the readers' view, it is important for writers, or representers, in this case, to view their texts from the readers' point of view, even before creating a table or generating any web pages.

The following instructional framework can help students organize their move from linear thinking to constructing an environment for their texts where readers can make decisions about the pathway of their viewing. Electronic portfolios provide a rich environment for thinking through relationships between visuals and readers' response to those visuals. Preplanning is recommended as a time-saver and a conceptual organizer. This instructional framework has two parts for preplanning the electronic portfolio. The first part is a storyboard framework that is not used to tell a story but used to brainstorm ideas for links between texts. The student can complete this part alone or in a group. The second part, not illustrated, is a type of card game where students transfer their storyboard ideas onto recipe cards and then use drinking straws or Popsicle sticks to show links between concepts located on the recipe cards. The card game provides a more three dimensional model of the writing/representing process for students and because it is a game of cards, changes can be easily viewed without spending hours creating a visual such as a web that may or may not work with artifacts added over time. Students will meet in groups, perhaps Viewing Circle groups, to discuss the reasoning behind and connections between the parts of their own writing/representing portfolio.

An Electronic Writing/Representing Portfolio Organizer

Purpose (Writing/Representing Objectives):	
Main Page and Elements:	
Elements: Transfer elements to cards.	
	URL: http://

(use recipe cards and straws in stage two of this instructional framework)

In this instructional framework, students choose portfolio artifacts from their ongoing writing and representing activities and they post these artifacts within their own electronic portfolio. Examples of artifacts may be essays, illustrations, flow charts, posters, movies and poems, to name only a few. The next step is for the teacher to set up an environment or container for student work to be produced. Examples of the electronic portfolio container are a WebCT shell-based portfolio, a portal project for student websites (Katz & Associates, 2002), student work presented through a CD, or individual student websites posted to the World Wide Web. The type of container will depend on the school policy regarding the posting of student work to the web and the overall purposes of the portfolio as a writing/representing activity. For example, a teacher can use a WebCT shell and have only guests and class members view the portfolios until the day they decide to make public their final product portfolios. A teacher may choose to exclude or include audience depending on the need to publish a final project that an audience can view.

The purpose of the representing instructional framework is to link and support the intermediality of a myriad of types of individual student work. Intermediality (Semali & Pailliotet, 1999) refers to the ability to critically read and write with and across varied symbol systems. Relating the varied symbol systems in a portfolio leads to critical media literacy analysis, authenticated in a visual text that, more often than not, has varied symbol systems, since the portfolio artifacts come from a varied history of student work. Having students plan the construction of the overall portfolio environment provides a reason for teaching critical media literacy in general, and intermediality in particular. Students will examine links between their artifact texts that may not necessarily be intertextually or semantically linked. Instead, they may be visually linked.

ASSESSMENT AND EVALUATION

When students apply their newly-developed backgrounds in deep viewing and Viewing Circles to their own work, lively discussion occurs because the viewing and representing activity is then personalized. The opportunity to blend Viewing Circles with the preparation of electronic portfolios provides a rich context for sharing, critique, praise and improvement. Student self assessment through discussion and commentary is at the heart of electronic portfolio development. It is important for pre-service teachers to sustain feelings of success through positive commentary about individual progress, noting that not all progress is made in a positive direction. Provocation often provides great challenges and points of discussion, leading to greater progress in the long run.

The good news about portfolio assessment/evaluation is that it may occur on many informal and formal levels and still be successful. Students learn to self-assess, set goals, express for an audience and demonstrate growth over time. For several years, classroom teachers have experienced the success of classroom-based writing portfolios that demonstrate student progress over time (Smagorinski, 2002). Now, however, there is some evidence that large scale writing portfolio assessments have some success as well (Hillocks, 2002). The success of portfolio assessment lies in instructional settings that do not restrain learning, in having a portfolio procedure that can structure the direction and at the same time free learners from the limitations of outcomes and expected products that challenge the notion of inquiry and utilized critique and discussion to expand definitions and concepts. In a media age when textual ideas are expanding, this allows for a needed dynamic in curricular thinking about new literacy forms.

FINAL FRAME

The activities in this chapter are linked together in the way they support social construction of knowledge in classrooms. Together they form a tripartite of viewing and representing activities that help pre-service teachers quick-start their way into viewing and representing, even if they themselves have little visual literacy background. The Road Map is a vocabulary builder and a critical analysis method that individuals and groups can apply to a variety of visual and media representations. The second activity, Viewing Circles, also helps to build vocabulary and supports social interaction for a deeper view of meaning construction. The third activity celebrates the activity of representation and is most valuable in a socially interactive context. All three activities allow teachers and students to respect the individuality and diversity of our classrooms today because they do not close the door on that celebration with pre-set limitations. These activities provide a structure for exploring new literacies and new notions of text that continue to develop as a natural part of the social construction of knowledge in English language arts.

Are you a pre-service teacher or do you teach senior years English language arts curriculum and instruction? As new notions of text continue to unfold, our classes would like to pen-pal with you, and hear about your ideas in exchange for our ideas about how to implement viewing and representing into language arts instruction. Please send an e-mail to Karen_Smith@UManitoba.ca so we can include your voice in our billboard of viewing and representing discussion. In this way we can keep the dialogue alive.

REFERENCES

Anderson, N. & Pungente, J. (1997). *Scanning television: Videos for media literacy in class.* Guide and 4 videos. Philadelphia, PA: Harcourt Brace Canada.

Close, E. (1992). Literature discussion: A classroom environment for thinking and sharing. *English Journal, 81*(5), 65-72.

Daniels, H. (1994). *Literature circles: voice and choice in the student-centred classroom.* Markham, ON: Pembroke Publishers.

Eisner, E. (1991). *The enlightened eye: Qualitative inquiry and the enhancement of educational practice.* New York: Macmillan Publishing Company.

Giles, J.K., Macaul, S.L., & Rodenberg, R.K. (2000). Inquiry-based learning and the new literacies: Media, multimedia, and hypermedia. In A. Watts Pailliotet and P.B. Mosenthal (Eds.). *Advances in reading/ language research: Reconceptualizing literacy in the media age* (pp. 155-183). Samford, CN: JAI Press.

Hillocks, G. Jr. (2002) *The testing trap: How state writing assessments control learning.* New York, NY: Teachers College Press.

Himley, M. (1991). *Shared territory: Understanding children's writing as works.* New York, NY: Oxford University Press.

Katz, R.N. & Associates (2002). *Web portals & higher education.* San Francisco, CA: Jossey-Bass.

Keegan, S. & Shrake, K. (1991). Literature study groups: An alternative to ability grouping. *The Reading Teacher, 44*(8), 542-547.

Landow, G.P. (1997). *Hypertext 2.0.* Baltimore, MD: Johns Hopkins

University Press.

Leu, D.J., Jr. (2000). Literacy and technology: Deictic consequences for literacy education in an information age. In M.L. Kamil, Mosenthal, P.D. Pearson & R. Barr (Eds.), *Handbook of reading research: Volume III* (pp. 743-770). Mahwah, NJ: Erlbaum.

Luke, A. & Elkins, J. (l998). Reinventing literacy in "New Times". *Journal of Adolescent and Adult Literacy, 42*, p. 4-7.

Manitoba Education and Training (1996a) *Senior 1 English language arts: Manitoba curriculum framework of outcomes.* Winnipeg, MB: Author.

Manitoba Education and Training (1998a) *Senior 2 English language arts: Manitoba curriculum framework of outcomes.* Winnipeg, MB: Author.

Manitoba Education and Training (1996b). *Success for all learners: A handbook on differentiated instruction.* Winnipeg, MB: Author.

Manitoba Education and Training (1998b). *Technology as a foundation skill area: A journey toward information technology literacy.* Winnipeg, MB: Author.

Rada, R. (1989). Writing and reading hypertext: An overview. *Journal of the American Society for Information Science, 40*, 164-171.

Semali, L.M., & Pailliotet, A.W. (1999). Introduction: What is intermediality and why study it in U.S. classroom? In L.M. Semali & A.W. Pailliotet (Eds.) *Intermediality: The teachers' handbook of critical media literacy* (pp. 1-29). New York: Longman.

Scott, J. (1994). Literature circles in the middle school classroom: developing reading, responding and responsibility. *Middle School Journal.* November, 37-41.

Smagorinski, P. (2002). *Teaching English through principled practice.* Columbus, OH: Merrill Prentice Hall.

The New London Group (Spring, 1996). A pedagogy of multiliteracies designing social futures. *Harvard Educational Review, 66*(1), 83.

Thoman, E. (1999). Skills and strategies for media education. *Educational Leadership, 56*(5), 52.

Tyner, K. (1998). *Literacy in a digital world: Teaching and learning in the age of information.* Mahwah, NJ: Lawrence Erlbaum Associates.

Vacca, R.T. & Vacca, J.L. (2002). *Content area reading: Literacy and learning across the curriculum* (Seventh edition). New York: Addison-Wesley.

Watts Pailliotet, A. (1995). I never saw that before: A deeper view of video analysis in teacher education. *Teacher-Educator, 31*(2), 138-156.

Watts Pailliotet, A. (1993). Understanding visual information through deep viewing. In *Visual literacy in the digital age: Selected readings from the annual conference of the International Visual Literacy Association,* ED 370560.

Watts Pailliotet, A., Semali, L., Rodenberg, R.K., Giles, J.K. & Macaul, S.L. (2000). Intermediality: bridge to critical media literacy. *Reading Teacher, 54* (2), 208-19.

An Asset Model of New Literacies

A Conceptual and Strategic Approach to Change

Margaret Mackey

The deficit model of media use is well known: too much television interferes with reading; too many computer games are bad for your brain cells; too much time online is detrimental to your social skills. A lesser-known variant of this model suggests that too much reading of series books or comics is developmentally pernicious and interferes with the appreciation of serious literature.

Many people who hold to these views sincerely want the best for today's young people. Yet very often, the young people they are trying to protect – the young people who watch TV, play computer games, spend hours online with their chatroom friends – perceive this model to be describing *them* as deficient. The result is not an increase in critical dialogue between the interested parties, but rather the development of defiance and defensiveness in teenagers and of a negative despair in many adults that may actually prevent them from seeing the real accomplishments of multi-literate young people.

Kathleen Tyner suggests an alternative model that opens the door for a more constructive approach: an asset model. "An asset model for media teaching assumes that mass media and popular culture content can work as a benefit to literacy instead of as a social deficit" (1998, p. 7). Tyner swiftly turns her attention to examples of pedagogy but I would like to take her phrase and use it more descriptively to develop the concept of an asset model for the contemporary literate.

The idea of literacy as solely or mainly involving the interpretation of print on paper is comfortably manageable. Once we attempt to compose a broader list of descriptors of all forms of contemporary literate experiences, it rapidly becomes very large. To create this particular asset model, my criterion for selection was that any item on this list had to involve some form of *interpretation of recorded symbolic representation* – a very broad category of literacy indeed, but one that can be defended

199

in today's society and that provides a useful opportunity to open up discussion. This broader list demonstrates one incontrovertible fact, that what we often regard as traditional literacy is only one small component today's interpretive experiences. The whole concept of an asset model needs to be flexible; we are going through a period of rapid transition and new entries will be necessary all the time.

The exercise of working out this list is itself a useful one. I offer my own suggestions in Table 1, but I am quite sure that others will be able to think of additions to this extensive list, and that time will alter it sooner rather than later. But, for the sake of developing a useful discussion, my asset model offers a provisional set of areas of contemporary literacy genres. Experience in any or all of these genres, either in reception or production, is an asset in terms of literacy development.

USING AN ASSET MODEL

My model is only an example (see end of chapter), supplied here in the hopes of grounding discussion and questions in productive way. My groupings are provisional, and the categories are highly porous. As various forms of multimedia production become easier (for example, both video-editing and website creation are markedly simpler today than they were five years ago), more and more people will take part in creating a variety of texts, in addition to interpreting the texts of others.

Some of my conceptual framework may be seen as contentious. There are many people who would quarrel with some of the entries, not prepared, for example, to consider an arcade video game as a kind of literate experience. My category of *interpreting recorded symbolic representation* is a wide one, and I think there is more to be gained than lost from an inclusive approach, but it is not entirely unproblematic.

There are many ways of using such a list. I have asked my own students to process it in a variety of ways. We have used it as a starter for discussion, exploring what should and should not be included on such an inventory. On one occasion I asked students to highlight all the items with which they had had experience. I might have asked them to sign these lists and kept them as a useful record for my own purposes; what I actually did on this occasion was slightly different. I collected them anonymously and redistributed them around the class. Then I asked the students, working in pairs, to produce a description of two individual readers, using the information on the list and dealing with the entries specifically as assets. The contrast between even two individuals was generally striking; what was even more noticeable was that the students, even with explicit instructions, still had difficulty in thinking in terms of assets. "It's so easy to notice what a person can't do," they said. That perception itself is food for productive discussion; what is our attitude to a textual world where many of us now feel incompetent, even disenfranchised, by the expanding demands of new media?

This kind of asset model provides the opportunity to gather a swift snapshot of an individual's or a group's media experiences. What are the advantages of having such a snapshot? English teachers can benefit from having a broader-based view of their students' experience and knowledge; it is also helpful to students to perceive that their numerous multimodal skills are acknowledged.

Such work would be interesting and appropriate both in junior and senior high school classes and also in pre-service education classes and other university settings.

THINKING ABOUT THE ASSET MODEL

At a more conceptual level, the model provides a useful outline for thinking in more depth about different kinds of literate behaviors and their importance for school, recreational and civic literacies.

For the rest of this chapter, I will tease out some of the implications of these different categories of literary experience. I will particularly focus on what this model might mean for the classroom.

TEXT ON PAPER

This is the category that would be recognized as literacy by everyone. However, even this category does not represent uncontested literary territory in many schools. I have met young people who voluntarily read every kind of text on this list from the fourth entry or even the third entry onwards. They look at sections of the newspaper, they have magazines for their hobbies, they read comics, graphic novels, manuals. But they do not read novels or short fiction and are therefore not perceived as real readers by some of their teachers or by their librarian, or even by their own parents. All too often these people are induced even to regard *themselves* as non-readers.

There are substantial issues regarding how readers are perceived and defined. An important question for all schools is the issue of the power of definition: who defines what "counts" as reading? If the teachers and librarians only truly value the reading of novels and biographies, how likely are they to misperceive a reader of comics and magazines as a non-reader? What are the chances that they will underestimate both the reading skills and the depth of thinking required to grapple with, say, a complex graphic novel? Will they even notice the quantity of reading and quality of imaginative engagement invested by some video game players in acquiring background knowledge for their game of choice?

I am a novel-reader myself and I value what extended narrative can offer in the way of insights into our complex lives. But I am concerned that an over-concentration on the virtues of fiction reading could result in under-valuing many other elements of contemporary literacy. Hall and Coles (1999) discuss this contradiction in gender terms, reporting on their survey of the reading habits of 8000 British school children:

> *Whilst acknowledging the success of teachers in promoting and sustaining reading habits amongst girls, it seems important to recognize the virtuous circle which is dominating patterns here. Cultural influences on girls are encouraging them to read and value narrative; school definitions of English and reading reinforce those patterns; girls feel positive and successful in these terms and tend to have relatively high self-esteem about their reading and to do relatively well in English examinations. But is this enough? We are arguing that it is not. (p. 88)*

Hall and Coles argue that both those who read mainly narrative (disproportionately girls) and those who read a wider range of texts but tend to avoid narrative (disproportionately boys) are both disadvantaged by a system that places particular value on one genre. The narrative readers need to be encouraged to branch out, and the non-narrative readers need to be acknowledged for the breadth of what they *do* read, not perpetually defined in terms of the one genre they do not read.

I have couched my asset model relatively neutrally (apart from the inevitable appearance of hierarchy that comes into play simply because items on the list have to be placed in some kind of order). But of course our perceptions of entries on this list are not neutral – and our perceptions of the values of particular kinds of print reading are often loaded with implicit overtones of moral judgement. Reading is good, and good for you, we say, but only on *my* terms of what constitutes "real" reading.

A related school question is one of visibility. What reading behaviors are manifested or even taught in school and which ones occur completely outside the school's purview? A great deal of official school reading is of print on paper and most of that falls under the first three headings on this list: novels, short fiction/poetry/drama, and information books. Even dealing with the third item on this list – how to read an information book in the most profitable way – is often not taught as carefully or thoughtfully as it should be. The occasional media studies class will look at newspapers or magazines but very often the approach is not one of increasing readers' pleasure in or skill with their chosen texts but rather one of unpicking the commercial apparatus – a worthwhile cause but not the only way of dealing with such material.

At the non-commercial level, underground materials such as zines (privately produced and circulated publications, often predominantly featuring a particular interest or topic) are often neglected entirely, even though they offer very interesting material for considering issues both of production and of reception. In zines, questions of content (often edgy, which creates both advantages and drawbacks for classroom use), writing, use of graphics, design and layout – all of these issues become more real in the context of materials often produced by teens themselves. The magazine *Broken Pencil* provides convenient access to many Canadian zines.

Zines, of course, are not the only texts produced by young people. One of the real advantages of print literacy is that it is so easy for any literate person to be a producer as well as a consumer. Any of these text forms could be produced by a keen school student.

AUDIOVISUAL TEXT

Television is often perceived as a major villain in any deficit model of literacy. It is, however, arguable that current formats of audiovisual technology, rather than being detrimental to the development of literary understanding, actually create opportunities for explicit media education.

A central tenet of critical media literacy is the idea that "all media are constructed." In other words, television is not a simple window onto the world. Rather, television and other moving images are often prearranged, always framed, nearly always edited, and always presented within a context that affects viewers' interpretation.

Understanding that media events are constructions even when they look totally natural is an important development in comprehending how media work. It can be a rather abstract idea. The past decade, however, has provided more and more numerous concrete examples of the very constructed nature of audiovisual texts. In roughly chronological order, we have seen the appearance of many books about the making of movies, numerous special interest niche magazines, websites full of background information, and alternative tracks on DVDs. Access to insights about what the producer intended, how the special effects were assembled, why certain casting decisions were made, and so forth, is now available on all sides. Thinking about such questions is close to being completely normalized as part of the regular viewing experience. In many ways it would now be quite a challenge to think of a Hollywood film as anything but a construction. Media teachers looking to explore the idea of the constructedness of texts are spoiled for choice in their examples, and, possibly even more importantly, are dealing with students who come into the classroom with a wealth of background experience in this very area to draw on.

Alternative tracks on DVDs are often crammed with information about how the story was constructed, but they offer rather less in the way of critical perspectives on the content and shaping of the film since they are produced by the same commercial organization that created the film in the first place. However, contemporary technology works dynamically and is less and less likely to involve a simple one-way street. A small story in *Wired* magazine provides an example of a step in the opposite direction, restoring a personal voice to a commercial format.

> *Obsessed fans – and critics – are recording their own audio tracks for DVD movies... They blab about loving or loathing a film, point out trivia or errata, and poke fun at bad acting or direction. Recorded as low-bit-rate MP3s, these audio tracks can be played on a computer and easily synced up with a film by cueing to specific frames in the footage. The files are so small, commentators can easily share their work over the Net. (Rojas, 2002, p. 43)*

Such a model of recording a personal audio track for all or part of a movie offers substantial potential for media literacy education. If a DVD player and projector are available, teachers can make good use of

the vast amount of technical and creative background information provided on many commercial DVDs of movies. Obviously the model of a
do-it-yourself commentary and criticism is an appealing one, with or
without the use of real MP3 files. There is also considerable educational scope in comparing and contrasting an independent and critical
soundtrack with the kind of background information tracks included
on many DVDs as part of a corporate package. Clearly the emphasis on
special effects works most effectively with the backing of the original
producer; but what kinds of commentary are missing on these commercial releases?

The creation of such additional soundtracks provides ample opportunity for incorporating different forms of writing and reading, listening and viewing into what has traditionally been simply viewing.
Furthermore, such activities supply a route to improving critical viewing acumen, a worthwhile aim in its own right.

Producing audiovisual texts is also easier than it has ever been.
There is not space here to go into great detail, but ever-cheaper cam-
corders and digital editing suites provide new and exciting opportunities for classroom video work. Many students now come to class with a
broad background of domestic experience in creating quite sophisticated video productions – yet another kind of asset. Roberta Hammett in
this book provides one example of such potential for valuable classroom
work that draws on the assets of students' previous media experience
and awareness.

AUDIO

In comparison with the complexities of electronic, digital and/or
wireless texts, plain old-fashioned audio materials can easily be over-
looked. After all, English teachers have been hauling out the record
player so classes could listen to LPs of Shakespeare productions for
many decades. For almost as long, students have been using tape
recorders for various creative purposes.

Audio materials generally fall into two categories: music and spoken
word. Over the past ten or fifteen years, the use of spoken word materials has soared, both in library loans and in purchases. Audio books are
now big business.

An audio recording of a novel or story is a modest form of adapta-
tion. As its label indicates, spoken word texts, like the printed page, are

verbal. The author's words are transferred to a new medium but not necessarily altered in any other way.

Yet no such transfer can occur without some decisions being made. Will the entire text be taped or just an abridged version? Or will the story be altered more radically to fit a relatively short time-frame? Will the words be read aloud by a single reader or will characters' voices be spoken by different actors? Alternatively, will the whole story be dramatized, with or without a narrative voice-over? If there is a reader, will the narrative voice be male or female? What kind of accent does the reader have? What is the effect if the author is the reader? Will there be background music? sound effects? If so, how elaborate will they be? Will new music be created or will the recording draw on the associations of familiar music? Each of these decisions affects the final impact of the recording.

Most of these decisions can also be made by students creating an audio text of their own. Audio recording is cheap and most schools have plenty of the right equipment. Turning a short story or a poem into a tape is often a satisfying project. Another audio project can be the simulation of a radio program, a project full of potential for talking about content, tone and register, local politics and democracy, marketing and many other lively topics.

There are other dimensions to audio in today's media world, many of which provide interesting topics for discussion. Where audio, mainly music, has led the way in computer file-swapping with Napster, Gnutella, et al., other media forms are now following. Pirate movies are the next big area of contention and copyright questions are a major public issue of the twenty-first century. The ethics of free access to other people's intellectual property, the nature of the commercial organizations that are opposing such free access, the divided opinions of the musicians themselves, all these are live topics for classroom debate. As with many media topics, the virtue of such a discussion is that it draws on students' experiences and genuine expertise.

ELECTRONIC IMAGES

The deficit model probably holds strongest in relation to all forms of digital video games, whether based in a computer, a game-playing apparatus such as PlayStation, a small handheld player such as GameBoy, or a video machine in an arcade. All kinds of pejorative adjectives are hurled at these amusements: they are perceived as mindless, violent, addictive and otherwise generally frightening. They are also extremely confusing to people who have never played them, and I suspect this confusion is part of why many people find these games so threatening.

My own personal experience with video games of all sorts is most kindly described as amateur. I can see coherence and organization in these games as I watch other people play, but once I get my own hands on the controls, disintegration and failure are only minutes away. I have not invested the hours of practice required for instantaneous and fine-tuned manual response to the tests of the game, nor do I have a good understanding of standard game conventions so that I can apply them to make sense of the immediate challenges of a particular plot. In short, I am hopeless.

Fortunately my experience of these games is not confined to my own limits as a player. I have video recorded a variety of young people playing at least the initial stages of more than a dozen games. Playing close attention to these videotapes has been very instructive. (See Mackey 2002 for one account of young players and the complex interpretive strategies they apply to their computer games).

Firstly, the skill question is very important. Many adult criticisms of these games are the equivalent of a very beginning reader complaining that reading is a mindless activity because all you do is struggle with one individual letter after another. Until a certain amount of automaticity is attained, a player's attention is so focused on the struggle for control that making any other meaning out of the story is almost impossible.

Secondly, there are fascinating questions of convention. There are the conventions necessitated by the technical limitations of the platform; there are the strategic conventions built up over previous games; and there are the narrative conventions of the kinds of fantasies created in many of the game stories. Watching an experienced game player tackle a brand new game is an impressive experience. A good player will take account of all these different levels of convention at once, and an articulate player will be able to explain them to an observer.

It is possible to concede every point I have made so far and still be disturbed by what is perceived as impoverished imagination, lame psychology, sexism and an over-emphasis on violence as drawbacks to many games. Certainly some are better than others in terms of what they offer to the imagination – but the same is true of all forms of literate experience. Playing a good video game well is a real achievement.

One of the things that surprised me when I first started to look more closely at digital games was the amount of print reading involved in many of them – and not just in the instruction manual and the help screens. In my prejudiced way, I think I had expected something like television cartoons, with the odd "splat!" as the only verbal element in the story. Certainly there are games like that, but many more than I expected include a verbal text as one of the multimedia ingredients in the whole experience.

The other issue of interest to those concerned with a broad picture of literacy is that adult categorizations of these games may be more hard-and-fast than those of young players. The most experienced gameplayer I have worked with so far is a young man of 23 called Damien. Damien likes to play his games in one or two extended sweeps of time. He says that it is often necessary to invest a great deal of energy in mental mapping of the game space and that you can lose that investment if you interrupt the game too frequently. He also says there is a flow to the game that enhances the experience. Thus he is ready to stay up, sometimes all night, to finish a game rather than interrupt it. Just as I was reaching for the usual stereotyped conclusions, he said, "It's the same with a book. A book has a flow. I'll stay up late to finish a book for exactly the same reasons."

Damien's connection between the game-playing experience and the novel-reading experience is a reminder that both represent sustained and complex immersion in a fictional universe. The idea of paying all our respects to one form and ignoring or despising the other may seem perverse and old-fashioned to some skilled and committed young gameplayers.

How can the English/media educator address the asset of many students' gaming experience in classroom work? One possibility is to have small groups creating the outline of a digital game, either electronically or on paper. What rules and conventions do they make use of to ensure that their game will be "playable"? Even those who never play such games have certain conventional understandings about them, and the reshaping of narrative forces into the paradigm of a set of alternative developments offers its own intellectual challenge. Even non-gaming teachers can organize class discussions about the pros and cons of digital games. With a projector, it might even be possible to have a brief "show and tell" of students' favorite games and a follow-up discussion of what makes them appealing and what makes the stories work successfully – an electronic cousin to the trusty book talk!

ELECTRONIC TEXT

The most common manifestation of offline and fixed electronic text, at least in 2002, is probably still the CD-ROM information text: the encyclopedia, the reading or mathematics game, the historical or geographical text that takes advantage of the disk's multi-modal potential. The memory limits of CD-ROM mean that it still relies extensively on text and still pictures, but the new generation of DVD replacements will probably increase the quotient of moving images and soundtracks. Already the requisite literacy for dealing with CD-ROM includes strategies for locating, selecting, cutting and pasting; as texts become ever more multimedia, the decisions about what is communicated most successfully in words and what in other media will become increasingly complex. Even with today's limited CD-ROMs, readers must develop a whole skill-set for tracking information and not becoming lost in hyperspace; the next generation of texts will tax these skills even further.

Meanwhile there is a great deal of electronic text that does not feature too extensively in schools as yet. The portable readers such as electronic books and the screens of personal data assistants (PDAs) are still too expensive to play much of a role in the lives of most school children. Microsoft Reader is freely available for downloading but it assumes extended access to a computer screen for any continuous reading. It is not at all clear how these formats are going to develop. I do know people who read whole novels on their PDAs but they are still very much in a minority, and we need to learn much more about both the practicalities and the aesthetics of this kind of experience. The marketing of the electronic book has been a dismal failure up to this point, but this fact does not mean that nobody will ever figure out how to sell us a truly portable and truly attractive electronic alternative to the paper page. At present, electronic ink on some facsimile of paper looks like one possible option, but again there will be both practical and aesthetic questions to answer.

Literary hypertext – the use of linked screens to tell a story or communicate a poem – is theoretically interesting but very much a minority interest at the moment. The popularity a generation ago of the *Choose Your Own Adventure* books suggests that a determined hypertext assault on the popular market might actually be successful, but at present most fictional hypertexts are much more literary than popular. It may be that when the questions about portable hardware (e-book, PDA, some new alternative) are answered, there will be more scope for experimentation with the software, the kinds of texts that can be mounted on our new electronic readers.

When thinking about the success or failure of such readers, it is useful to remember the history of the DVD, which had its own format fights before its current astonishing success. There was a long period when DVD was hyped but not actually selling; now it is widely recognized as the fastest selling consumer electronic item in history. The mistakes and experiments in the development of the electronic book may yet culminate in the critical mass needed for take-off, even if it is not presently clear what final form may actually succeed. When that happens, all kinds of *Choose Your Own Adventure* hypertexts may be the result. Another possibility, one alluringly outlined by Janet Murray in *Hamlet on the Holodeck* (1997), may be the development of many forms of hybrid text, where readers assemble their own stories from a variety of sources. Relatively clunky prototypes of this kind of approach to story already exist and I shall return to them later.

E-zines, the electronic equivalents of paper zines, also provide scope for considering many issues of communication. It would not take a very large collection of print and electronic zines to raise genuinely important questions about how all the elements – content, writing, use of graphics, design and layout – are affected by the decision to communicate on paper or on computer. As assets for a discussion on questions of how best to communicate in a particular format, they provide many advantages for school classrooms; they are current and can be selected to appeal to students' own interests.

WIRELESS TEXT

Europeans pay far more than North Americans for local telephone calls and have turned far more enthusiastically to cell phones. As a result, European young people have been quicker to adopt text messaging (typing interactive messages on the screen of the cell phone) as a prominent feature of their lives. The small screen available on a cell phone and the awkwardness of typing on the cell phone's keypad means that brevity is important and teens have developed a new shorthand for use on their phones. Acronyms, abbreviations and contractions abound, to an even greater extent than on chat lines.

Whether the text messaging phenomenon ever catches on in Canada to the same extent remains to be seen. As a literacy exercise, it is the site of some teasing ambiguities. Does such a severely truncated form of expression lead to creativity under pressure, or does it encourage predictable repetition of the phrases that have already been boiled down to a few letters – or a mixture of both ingredients? How many users actually communicate new information to their correspondents and how many of their exchanges are simply a new incarnation of that old telephone slogan, "Reach out and touch someone," an interaction more concerned with sociability than with content? And how long will it be before somebody writes an epistolary short story entirely in text messages – much as Wuther Crue in 1932 wrote a "short story" that was told entirely in the form of bank cheques (Vacca & Vacca, 1999, pp. 20-23)? Or, indeed, how long before somebody sets an English assignment to demonstrate how text messaging might have saved Romeo and Juliet!

Although they may never become a dominant element in North Americans' literate lives (though an explosion in text messaging may actually be imminent), in many countries text messages form a vibrant vernacular literacy (Barton & Hamilton, 1998, p. 10), an informal channel of communication with a home-grown structure and etiquette.

ONLINE TEXT

The Internet has changed our literate lives in ways too vast to enumerate comprehensively in a brief chapter. Speaking more generally about the lengthy list of activities outlined in the asset model, it is noteworthy that one major transformation wrought by the Internet is the addition of enormous amounts of reading and writing to other media encounters that previously existed without the carapace of added literacies many young people now take for granted.

For example, back in the olden days not that long ago, people used to watch a movie or a television program and that was more or less the end of it. They might talk about it with their friends, or possibly read a magazine interview with the star. Nowadays, of course, there is a huge apparatus of commentary on the most ordinary film or TV show. Viewers are online exhanging opinions in chatrooms, sometimes even as the credits roll. It is worth picking a television program and doing an online search on a search engine such as google.com for related websites; the results are usually instructive. I have been exploring websites related to the television series *Felicity*, a modestly successful WBTV teen series about a group of college students (Mackey, in press). The results are astonishing to me, though not to the young people I know. A sampling of the available sites includes the following:

- official background information from WBTV, including some snippets of tape not seen on the original program;
- complete unofficial transcripts of each episode;
- capsule summaries (some with and some without added opinions from the summarizer);
- numerous chatroom exchanges among fans;
- campaigns to persuade WBTV to schedule better;
- campaigns to persuade the scriptwriters to pursue one plot development or another;
- listings of the soundtrack for each episode, complete with links to MP3 files in some cases;
- photo collages of the characters;
- fan fiction, in which the characters of Felicity are featured in new stories;
- a website "belonging" to one of the fictional characters (giving no hint on the site itself that the creator doesn't really exist)

I chose *Felicity* deliberately because it is not a runaway mega-hit like *Buffy the Vampire Slayer* or *The Simpsons*. Even so, the quantity and range of available material, mostly written though some is visual or audio, is truly startling to those who have not been paying attention. It is also interesting to see how the chatroom exchanges support more complex viewing; the final season of *Felicity* ended with several complicated time travel episodes in which Felicity revisited a moment in the past and made a different decision, which led to whole new plot-lines. Fans answered each other's questions and sorted out potential confusion; it is worth asking if the producers would have been able to risk such a radical turn to the series without the knowledge that such a support network was available.

It is not just audiovisual texts that foster such an expanded online literacy. Computer games of all sorts lend themselves to online support – game players correspond in a variety of different ways:

- in role as characters of role-playing games;
- as players, conducting strategic discussions;
- as merchants (though this is often frowned on), selling characters with advanced skills to other players;
- in many of the ways described with regard to *Felicity*.

Likewise, print texts (especially those published in series where building up a following is part of the experience) lend themselves to an amazing quantity of online discussion. *Harry Potter* is closing in on two million sites listed on google.com (1 840 000 sites listed as of May 8, 2002). Even allowing for a certain number of duplicates, dead-ends and so forth, this is a lot of added reading and writing. How much of it is worth the trouble is a different question, but it is not all dross by any means; I have explored many lively and informative sites.

Nobody reads it all, of course. However, it is not merely the scale of extra reading that affects our literate behaviors very profoundly; it is also the potential for readers to be writers as well. Many of these sites are open for readers to make contributions of their own. Correspondence between readers is commonplace and encouraged. Access to computers can be an issue, but once that barrier is crossed the web is in many ways genuinely democratic.

The variety and prolixity of the web lends itself to extensiveness. Its users will need to develop corresponding skills in selectivity and critical reading. If you are a *Felicity* fan, how do you decide whether and when you will sample the extra information on the web, and where do you stop? What do *Felicity* websites contribute to developing a more informed and critical awareness of the strengths and limitations of the program?

For teachers, this last question is a crucial one. The web is highly participatory but also very short of gatekeepers. The enthusiasm of its many, many creators and contributors is a salutary reminder that literacy is a very long way from dead, though it may be mutating. But access to the Internet is no substitute for a thoroughly thought-out approach to critical literacy.

The other key attribute of online text is its openness to interactivity. This quality is its revolutionary contribution to new literacies, but it is also the area of greatest risk. Pornography, hate sites, malevolent strangers posing as friends, commercial exploitation, all are hazards of the Internet. Nor can it safely be said that all evil is externally imposed on innocent children; online bullying, local hate literature (sites listing the ugliest girls in a particular junior high class, for example), and various kinds of flaming all flourish out of reach of adult supervision. All playgrounds have their nasty corners and tyrannical cliques; the Internet is no different.

Canadian teachers and librarians are very well served by the Media Awareness Network (www.media-awareness.ca) which provides both information and teaching strategies for dealing with this new and potent interactive giant that has suddenly intruded into our teaching and domestic space. Strengthening the defences of young Internet users is now an essential part of education, and the Media Awareness Network is a useful ally.

CONCLUSIONS

The asset model provides one lens for exploring the world in which North American young people are learning about literate behaviors. No doubt it can readily be expanded, either right away or in the near future. It remains a highly provisional list, and will go out of date before it can be refined to any state of comprehensive perfection. However, I hope it does serve a purpose in contributing to an awareness of the complexity of the challenges facing both students and teachers at the start of the twenty-first century. "Know your enemy" is a cynical warning; in this case, I would argue that there is at least a comparable case to be made for "Know your opportunities." Many of today's students are coming into class with experience in a rich matrix of multimedia engagements. Acknowledging and building on these new literacies is both constructive and essential.

REFERENCES

Barton, David & Mary Hamilton (1998). *Local literacies: Reading and writ-*

ing in one community. London: Routledge.

Broken Pencil: The Magazine of Zine Culture and the Independent Arts. PO Box 203, Stn. P, Toronto, ON M5S 2S7. Available: http://www.brokenpencil.com)

Hall, C. & Coles, M (1999). *Children's reading choices.* London: Routledge.

Mackey, M. (2002). *Literacies across media: Playing the text.* London: Routledge/Falmer.

Mackey, M. (in press). Television and the teenage literate: Discourses of *Felicity. College English.*

Media Awareness Network. [Online]. Available: http://www.media-awareness.ca.

Murray, J. H. (1997). *Hamlet on the holodeck: The future of narrative in cyberspace.* New York: Free Press.

Rojas, P. (2002). Everyone's a critic. *Wired*, May, 43.

Tyner, K. (1998). *Literacy in a digital world: Teaching and learning in the age of information.* Mahwah, NJ: Lawrence Erlbaum.

Vacca, R. T. & Vacca, J. (1999). *Content area reading: Literacy and learning across the curriculum.* 6th ed. New York: Longman.

END NOTE

The author would like to acknowledge the Social Sciences and Humanities Research Council of Canada whose generous assistance made this work possible.

Table 1: An Asset Model of Contemporary Literacy Experiences

Text on paper
novels
short fiction/poetry/drama
information books
newspapers
magazines
    fashion/self-help
    sports/games/hobbies
    general information/news
    other – specify
comics
graphic novels
zines (home-made/small-circulation
    magazines/newsletters)
picture books
computer manuals
games manuals/help books
letters/newsletters
educational assignments
other – specify

Audiovisual
television
video
    viewing
        timeshifting TV programs
        for later viewing
        pre-recorded movies
    producing
        screenwriting, etc.
        camerawork
        editing
DVD
    viewing movies
    viewing alternative tracks
        production information
            special effects
            director's commentary
            trailers, etc.

alternative playback
    different soundtracks
    different camera angles
    other – specify
producing alternative
    soundtracks
cinema
    viewing movies
    viewing IMAX features
    other – specify

Audio
radio
    local
    distant (short-wave or Internet)
    CB
    music
    talk
audiocassette
    music
    spoken word
CD
    music
    spoken word
MP3 or other form of online sound
    music
    spoken word
other – specify

Electronic images
computer games (on CD-ROM
    or DVD)
    played alone
    played against face-to-face
        opponent
    played online
video games (PlayStation, Nintendo,
    etc.)

hand-held electronic games
(GameBoy, etc.)
arcade games
other – specify

Electronic text
e-books
PDAs (personal data assistants such
as PalmPilot)
on-screen readers such as Microsoft
Reader
e-mail
CD-ROM information texts
e-zines
literary hypertext
other - specify

Wireless text
text messaging
other – specify

Online text
Internet – reading
surfing/browsing websites
searching for specific
information
revisiting bookmarked sites
listservs
chatrooms
Instant Messages
Internet – producing
contributing to chatrooms
related to specific topics
computer games
in role
as a player
television programs
movies
particular hobbies
other – specify
general chatrooms
other – specify

instant messaging
with personally known
friends
with Internet-only friends
writing to listservs
specific topic-related
general
blogging (web logging)
on a specific topic
general
creating websites
personal – e.g. home page
topic-related
text-only
text and still image
text and moving image
audio
contributing to other websites
in writing
opinions
fan fictions
other – specify
in visual forms
still images
moving images
by adding links
Internet – learning
Internet – helping others
Internet – other – specify

CONTEXTUALIZING MEDIA
AND ICT LITERACIES
WITHIN AN ECONOMIC
IMPERATIVE DISCOURSE

BARRIE R.C. BARRELL

Many areas of endeavor in America pressured by technological change have already had to decide what business they were really in, and those making the narrow choice have usually not fared well. The railroads had to decide whether they were in the transportation business or the railroad business: they chose the latter and gradual extinction...For all its fastidious self-distancing from the world of affairs, literary study faces the same kind of decision. If we are not in the codex book business, what business are we really in? – Richard Lanham

I close this book with two personal anecdotes. Recently, my Mexican made IBM laptop's keyboard developed problems. I called IBM Canada in Montreal from a ranger station in the Canadian Rockies where I was writing. After a discussion that had me following instructions and acting much as an IBM repair person, the technician, who did not know or care where I was, told me the machine would need to be taken "in." I was given the number of GE Capital (another multinational corporation) in Calgary. GE Capital told me to bring the computer in, but first to call India to get a work order number. I called the 1-800 number and laughed with the voice on the other end of the line about it being the middle of the night for him. A check was done on my computer's serial number and then an e-mail sent to Calgary giving permission for the needed repair. GE Capital then informed me they had to order "in" (location not given) a new keyboard and that it would take about a day or two to arrive. The story ends a month later when I received a call from Minnesota inquiring about the quality of the service that I had received from GE Capital.

This one small example of my life in a globalized world makes clear, if nothing else, the interconnectedness of corporate communications, the shifting notions of corporate time and space and the limited importance of distances. It also demonstrates my ability to write and communicate within the physical isolation of the Rockies and yet still have access to worldwide communications, goods and services.

THE SECOND ANECDOTE

As an English schoolboy it was my job to hand out the ink while my friend, Martin, distributed the nibs and blotting paper before cursive writing classes. Maybe it was India ink, I'm not sure. What I am sure of is the immense technological distances I have traveled in the last fifty years and the transitional journey I have made from pen and ink communications to all the capabilities that a connected laptop provides. I *see* the technologies and texts that are evolving around me. I have lived through a great deal of their development and integration into society. I have seen computers shrink from the size of boxcars to juice boxes while their power has dramatically increased, giving me access to multiple texts and representations. I have been afforded the luxury of having stood on both sides of the digital divide.

Today's young people are rather blasé about technology and various media. Unlike me, they do not *see* technology, even though it encompasses much of their daily lives. As Tapscott (1998) informs us, they merely read it, view it, listen to it, talk and write into it, play with it and even wear it. Indeed, fashion and communications have recently been blended into a single media event when Roots Clothing and Nokia teamed up with Radio Shack to produce a fashionable mobile phone complete with "wearable" carrying case and corporate logo.

The young might view my pen and ink anecdote as cute or as proof of just how old I am. The laptop anecdote would most probably leave them wondering "so what's the big deal?" since they operate in a world where the media, modern technologies and communication systems are rather opaque; the young take technology for granted much as electric lighting is taken for granted by many of us. Indeed, it is only when the lights fail to come on or heat does not issue from heating ducts that we are reminded of their relevance to us. Likewise, today it would be the *absence* of computers and VCRs in Canadian schools that would gain our attention, certainly not their presence.

There are signs we are becoming somewhat like the young. We assume Internet connections are readily available to us in our cities, homes, hotels, airports and work places. We ask, "Where is there a bank machine?" or "Where can I check my e-mail?" all the while assuming that account access is just around the corner or across the lobby. We are in the midst of deep systemic and historical change. New social orders are emerging. Writing projects can be truly communal and inter-provincial. We can expect film text to follow the same route as the cost of computing moves toward $.02 a megabyte.

Thus my own educational experiences that started with pen and ink communications and the text-bound literary studies that followed have since run to all the power of a connected laptop. Of course, I cannot help but drag prejudices from the world of print into my online communities and ask, as Bass (1996) does, questions like, is hypertext a style, a theory, a concept, a typography, a rhetoric? My online experiences lead me to ponder where the line between the "real" world and the "virtual" world is situated and what aspects of "real" communities do I replicate in electronic ones? Do electronic archives re-shape or change the primary texts I study? And like Lanham's quote used at the beginning of this chapter, I continue to ask into "what business" is ELA teaching moving?

My questions will quickly be eclipsed by this generation's experiences with technology and the digitally integrated texts they construction and into which they pour their identities. The young will shortly engage new and expanding media and evolving information and communication technologies (ICT). These technologies will collapse and blend audio, video, print and data recording and retrieval systems within the broadcasting capabilities of hand held devices. With these devices, and their bundled applications, come opportunities to engage with a multiplicity of new problem solving and creative endeavors. Further, their proficient use and integration into a broad array of daily educational experiences will be an expected part of the knowledge economy. Both civic and corporate communication practices will shortly assume students have used all kinds of digital technologies and have a working familiarity with a broad spectrum of ICT applications.

Educational history is in a transitional phase. Schools are losing their monopoly over information and its decimation. Students often have the edge over teachers in their acquired computer skills. Their homes provide faster access to primary sources, media texts and electronic archives; their computers are often more advanced than those found in the classroom. It is apparent that in the coming decade schools will need to retool, rethink and reinvent themselves as they go about looking at the literacy and educational experiences that will help young people live a competent life in the digital age. Schools will need to look closely at changing skill sets and literacy requirements.

THE LITERACY DEMAND OF KNOWLEDGE WORKERS

Information and communication technologies are now invaluable tools to most civic, business and university endeavors (see R. Reich, 1992). From robotics to computer-aided designs, from the use of synthesizers in music production to animated film-making, from nanotechnology to biotechnology, and from census databases to collaborative writing projects, information and communication technologies are essential for the completion of both routine and complex calculations, predictions, procedures, productions and diagnoses. These advancements will change the structures of what will be expected of ELA teachers.

In the past, high school diplomas have signified that the bearer could complete a set curriculum, arrive on time, sit for long periods, move about independently within a highly structured environment, pass standardized tests and do whatever was required to satisfy the rules and regulations of a large institution. For a century or more economic and industrial requirements have kept public schools riveted to established traditions and have dictated normative patterns of organization and instruction. Now pressured by the realities of globalization, corporations are requiring different skill sets and worker attributes.

Transnational corporations have an insatiable need for flexible knowledge workers and thinkers. These workers need to come armed with the "new ELA basics" – an understanding of teamwork, a command of multiple literacies, an ability to use the power of digital technologies to solve a variety of complex industrial problems and an understanding of integrated text communications. All transnational corporations with global information and communication networks are re-engineering their networked enterprises, research and development processes, delivery routines, manufacturing procedures and service systems. The Web has dramatically changed corporate organization and communication structures. Indeed, Intel's Andy Grove has driven this point home when he bluntly stated that "all businesses will be Internet businesses – or they won't have a business."

Widespread worker flexibility is already a mainstay of many financial institutions where teams of teams are assembled to solve particular client problems or to devise new products and services. Once solutions are found or particular products designed, the conglomeration of workers is dissolved. Later, they are reassembled into new teams containing different players ready to take on projects that demand different skill sets and worker characteristics. Whatever the civic or corporate structure, one common requirement of skilled workers stands out: an ability to cooperate together in interdisciplinary teams, using various media and communications technologies to solve increasingly complex problems.

Guiding this work is a "just in time" mentality where solutions are directly applied or products brought immediately to market. In these environments there is an understanding that solutions to problems come from the fluidity of blending information from multiple sources and experiences. It is the intangible "problem solving" capability that moves about and within the ether of the teams' work environment that is a value added byproduct of this kind of work. The ability to juggle information and cascade multiple solutions through corporate or civic structures becomes a key attribute of players/workers and represents a significant shift from industrial models of corporate worker engagement.

The new environments in which these employees work does not rely on people working individually around discrete crystallized discipline knowledge where memorization and routine problem solving skills play a large role. As Waks (2000) tells us, schools, as we have known them, are *not efficient* suppliers of workers capable of meeting the skill sets needed by knowledge workers in globally networked environments.

Schools *have been* efficient suppliers of routine workers. However, there is a glut of routine workers (women, recent immigrants and minorities are disproportionately represented in this group) who more and more are being pushed into temporary or part time contractual, non-union jobs with limited pensions and benefits. Globalization allows routine office work, component assembly, 1-800 call centre work, etc. to be drained from a particular region and exported to countries (India) or province or states (Minnesota) with the lowest overheads or with abilities to give corporate tax incentives. A swelling of the ranks constantly pressures routine workers during periods of economic downturn and disruption. Economic pressures force routine workers to drastically limit their compensation demands because their work can be exported out of their community and/or country.

A reality of globalization and free trade is the threat of exportation of any commercial work that is sequential, linear, concrete and/or routine to locations anywhere in the global economy. With limits placed on the need for routine workers, students will need to develop other ways of earning a living or face diminished opportunities. Survival reading and writing competencies are no longer enough for effective participation in the economic and social mainstream of the nation (see Lankshear, 1998). Growing percentages of workers are now required to move about in electronic formats. The Canadian economy has difficulty finding enough knowledge workers while at the same time experiencing a glut of routine workers. The contributors to this text have offered a glimpse into how ELA can meet and contribute to the textual and creative demand of a changing world.

GLOBALIZATION SHIFTS POWER RELATIONSHIPS

Globalization is not a new phenomenon, as any study of the Roman or British Empires would demonstrate. However, while Hadrian waited months to hear from the corners of his Empire, this time around the speed and ease of networked communications dramatically alters power relationships. Public schools are no longer the sole purveyors of knowledge and information in a globalized networked environment. Digital access to information and communications technologies within globalized communities challenges the government's monopoly over fixed curricula and its power to determine specific curricula outcomes. Classroom textbooks are no longer the lifeline back to discipline knowledge and information. Indeed, on-line sources can be primary sources. In the case of science, real time pictures and information are often available via the Net. In either case the materials can be more up-to-date, more comprehensive, and much broader in scope. The availability of primary sources and original materials are powerful enough to both force and support radical changes to existing instructional traditions and practices. Students now have the opportunity to engage with various media and publish those engagements, extensions, and challenges directly to other connected scholars (see Barrell and Hammett, 2002 and 1999, and Cameron and Barrell, 2001). I believe a growing ICT base that spreads information, knowledge, collaborative engagements and artistic constructions to individuals, societies and businesses is powerful enough to begin to destabilize the staid internal institutional traditions that maintain public schooling.

The technologies that sustain globalization are profound. They will continue to advance even if Moore's Law is repealed in the coming decades and evolutionary computer capabilities decrease. Bluetooth technologies, gene mapping, the creation of DNA bar coding, the capability to grow body parts (except the eye and the brain) and computers able to pass the Turing test (human-level intelligence) are going to force public schools to engage with new issues and invite students to make more value-laden decisions about human interaction than ever before. To help students come to ethical and moral decisions about a range of new scientific and social issues will require that students read more broadly, view more critically and think more deeply than they have in the past. It will require that they gain experience working on very complex problems situated in complex environments. Their responses and representation will call on various ICT applications and media constructions to make their case, display their evidence or express their suggested courses of action.

Public education needs a very specific campaign to explain to citizens why it needs to have a new guiding vision that is inclusive of digital technologies and media. For teachers, hypertexts and multimedia authoring tools open up the nonlinear world of textual creation and bring visual expressions into a student's compositional capabilities. For ELA teachers this means textual engagements need to become broader ranging and thus more complex. These engagements need to encompass a mixture of different media that both challenge and change the traditional textual positioning of readers and viewers. Advances in technology and communications have constantly disrupted the current conception of literacy and institutionalized ELA practices. Given the variety of new media and textual events that are appearing, ELA teachers can no longer simply limit their teaching to traditional reading and writing practices. We now need to think more in terms of composing texts using various multimedia in nonlinear formats rather than just simple acts of writing. We also need to move beyond the traditions of sociological and textual criticism and to be more inclusive of such things as art criticism or film editing and analysis as various media are engaged.

Gained will be new perspectives and interpretative fields that were previously given little attention (Burn, Brindley, Durran, Kelsall, Sweetlove and Tuhey, 2001). It would also be helpful to start conceptualizing, in more detail, what specific encoding and decoding practices make good sense for students to experience before graduation from high school. As Galileo Educational Network's Sharon Friesen (2002) carefully reminds us, "we need to provide students with an education for their future not for our past."

In order to do so we need to better understand the nature and requirements of new textual events within the context of a rapidly changing world. A picture has begun to emerge in this text of the particular composing, representing, viewing and digital experiences that will allow citizens to construct knowledge, earn a living, contest injustices, tackle compounding environmental problems, enjoy all the wonders that modern democracies provide and navigate an emancipatory path through an increasingly complex world. The power of new media and technology is in what it can reveal, uncover, connect and bring forth into the world. Ignacio Götz (2001) says, "technology is the instrument through which the made world is made manifest" (p. 24). However, Götz got it only partly right. His definition needs to account for the virtual spaces and worlds into which people now pour constructions of their identity, seek and give help, and generate a sense of community. The construction of texts through various digital media, after all, can extend our sensory modes of knowing and creative possibilities.

The point of having digital technologies in schools is not to make things easier for students or to electronically enhance traditional lectures and teaching practices or to make provincial testing programs more efficient. New technologies allow us to do things differently. They allow us to search a little further, dig a little deeper, and publish our investigations to broader audiences. We can do schooling much better. ICT allows us to ask more authentic questions of our students that are connected to real events and problems. The harder questions we ask often have multiple and complex solutions. Students need more interrelated practice with the complexities of the world. Their answers can demand the blending of data from various sources. Technology can bring more clarity, precision and pride to a student's investigations or creative constructions. There is a great deal of work to be done in this world. Just as the metaphors and images of writers and painters help us make sense of our lives and experiences, so too can the wise use of technology help further civil liberties, protect the right of descent, improve communications and spark the imagination.

The anecdotes used at the beginning of this concluding chapter and the skills needed by knowledge workers are presented to put the work ELA teachers do in a larger context. The weaving together of a story and imagination is now able to take on new forms and structures. Classes can communicate and publish to a wider audience using more textured constructions. The last stanza of Marge Piercy's "To Be of Use" is helpful to me in thinking about the power of English language arts, media and ICT to help us do more authentic, more meaningful work and to help us strive to live better with our students.

The work of the world is common as mud.

Botched, it smears the hands, crumbles to dust.

But the thing worth doing well done

has a shape that satisfies, clean and evident.

Greek amphoras for wine or oil,

Hopi vases that held corn, are put in museums

but you know they were made to be used.

The pitcher cries for water to carry

and a person for work that is real.

REFERENCES

Barrell, B. & Hammett, R. (2002). A critique of a critical social literacy project: Newfoundlanders confront *The Shipping News*. *Interchange: A Quarterly Review of Education, 33*(2), 139-158.

Barrell, B. & Hammett, R. (1999). Hypermedia as a medium for textual resistance. *English in Education, 33*(3), 21-30.

Bass, R. (1996). A bigger place to play, or, texts, knowledge and pedagogy in the electronic age [Online]. Available: http://otal.umd.edu/cgi-bin/imagemap/~googie/bass/bass.map, Retrieved August 25, 2002.

Burn, A., Brindley, S., Durran, J., Kelsall, C., Sweetlove, J. & Tuhey, C. (2001). "The rush of images": A research report into digital editing and the moving image. *English in Education, 35*(2), 34-48.

Clifford, P. & Friesen, S. (2001). The stewardship of the intellect. In B. Barrell (Ed.). *Technology, teaching and learning: Issues in the integration of technology.* Calgary, AB: Detselig Enterprises Ltd.

Freisen, S. (2002). Once more it is time to begin. A paper presented to The Centre for Leadership in Learning Annual Seminar Series, University of Calgary.

Götz, I. (2001). On technology. *Interchange: A Quarterly Review of Education, 32*(1), 17-37.

Lankshear, C. (1998). Meanings of literacy in contemporary educational reform proposals. *Educational Theory, 48*(3), 351-372

Piercy, M. (2000). To be of use. *Circle on the water: Selected poems of Marge Piercy.* New York: Alfred A. Knopf.

Reich, R. (1992). *The work of nation: Preparing ourselves for 21st century capitalism.* New York: Vintage.

Tapscott, D. (1998). *Growing up digital: The rise of the net generation.* New York: McGraw-Hill.

Waks, L. (2000). Why globalization will cause fundamental curriculum change. A paper delivered at the annual conference of the American Educational Research Association, New Orlean, LA.